D0938107

"As Editor of *Kosmos Journal* I have selected *MEMEnomics* as one of two recommended books in our current journal. In addition to a pioneering effort to place economics within a memetic continuum, it is valuable as a text on the whole field of economics as it has developed through time. This will be a classic in the new field of Memenomics and should be accessible to all university students. It is a major contribution to the field of transformational economics as we search for new ways of sharing resources in a new economy."

Nancy Roof
Editor, *Kosmos Journal*

"We are in a world of crisis. Earth is experiencing the Sixth Great Mass Extinction of life, an event science attributes to civilization living out of alignment with the wisdom of Nature. Modeling our existence and behavior on the outdated Darwinian philosophy of 'survival of the fittest,' while ignoring our responsibility to the whole of humanity *and* our supporting environment, threatens our existence.

In *MEMEnomics*, cultural creative Said E. Dawlabani provides a resource to help us safely navigate this dark passage to a healthier future. Dawlabani, a macroeconomics expert, exploits the frontier science of biomimicry to offer a pioneering value-system's approach to modeling the conscious evolution of business. I highly recommend *MEMEnomics* as an important contribution that presents a compelling and sustainable economic model to guide the future of human evolution and help save our biosphere."

Bruce H. Lipton, PhD
Cell biologist and best-selling author of *The Biology of Belief*
Author of *The Honeymoon Effect: The Science of Creating Heaven on Earth*
Co-author of *Spontaneous Evolution*

"Creating a world that works for all requires understanding the complex kaleidoscope of human value systems across our country and our planet. In no arena is this more important than in the world of business and economics. Said Elias Dawlabani has opened the door to this crucial topic with a groundbreaking conversation about the stages of development of people and societies, and the emerging economic systems needed to fit the life conditions we face. As we learn to apply next-generation thinking we can create a thriving future for humanity. Read this book—and join the conversation about healthy change."

Cindy Wigglesworth
Author, *SQ21: The Twenty-One Skills of Spiritual Intelligence*
President, Deep Change, Inc.

MEMEnomics

MEMEnomics

The Next-Generation Economic System

SAID ELIAS DAWLABANI

Foreword by Don E. Beck, PhD

SelectBooks, Inc.
New York

This edition published by SelectBooks, Inc.
For information address SelectBooks, Inc., New York, New York.

First Edition

ISBN 978-1-59079-996-3

Library of Congress Cataloging-in-Publication Data
Dawlabani, Said Elias.
 Memenomics : the next-generation economic system / Said Elias Dawlabani ; foreword by Don E. Beck, PhD. -- First edition.
   pages cm
 Includes bibliographical references and index.
 Summary: "Economist and founder of The Memenomics Group presents the emerging science of Memenomics that redefines cultural evolution by examining the long-term effects of economic policy on society through the prism of value systems, reframing economics through a whole-systems' approach to economic development to provide an integral view of the future of capitalism"--Provided by publisher.
 ISBN 978-1-59079-996-3 (hardbound : alk. paper)
 1. Economics--Sociological aspects. 2. Capitalism--Social aspects. 3. Economic development--Social aspects. 4. Values. I. Title.
 HM548.D38 2013
 306.3--dc23
                              2013008910

Interior book design and production by Janice Benight

Manufactured in the United States of America

10 9 8 7 6 5 4 3 2 1

TO MY DAUGHTERS, CHLOE AND QUINN,
AND TO MY PARENTS, JAMILEH AND ELIAS.

TO MY COLLEAGUE AND FRIEND, DON BECK, WHOSE GENIUS
HAS INSPIRED ME EVERYDAY FOR THE LAST TEN YEARS.

AND TO MY BRILLIANT AND LOVING PARTNER, ELZA,
WHO SHOWED ME THE WAY TO THE NEVER-ENDING QUEST.

CONTENTS

6 THE THIRD MEMENOMIC CYCLE:
The "Only Money Matters" Meme 125

7 IN SEARCH OF A NEW PARADIGM 153

PART THREE

The Platform for Functional Capitalism 165

8 VALUE SYSTEMS AND FUNCTIONAL FLOW 167

9 EMBRACING THE VALUES OF THE KNOWLEDGE ECONOMY: ƒ(KNOWLEDGE) 195

10 THE CASE FOR FUNCTIONAL FINANCIAL SYSTEMS: ƒ(FINANCE) 209

11 DESIGNING FOR THE FUTURE OF MANUFACTURING: ƒ(MANUFACTURING) 221

12 DEFINING THE SUSTAINABLE CORPORATION FROM STOCKHOLDER TO STAKEHOLDERS: ƒ(CORP) 233

Foreword

By Don Edward Beck, PhD

Books about subjects like economics are rarely written from the perspective of human or cultural evolution. Seldom, if ever, does a reader come across a narrative with pioneering methods that reframe a specialized discipline through a wide-cultural whole systems approach. This is precisely what Said E. Dawlabani has done in the book *Memenomics: The Next-Generation Economic System.* This is a book that reframes the issues of competing economic and political ideologies and places them into an evolutionary new paradigm. This is a book about change done right.

It is no secret that today we are dealing with a great political divide that threatens many of our democratic institutions. Right and left ideologies have becomes polarized camps that seem to be worlds apart. If we were to do a content analysis of all the speeches, books, and articles from the last few years, and consider the arguments presented in academic or think tank settings on these issues, we would see several clear and distinct patterns. Capitalism is great or greedy. Socialism is humane or harmful. The rich are that way because they worked hard or simply won life's lottery. The poor are that way because they are undisciplined or oppressed by the rich. Economic redistribution will level the playing field or dumb-down global intelligences. Which is it?

Most of these conventional discussions center around competing economic models, open political access, mandated equality of opportunity and results, and a host of other external, top-down solutions. Arguments have grown in emotional intensity around the size and distribution of government budgets. Money becomes the magic elixir that will cure all ills. New rules and regulations will transform hearts and minds or anger those who believe in the invisible hand of the free market. Everybody benefits from the largess of big government, as it bails out bigger and bigger "too big to fail" enterprise and uses taxes to fund social work schemes. And, of course, the knowledge economy will bring brilliant technological innovations to the most remote village in Africa, with or without electricity. Right.

There is a formidable challenge that awaits thinkers who are shaping the future of humanity—one of monumental proportions that will call on our collective ability to create political and economic systems that can best handle the complex conditions confronting life on our planet. When the Scottish moral philosopher Adam Smith penned his views on the evolution of human morality and trade over two centuries ago, he captured the hearts and minds of people the world over. But today, after guiding the free enterprise system to unimaginable heights, his teachings are being questioned at their core. Current global economic and governing systems can no longer run on fixed or rigid ideologies regardless of how virtuous or inspiring they were in the past.

Today, the hubris of command intelligence that prescribes to fixed structures in economic and political leadership is waning and models empowered by open systems and distributed intelligence are on the rise. As economic activity languishes from one recession to the next the search for more sophisticated leadership models is intensifying. The diversity of human systems cannot afford to rely on contrived designs by the entrenched elite as a sole approach. This old paradigm of trickle down knowledge and policy formulation represents industrial age values that shaped both political and economic life for centuries, but have become increasingly obsolete in the last few decades. These relics of values past continue to be the dominant source of solutions that are proving to be less effective with every passing day.

In order for new leadership to emerge to answer our challenges, new paradigms must be created. Today, a new paradigm for leadership is being born and the conceptual revelations on how to design for the future of political and economic complexity are beginning to take hold. In order for a new model to succeed it has to be able to explain more variables, account for more contingencies, and solve more problems than the one it will ultimately replace. Since life is constantly changing, this emerging paradigm must be an open system rather than a closed state. It must subsume that all previous ideologies are legitimate for different times, circumstances and developmental stages. It must also possess the distributed intelligence that gathers information from the deep reaches of every corner of society in order to design effective long-term solutions. Those solutions must be equally relevant for individuals, organizations and society at large. They must accommodate the full texture of human cultural differences as they evolve over time while addressing multiple bottom-lines on issues regarding standards of living and the quality of life.

Today we stand on the cusp of much advancement in the fields of physical and biological sciences and should learn how to incorporate complexities from these systems into the field of social sciences. Areas of study in biomimicry and evolutionary biology are providing a rich reservoir of knowledge that helps us design for a future that follows natural order to accommodate complexity. Governing systems of the future will be rich with designs that mimic nature where power is distributed to the highest degree of function. Decision-making processes will be empowered by the confluence of knowledge that rises up, policies that trickle down, and values and intelligences that move in every direction based on the function they need to satisfy. Economics has to examine concepts such as human and cultural emergence and Complex Adaptive Systems as ways to create a diversified approach towards reframing global economic challenges.

The field of complexity in social science has been around for decades. My late colleague and friend Dr. Clare W. Graves first mapped the levels of human existence and pioneered methodologies that deal with the understanding of the bio-psycho-social stages of development. His research lent much to the understanding of complex adaptive systems in culture. A considerable part of my post academic career has been focused on the development of Grave's research into models that help governments and businesses throughout the world in breaking through logjams and managing the complexities that lie ahead. From South Africa to the Middle East and Iceland we have proven that meaningful change is possible if policymakers are informed by the unique, DNA-like construct of societal complexity if seen through a prism we call value-systems. Many decades after Graves laid down his framework of understanding culture at the large scale, research in the field of life sciences along with the information revolution are proving that culture mimics life in its construct and that simple fixed ideologies will no longer provide the sole solutions for a future full of complexity.

Nowhere are these ideas brought to contemporary life applications better than in this book. The work that Said E. Dawlabani has penned here is nothing short of a genius adaptation of the Gravesian technology to the field of evolutionary economics. His approach and analysis, combined with his deep understanding of this theory, make him a contemporary Third Generation Gravesian presence on the economics stage today. He was among the first to challenge the conventional thinking of economists past and present prior to the onset of the financial crisis in 2008. He has continued to methodically articulate the reasons the current expression of capitalism is in decline and why a far higher form of economic order needs to emerge. Since human existence spirals in an upward trajectory towards higher levels of expression, Said's approach to defining economic emergence is among the freshest approaches I've seen. He is a member of a worldwide constellation of thinkers who are influencing the conscious evolution of a new worldview. Based on our decades of research and worldwide applications of this integral bio-psycho-social theory of human development we know that this approach works. We know that cultures, as well as countries, are formed by the emergence of value systems or social stages in response to life conditions. Such complex adaptive intelligences form the glue that bonds a group together, defines who they are as a people, and reflects the place on the planet they inhabit.

These cultural stages of development have formed over time into unique mixtures and blends of instructional and survival codes, myths of origin, artistic forms, life styles, and senses of community. While they are all legitimate expressions of the human experience, they are not "equal" in their capacities to deal with complex problems in society and herein lies the challenge that prevents politically correct leadership from designing effective solutions. Yet these detectable social stages within cultures are not deterministic scripts that lock us into choices against our will. Nor are they inevitable steps on a predetermined staircase, or magically appearing like crop circle structures in our collective psyche. Cultures should not be seen as rigid types, having permanent traits.

Instead, they are core adaptive intelligences that ebb and flow, progress and regress, with the capacity to lay on new levels of sophistication when conditions warrant. Much like an onion, they form layers on layers on layers. There is no final state, no ultimate destination, and no utopian paradise. Each stage is but a prelude to the next, then the next, and the next. Each emerging social stage or cultural wave contains a more expansive horizon, a more complex organizing principle with newly calibrated priorities, mindsets, and specific bottom-lines. All of the previously acquired social stages remain in the composite value system to determine the unique texture of a given culture, country, or society. Once a new social stage appears in a culture, it will spread its instructional codes and life priority messages throughout that culture's surface-level expressions: religion, economic and political arrangements, psychological and anthropological theories, and views of human nature, our future destiny, globalization, and even architectural patterns and sports preferences.

Here's the key idea behind this new paradigm for dealing with complexity that will help define the future of leadership that is so eloquently described in this book: We all live in flow states; there is always new wine, always old wine skins. We, indeed, find ourselves pursuing a never-ending quest and that is true in how politics and economics emerge. Different societies, cultures and subcultures, as well as entire nations are at different levels of psycho-cultural emergence, as displayed within these evolutionary levels of complexity. So many of the same issues that confronted us on the West Bank can be found in South Central Los Angeles. One can experience the animistic worldview on Bourbon Street as well as with the Zulu tribes we worked with in South Africa. Matters brought before city council in Minneapolis are not unlike the debates in front of governing bodies in the Netherlands.

So-called Third World societies are dealing, for the most part, with issues relative to challenges within their developmental zones, thus the outcome is higher rates of violence and poverty. Economic and political leadership models designed for these stages of developments cannot be the same as the First World. Staying alive, finding safety, and dealing with feudal age conditions matter most. Challenges facing Second World societies are also different. They are characterized by authoritarian one-party states, whether from the right or the left. It makes no difference. They too, must have different models to best accommodate their cultural transition from these developmental stages.

So-called First World nations and groupings have achieved the highest levels of affluence known to man, with lower birth rates and more expansive use of technology. While centered in values that are strategic, free-market driven, and individualistic, they believe this is the final state, the "end of history." While that seems to be the dominant belief today, new value systems are emerging in the post "postmodern" age. Yet we have not fully developed the language to intelligently articulate anything beyond First World. Further, there is a serious question as to whether the billions of people who are now exiting Second and Third World life styles can anticipate the same level of affluence as what they see on satellite TV and through social media. And what will happen to the environment if every Chinese family had a two-car garage?

As Said contends so movingly in this book, the answers to so many of these questions become less overwhelming once solutions start being framed through a stratified approach that considers different remedies for different stages of emergence. Under this model, flow state perspectives replace final state paralysis. Simplistic car-wash solutions evolve to a richer understanding of people, uniqueness in situations, and inevitable steps and stages in human emergence. Rigid rules, a product of fixed state ideologies, will be supplanted by fluctuating algorithms that engage a world full of variables, life cycles, wild cards, and other complex dynamics that lie at the core of life itself. There are no guarantees, no eternal road maps, no inevitable destinations, no blue print etched in permanent ink. Yet there are equations, formulas, big data, analytics, fractals, consequences, flows, and processes. Each new solution will, over time, create new problems. Human motivations will change as our life conditions get better, or get worse. There are systems within us rather than types of us—stratified decision-making stacks that constantly rearrange themselves in terms of priorities and a sense of urgency. Different cultures and subcultures become recognized as organic entities that lay on new levels of complexity as changes in life conditions warrant.

This new paradigm for human and cultural emergence is beautifully detailed in this book. *Memenomics* makes the case for how artificially imposed systems in economics become closed and toxic. By using processes that were pioneered through five decade of research and global applications Said repeatedly makes the case for why the future of economics must consider a values-systems approach if the field should emerge into a whole-systems form of leadership in the future. Through technologies such as Natural Design and life cycles of values systems, Said pioneers a fresh reframing of economic history that uncovers the blockages of trickle-down approaches of the past. He then offers remedies that set a new standard for sustainable practices, ones that are based on functional platforms designed to address the needs of people and cultures at their particular level of economic emergence. This book is a brilliant primer on the application of the values-systems theory to economics. It is a field guide for anyone looking to establish a cultural values-systems understanding not only to economics but also to the applications of the theory of Spiral Dynamics and the seminal work of Clare W. Graves. It represents the evolution of the Gravesian model into a field that rarely considers the different needs and motivations of the different stages of human and societal development.

Finally, a word of caution. The real intent of this approach to leadership is to shape both interior and exterior dynamics—the expansion of capacities in the brain as well as in culture, politics, and economics. Its purpose is to expedite the natural principles that appear to drive societal transformation. These dynamics rely heavily on self-organizing principles and processes rather than ones that are mechanistic or artificially mandated or commanded. With the help of the knowledge economy and social media, the change we seek under this model has begun. It is messy, chaotic, often violence-prone, and uncertain with false starts, regressions, quantum leaps, advances, and retreats. This change is systemic and integral and by nature is designed to dredge out imbedded practices, expose corruption, and make full transparency the norm. It drains stagnant backwaters, unblocks tributaries, navigates white water rapids, and maintains the ongoing movement of ideas, energy, and the human spirit through time and space that are becoming increasingly condensed with every passing day. It is in the proper management of that tension between chaos and order spiraling upwards on an endless human journey that we become co-creators with *The Prime Directive* in crafting the human story.

—Don E. Beck, PhD
Founder, Global Centers for Human Emergence
Coauthor of *Spiral Dynamics: Mastering Values, Leadership, and Change*
Denton, Texas

PART ONE

MEMEnomics

*The Whole-Systems View
of the Evolution of Economies*

Introduction

It is claimed that Albert Einstein said: "We can't solve problems by using the same kind of thinking we used when we created them." Anyone who is familiar with the current political and economic divide in this country knows we are facing problems of significant proportions that the old system cannot solve. Innovative ideas don't see the light of day as they become polarized into the two political camps of the left or the right. We elect politicians who promise change, yet the political machinery renders their visions obsolete. In frustration, we elect new politicians and send them to the same politically divided system expecting different results. Opposing economic and political ideologies are driving a deep wedge into the fabric of American culture, but things don't have to be that way. What if the current political and economic stalemate could be reframed through a theory that attempts to "explain everything"? One that has been used to help South Africa transition from Apartheid, inspire the Palestinian people to build the infrastructure of their future state, and inform the designers of the new Icelandic constitution? These are some of the successes that global change- agents have been able to achieve by applying the same theoretical framework on which the memenomics framework is based.

The impetus behind the concepts that are laid out in this book comes from the seminal work of two prominent developmental psychologists, Clare W. Graves and Don Edward Beck. Graves, who was a contemporary of Abraham Maslow, authored the theory known in its abbreviated form as *the theory of human existence*. In this theory, Graves laid out his views that differed from those of his contemporaries about the very nature of the development of the mature human being. While others contented that a mature human or a mature culture is a desired final state of existence, Graves argued that it is embedded in human nature not to have a final state. He described the human journey as an endless quest and that human values shape culture, and culture in turn shapes human values. It is the coupling of these two factors into what Graves termed as a "double helix" model where psychological human capacities can recalibrate higher or lower levels in response to changing life conditions, which is culture or the social part of the model. Unlike many of his contemporaries in the humanistic psychology movement at the time, he firmly believed that society, or social factors, play

3

a critical role in how humans and cultures evolve. He was the first academic researcher to incorporate the "social" aspect of human development into a model that became identified as the "bio-psycho-social" model of human and social development.

Beck met Graves in 1974 and left his tenured academic career as a professor to pursue Graves's application of his research. In 1996, along with Christopher Cowan, he authored a book titled *Spiral Dynamics* that became the most authoritative container of Graves's methodologies and research. Spiral Dynamics is the theory that Beck and Cowan created, of which I have been a student for the last decade. This is not only because of the theory's appeal. It is also because I have been one of the luckiest people in the world to work closely with the brilliant mind of Don E. Beck.

Memenomics is a composite of two words. The first is "meme," which is a term originally coined by evolutionary biologist Richard Dawkins. It rhymes with gene and just like a gene that carries the codes that define human characteristics, a meme carries the codes that define cultural characteristics. The second word is based on "economics." It is the coming together of the two fields, economics and memetics that form this new and innovative area for study that is presented in this book. Memenomics is based on natural evolutionary concepts that define individuals, institutions, and cultures as value systems memes or ᵛMEMEs and offers economic solutions that are congruent with these memetic codes.

Memes involving music, fads, fashion, and so forth, will be explained in more detail in an upcoming chapter. Memes define our lives. As they become classified into cultural groupings such as religion, philosophy, politics, and sports, they come together to form a values-system meme or ᵛMEME. Graves was the first person to use the term values-system to refer to the varying preferences and priorities that humans have in their lives depending on their level of development. Over many decades of research Graves identified eight levels of value systems. Beck and Cowan gave the term a more contemporary name by calling it a ᵛMEME. Their work also expanded on the definition of the "double helix" aspect of the model into two distinct principals: the first is the human capacity to create ᵛMEMEs, and the second is the life conditions that awaken ᵛMEMEs. A more detailed discussion of these two important aspects of this framework will take place in chapter 2. Throughout the book, the terms value systems and ᵛMEMEs are a reference to the bio-psycho-social stage of development of a person or a culture. Regardless of which term is used, the important distinction that is made in this book is that the decision-making process of leaders is a quantifiable one based on which value-system a decision maker belongs to, since each of these eight known levels of human existence has its own rules and views about which governing systems are the best to use to run social and economic systems. This is how *Memenomics* reframes the past, present, and future debate regarding economic policy.

The reader will repeatedly see my use of the term "human emergence." The genesis of this term should be explained since it has direct relevance to the very nature of the Graves/Beck conceptual framework and to that of memenomics. In the late 1960s and early 1970s, while Graves's academic contemporaries were busy defining the steps needed for a human or a culture to reach a mature or utopian state, his research was pointing away from this direction. Graves believed that there is no end state and that what might be a utopian existence today might not be that in a decade. To him, the human growth phenomenon was a leaf-like enfoldment on an endless journey towards higher levels of maturity, personality, and culture.[1] He called his theory the "Emergent, Cyclical, Levels of Existence of human behavior" and referred to it as ECLET. Below is a transcription of Graves's own words from a 1974 conference, in which he distinguished the use of the term "emergence" as an endless natural process to describe his unique approach in explaining human nature:

> I call this theory today the emergent, cyclical levels of existence theory of human behavior. Now, I call it that because certain things have come out of the data with time that require that particular terminology. One is the psychology of man seems to be ever emerging which is a point of view which is extremely different from what you have in so many psychologies of man where they talk about trying to move man toward The mature human being, The healthy personality. Or they try to move a society toward becoming a utopian society, and my data doesn't support that kind of thinking at all. My data says that there is no such thing as a mature society or the psychologically mature human being. It says that he infinitely changes. So the idea of "Emergence" came out of that.[2]

In several conversations I had with Beck about the genesis of the term, he agreed that the elegance through which Graves's data presented itself is more akin to an "enfoldment" of human development, than the evolution of it. According to Beck, the two additional factors that might have lead Graves to use the term *emergence* was Graves witnessing the academic and the institutional resistance that his colleague Maslow experienced in using terms such as *"hierarchy"* and *"evolution."* The 1960s and 1970s were times of egalitarian values and anything that used these two terms was frowned upon. In the late 1990s Beck established the first Center for Human Emergence (CHE) with the following mission: "The Center for Human Emergence will help facilitate the conscious emergence of the human species using a synthesis of profound breakthroughs in human knowledge and capabilities, encompassing natural pattern coherence, mega-integration, unification, expanded whole mind capacity, deep intelligence and consciousness"[3]

Today, there are more the a dozen CHEs around the world whose primary mission is to reframe human and cultural challenges through the prism of values systems and provide solutions that are naturally resilient.

My inspiration to write this book came from my decade-long work with Dr. Beck who is one of the pioneers of the values-systems approach to solving problems. As a renowned geopolitical advisor, Dr. Beck has left his mark around the globe from his hometown of Dallas to Johannesburg, London, and Ramallah, and everywhere in between. By applying this framework to real life applications I learned much of the intelligence behind the principles of Spiral Dynamics and large-scale change. My first experience with the applications of values systems to economics came at The Center for Human Emergence Middle East (CHE-ME) where as COO I helped its founders, Dr. Beck and my wife, Elza Maalouf, design the economic development elements of the *Build Palestine Initiative*. The culture that was created under Beck's leadership at the CHE-ME instilled a completely different approach to our research and design than the ones commonly used by Western think tanks, consultants, and the endless number of NGOs. Elza, who is the CEO of the CHE-ME, is writing a book about these methodologies that are based on a Spiral Dynamics concept called *Natural Design*. This is a large-scale systems change model of the Graves/Beck framework that naturally aligns people, resources, institutions, and processes to serve a superordinate goal that speaks to all the stakeholders in the culture. Much of the last part of this book will use these Natural Design processes to create a unique, culturally fit and resilient economy of the future.

What added to my resolve to write this book, were the tools that I acquired from this framework that I applied in my professional field as a real estate developer and investment advisor. The ability to perform "thin-slicing" on culture was a tool that helped me anticipate the housing crash and the subsequent financial crisis. At the end of 2005, to the surprise of my colleagues, I wound down development operations while they continued building homes. By the end of 2008 the housing bubble had left most builders in the country restructuring their debt or seeking outright bankruptcy protection. By the time the financial crisis was in full swing I was urged by a small circle of friends, including Don Beck, to let the world in on how this whole-systems approach to economic values can provide effective tools in predicting economic change and designing for a sustainable future.

In 2008 and 2009 I authored several papers that offered a memetic analysis on the causes of the financial crisis.[4] It is that paradigm shift of seeing the world through the stratified lenses of value systems as presented through the theory of Spiral Dynamics and the Graves methodology that I wish to bring to the perception of the reader. It is my hope that policymakers dealing with all aspects of our geopolitical challenges and not just economic policy bring this emerging science that recognizes various value systems that exist in the world into their decision-making framework.

I describe memenomics as the study of the long-term effects of economic policy on culture as seen through the eyes of the emerging science of value systems. The theory is about using a whole-systems approach to viewing and solving economic challenges. I have applied its concepts and principles in the field, and I have been teaching it at graduate transformational leadership programs for several years. It starts where evolutionary economics ends and borrows from all economic principles, but is not a part of the economics mainstream. An entire chapter is dedicated to detailing the main principles on which the memenomics framework is built. This is where complexity theory meets economic policy.

The concepts presented here are not about faulting certain aspects of economic theory and practice or the premise of one ideology over the other. It will not help a reader in the process of choosing certain stocks or aid a brokerage house in enhancing its hedge fund strategies. It's more about creating a paradigm shift away from the theoretical silos and the empirical nature of economics to the wider view of the role that modern day commerce plays in the emergence or stagnation of humanity. Over five thousand books have been written since the 2008 financial crisis that offer different views on the failure of past economic policy and what to do going forward. Some offer strategies on how to take advantage of the recessionary aftermath, while others look to point the finger of blame at whoever is in the cross hairs of their beliefs and value systems. Competing thought-leaders make compelling cases for why we should return to Keynesian economics and have government play a greater role in directing economic policy, while others want to revive the virtues of the Reaganomics era of laissez-faire capitalism. There is no single book on the market today that offers an evolutionary perspective on macroeconomics. This book is at the confluence of contemporary ideas on emergence, complex systems, and sustainable economic policies.

In *Memenomics* I explain from a unique perspective the role that cultural value systems play in defining the success or failure of economic policy. Through better knowledge of this emerging science that examines psychology on a large scale, the behaviors and ideologies emanating from certain value systems are easily detected and put through a new prism that determines their potential for either long-term sustainability or short-term exploitation.

The theory of memenomics peels away the layers of econo-speak and returns the core of this discipline to its origin as a social science. It creates ways for the reader to understand how government economic policies can be made wiser and how government itself can "run smarter." It shows how business can be made to have healthier practices and how to design for a future economy from a unique value-systems perspective. By reframing the issues through the prism of memenomics, a far more integral view emerges about the hierarchical nature of human development, which then opens the space to reframe human behavior and cultural development at a far deeper level. This is a unique approach that enables the reader to see the different value preferences of the vast numbers of people who roam the planet based on their level of development and offers a differentiated way to handle their needs that is naturally sustainable.

The first part of the book introduces the concept and the history of value systems and the different uses of its principles around the world in order to gain insights into why this approach is different. The first chapter chronicles the life of one of the most powerful men in modern-day capitalism. It follows the career of the former Chairman of the Federal Reserve Alan Greenspan, and examines the forces that shaped his life through a prism that sets the tone for the book. It describes his early childhood and his rise to power, as he became one of the most influential global leaders, and the final days of his career when he acknowledged the fallacy of his ideologies and the demise of his once pioneering worldview. On A *New Day of Infamy* the maestro of global commerce admits to faulty thinking that exposes vulnerabilities in the direction capitalism has taken over four decades, which becomes the catalyst that sparks the search for a new paradigm. This sets the stage for the reader to understand that the Enlightenment Era, a ˅Memetic code of one of the value-systems levels, was just a stop along our journey of human emergence in an endless quest towards higher values. It opens the doorway to begin thinking in terms of evolving systems that alter in response to a changing reality instead of being frozen in ideologies beholden to values fixed in time.

The second chapter details the main principals behind the emerging science of value-systems on which the concept of memenomics is built. Based on a bio-psycho-social approach to measuring human values, it describes how cultures emerge and why. The history of this conceptual framework is relayed, as well as the background of the reasons I developed my ideas that support the theory of Clare Graves, that was described by the Canadian publication *Maclean's Magazine* as *the theory that explains everything.*[5] It briefly introduces the groundbreaking research of Clare W. Graves whose seminal work represented the most ambitious effort by an academic on the mapping of human existence. The reader is then introduced to the theory of Spiral Dynamics developed by Graves's successors, Don Edward Beck and Christopher Cowan. Through my decade-long work experience with Beck, I reintroduce parts of the theory in this chapter that apply to value systems in economics. I then describe the eight known levels of human existence with distinct value systems and the characteristics unique to each level, such as social and economic preferences, life priorities, ways of thinking, and many other characteristics. The reader can gain understanding of what research now confirms: value systems exist as structures in the brain, as well as on psychological belief systems and behaviors and levels of existence within culture. There are examples in the chapter of different economic value systems around the world with analysis that demonstrate how we've been approaching economic development from what Graves called "subsistence values" which sets forth the urgent need to alter our approach.

The third chapter explains what memenomics is and presents the methodologies used through this approach. It explains why they are different from what most economists use in their approaches and why advancements even in the field of evolutionary economics fall short of providing a whole-systems approach to solving economic problems. It clarifies the difference between economic cycles and memenomic cycles and describes the different phases of a cycle. In this way, it can be understood how visionary ideas are born and come to define our culture for decades and how they mature, decline, and eventually decay, and become a part of the DNA of future cycles. The chapter also provides a new way for viewing technological cycles and how they affect human emergence. Finally, we look at the nature of change through the prism of value systems that enable the reader to acquire the knowledge needed to distinguish between *aesthetic change* and *systemic change* and know when and how to design for each.

The fourth chapter concludes the first part of the book by looking at the ᵛMemetic role that money historically played in the emergence of cultures. Before the appearance of any of the Abrahamic religions, which are codes of the fourth-level value system, something emerged much earlier in human history that made us abandon our impulsive hunter-gatherer existence and adopt more tempered values. This became the codification of trade into monetary systems of exchange. This chapter looks at the history of money through a value-systems lens in order to establish its functional role as an agent of the fourth-level value system. As we examine its evolution from its earliest form as grain to its current status as a fiat currency, we get a critical ᵛMEME perspective on the challenges facing Western economies today. This time is indeed different, not just because of what econometrics tell us, but because we have perverted the historic representative of productive output. This chapter gives many examples to make clear the consequences we must face when we corrupt one of the oldest and most common ᵛMemetic codes of the fourth-level value system: Money.

In the second part of the book the economic history of the United States is reinterpreted through the memenomics framework. Analysis of the competing value systems is made as history is reframed through a concept of memenomic cycles. Normal economic cycles and super economic cycles have framed the debate of modern economics, but memenomic cycles show us the unique nature of human values as they evolve in levels and waves to provide new tools for the reader to understand how and why complex economic ideologies rise and fall. Once this whole-systems approach is understood, the reader will have a new understanding of how events like the financial crisis of 2008 are the necessary transcendence of a lower value expression in order for the evolution of capitalism to continue on its endless quest along the upward spiral of human existence.

While there are eight known levels of existence or ᵛMEMEs that are the eight levels of value systems under the Graves/Beck model, this book focuses on the economic life cycles of only five of these levels. These historic periods I call memenomic cycles take place within the time frame that five of the eight known levels dominated our values and beliefs. The first two value systems don't have much of an economic system that is relevant to today's economy and are therefore not discussed. The first value system is of early human survival, which had no economic system to speak of. The second is the tribal value system that represents simple agrarian trade, which has a minor influence on today's complex global economy. The third ᵛMEME, which started with the spread of the values of "Empire" and ended with the beginning of the "mass production and allocation" of the Industrial Revolution, represents our entry into modern-day economics. This end phase of the third known level of existence, the egocentric value system, defined the adolescent stages of modern economics in the United States. This is the era that represents the first significant economic activity in cultural evolution that I call the first memenomic cycle.

Since the end of the Civil War the United States has been through three memenomic cycles. Chapter five examines the first two cycles. We will briefly look at the economic codes of the third-level value system that defined the first cycle that I call *the Fiefdoms of Power meme*. It is symbolized by the rise to power of feudal and egocentric values that were prevalent from the end of the Civil War to the onset of the Great Depression. The years from the 1930s to the 1970s are reframed through the theories of memenomics as the era that represents the second memenomic cycle and is called the Patriotic Prosperity Era. This is when values of the fourth-level system come to define America. This value system is represented by a society that thrives under the codes of law and order and of national patriotism. This is the time when institutions are built. We can see how memes of every type—economic, political, cultural, and educational—came to define the American middle class under an umbrella of the fourth-level system.

We also arrive at an understanding of the role that superordinate goals play in inspiring common economic activity, a tool that will become essential in designing economic policies in part III of the book. Simply put, a superordinate goal is a goal or a value that everybody wants and needs to realize, but no individual or group can achieve unilaterally. It's based on Beck's seminal work in conflict resolution and has been applied in large-scale design in South Africa and the Palestinian Territories. Winning wars was the dominant superordinate goal during the second memenomic cycle. Throughout the chapter we see through a new lens the different phases of a memenomic cycle that are usually ignored by economists, but make the compelling case for policymakers to design from a whole-systems perspective.

The sixth chapter examines the third memenomic cycle that started with the election of Ronald Reagan and is going through the entropy and collapse phase today. We will see how this cycle came to represent the values of the *Strategic Enterprise* fifth-level system, which emerged as a higher expression of economic evolution out of a system burdened by antiquated rules and regulations. We can see how finance evolved and became the tail that wagged the dog and how the promise of the post-industrial society was derailed. In a series of events that are reinterpreted through the prism of value systems, we learn how the perfect storm for the 2008 financial crisis came about. The reader will learn the value-systems reasons for why the Clinton Administration was far more complicit in causing the financial crisis than any other administration. The chapter concludes with an analysis of why the bailout represents the final phase of this memenomic cycle.

Part II of the book concludes with chapter seven and is about the long search for new paradigm. Long after Alan Greenspan testified to the US Congress about the shortcomings of the ideology of the era, predatory value systems are still running the global economy today. This chapter analyzes the value systems' cost of replacing productive output with financial innovation. It discusses the memenomic meaning of bubble economies as we linger in a prolonged malaise in the final phase of the third memenomic cycle. We also see the appearance of a new paradigm that is informing the next cycle and learn how the Egalitarian values of the sixth-level system are redefining the economic landscape. We see how the emergent fourth memenomic cycle holds so much hope for the future because it has the democratization of information and the deepening of human understanding at its core. These are all values of the sixth-level ᵛMEME.

Part III of the book serves as a unique guide for the United States to resume its role as a leader in defining the economic philosophy of the future. This is where we set a new superordinate goal that harnesses America's potential. We learn about the four essential pillars that create The Platform for Functional Capitalism; a seventh-level platform that is in its embryonic and introductory phases that will continue to differentiate its memetic characteristics over the next few decades. Adopting "functional" forms of management is a concept for large-scale change based on the unique cultural DNA codes of the seventh level of the values-systems framework. This is a ᵛMEME that aims to synthesize and integrate the best expression of past value systems into a functional flow while scanning the horizon for constant change. This is the distributed intelligence of biological systems being pioneered in culture.

Chapter eight further defines the characteristics of the value systems of the seventh level of human existence and the fifth memenomic cycle. This is where Graves's vision of "humanity's momentous leap" comes to fruition. It is one of systems integration and functional flow. This is the first chapter in what I refer to as the design section of the book in which we examine the values of the seventh-level system in greater detail. These are no longer *"subsistence"* values. These are the values of "being." By understanding the reasons why this is the most difficult phase for humanity to emerge into, we'll start to understand the systemic dysfunction we are experiencing today. The qualities of seventh-level leadership are described and examples given of these types of leaders today in government, business, the media, and the knowledge economy. Readers are then introduced to the *Natural Design* tool kit, which will enable us to reframe the issues and challenges facing society today through an easy to understand natural approach that will enable us to set a systemic superordinate goal for the future.

The ninth chapter offers a comparative analysis between the economic values of the fifth-level system, a system of scarcity, and those of a maturing sixth-level system, one of democratization of resources. These are the third and fourth memenomic cycles respectively. There is then an examination of what is needed to transition into the systemic seventh level, the fifth cycle, one of prudent abundance. A maturing knowledge economy is one of the four pillars of The Platform for Functional Capitalism. We follow the trajectory of the knowledge economy as it continues to create self-empowerment tools of a seventh-level system called "Distributed Innovations." We also examine the nature of the values systems of a new entrepreneurial meme that is re-empowering communities and bringing back the local business owner. It will be understood how the knowledge economy provides the first real example of an open system that accepts the diverse nature of other value systems, and how we can plug them on to a platform of a healthy and sustainable business expression that can revolutionize the very nature of how business gets done.

The tenth chapter focuses on creating functional financial systems of the seventh-level value system. It provides a new understanding of money, the second pillar of The Platform for Functional Capitalism once it is redefined through its role as a tool for social emergence. The often-unseen problem with the field of financial innovation is that it has decoupled from any reasonable measure of productive output. The tools of the seventh-level system that will realign finance and productivity are explained as we are introduced to a seventh-level monetary system that is more congruent with the proven functional history of money, but has an expression that keeps up with the times in being a catalyst for productive pursuits. We will also examine the very nature of central banking and the functional reforms needed in order to restore the Fed's role as the facilitator of distributed prosperity. The design elements needed to create functioning seventh-level capital markets are examined as well as details of plans on how to steer investment banking away from non-productive pursuits that remain the main cause behind every financial crisis.

Manufacturing is retuning to the West and it's looking nothing like it did when it left. In the eleventh chapter we see why the return of manufacturing, this third pillar of The Platform for Functional Capitalism, presents the United States with the rare opportunity to design an entirely new economic sector from the seventh level. We'll see why each relevant value system in today's culture must be heard and allowed to contribute to the design. We'll understand the reasons systemic involvement is needed to make this dream a reality. From teachers and community leaders, to government agencies and research universities, we'll learn how this design scheme can serve as a template for a sustainable economic future. We'll also get to understand why *smart government*, one that is designed from the seventh level, must increase expenditure on R&D at times when an economy lingers in the final phases of a memenomic cycle like the phase we're in today. Finally, we'll evaluate additive manufacturing and elements of the Third Industrial Revolution as viable tools of the seventh-level system.

The fourth pillar of The Platform for Functional Capitalism is a value-systems' examination of United States corporate culture, which is the focus of the twelfth and final chapter. Here the value-systems differences will be described between open system and closed-system corporations. It will be explained how changes in values and technology force the two types in different directions. I also examine the current functional misalignment of corporations and the hard road they face in regaining public trust, as well as the value-systems evolution of the term "ownership" in corporations and the stark differences between the Founder-CEO ethic and the professional CEO ethic. There is also a detailed discussion of the characteristics of a seventh-level CEO and what it takes to establish a seventh-level corporate culture.

I offer my analysis based on my research of the two distinct types of seventh-level corporations that are on the cutting edge today. Google and the disruptive nature of the knowledge economy represent the first emerging model. Whole Foods and its conscious evolutionary model represent the second. On the final pages a value-systems analysis is made of the concept of Conscious Capitalism and the reasons why it holds the promise for the systemic spread of seventh-level values in business practices.

Memenomics offers a unique view of the evolution of capitalism and economic systems. Throughout all sections I present the reader with new tools for how to detect unhealthy practices of each value system and its relationship to other value systems in order to deepen the understanding of this unique approach to economics. Unlike other economic theories that address specific segments of the economy in absence of other segments, I present an integral, whole-systems approach and lay out a comprehensive road map that addresses structural reforms. This includes best practices from previous systems but remains futuristic in its outlook.

The memenomics framework is based on the belief that whole-systems thinking is the way of the future, and by applying the unique principles of the emerging science of value systems we begin to see what that future looks like. As we develop more measurement techniques we continue to confirm the genius behind the Graves/Beck framework of the nature of human existence. Brain fMRI research concluded recently at the University of Cologne, Germany by scientists who are familiar with Graves's work, confirms the research behind the levels of human existence theory.[6] Much of the emerging qualities of the knowledge revolution are confirming Graves's characterization of the seventh and eighth levels of existence, which he described at a time when he could have not possibly foreseen the changes the information age would bring. This is similar to Beck's experience in South Africa after he helped design the transition from Apartheid. After the transition much of Beck's advice was ignored, resulting in the downshift in cultural values we see there today.

The memenomics framework is based on the same general principles of the Graves/Beck construct, which provides for a stratified view of the human experience. It is my hope that by offering an economic content for these stratified views I present a comprehensive way to reframe past and future values of economic activity and give the reader the tools to understand where we've been and where we are headed.

ONE

The Last Son of the Enlightenment

When I say 'capitalism,' I mean a full, pure, uncontrolled, unregulated laissez faire capitalism, with a separation of state and economics, in the same way and for the same reasons as the separation of state and church.[7]

—AYN RAND, Founder of *Objectivism* philosophy, from *The Objectivist Ethics*

A NEW DAY OF INFAMY

Most people around the globe attached no significant meaning to the day of October 23, 2008. It was just another ordinary day in a world that had become extra-ordinarily complex. Along the eastern seashore of the United States the warm rays of the morning sun mingled with the cool autumn breeze. Throngs of people crowded the streets and sidewalks of New York City attending to their hurried lives. From the observation deck of the Rockefeller Center beyond the Manhattan skyline, Central Park was set ablaze with the warm hue of red and orange leaves. Abandoned office towers that used to house Lehman Brothers and a number of other failed brokerages still stood in proud defiance of a once-in-a-hundred-year storm. On the other side of the planet spokesmen for the Chinese Communist Party announced with a good measure of certainty that China's roaring economy has shaken off any talk of instability as a result of faltering US financial markets. At the Tata Motors Headquarters in Mumbai India, executives still teeming with pride from the acquisition of Jaguar and Land Rover were busy acquiring large plots of farmland to build one of the biggest auto manufacturing facilities in the world. In the United Arab Emirates, the Ruler of Dubai pressed the more than 12,000 construction workers at Burj Dubai to keep up their frantic around the clock pace to get the tallest man-made structure ready for its grand opening on time. Back on the floor of the New York Stock Exchange the Wall Street establishment had successfully fended off the attacks of its critics, as its most revered pundits took the airwaves to assure the herds of followers around the world that recent market volatility was purely fear-driven, and the September market correction was firmly behind us.

Just below the surface of this business as usual day, or as Wall Street then called it, "the new normal," things were anything but. The cracks that started to form in the global financial markets at the end of September of that year were beginning to morph into major structural fault lines. The unease with doing business as usual was becoming more palpable by the day. Beyond the rhetoric of Wall Street, beyond the pomp and pageantry of China's central planning, and far past the glitz and glamour of Dubai's skyline, the entire global economy was teetering on the edge of collapse. Only one man in the world understood with great detail the devastation that was unfolding before modern humanity. He understood it far deeper and wider than anyone else in the world because he was the one behind it all—the one who built it and the one who was now watching all crumble.

THE RISE OF A GLOBAL LEADER

On that Thursday morning in October 2008 Alan Greenspan prepared to testify in front of the US Congress about the causes of the financial crisis. Millions around the world wondered what this day would be like for the man long considered one of the most powerful men in the world. During his tenure as chairman of the US Federal Reserve Bank Dr. Greenspan presided over policies that have created massive levels of wealth, the extent of which the world had never seen. Tall and strikingly confident with sharp intellect and a stately presence, he rarely uttered a word out of place or showed much emotion in public. No one in the history of the United States has been as involved in economic policy setting at the highest levels as Dr. Greenspan. His tenure of influence lasted over three decades and the effects of his policies will be felt around the world for many more decades to come. Before being appointed by President Reagan to the most powerful banking position in the world as Chairman of the Federal Reserve in 1987, and which he continued to hold during the administrations of Presidents George H. Bush, Bill Clinton, and George W. Bush, Dr. Greenspan's influence on shaping economic policy began in 1974 when he served as a close economic adviser to President Ford.

Fittingly, government and business leaders everywhere had bestowed upon him the designation of *maestro,* because when he spoke, the entire global economy fell silent. Then, for a few hours after the conclusion of his speech, they frantically analyzed and dissected his every word and phrase. Every pregnant pause was given to a speech specialist or a forensic psychologist to determine the deeper meaning of how the chairman felt about the condition of the global economy. When he testified on Capitol Hill, politicians eager to claim credit for his policies would swoon over him like teenage girls over their latest heartthrob. Members of the US Congress, regardless of party affiliation, had elevated this pioneering figure into the mythological stratosphere as the modern day oracle of capitalism.

In December 1996 his simple utterance of the phrase "irrational exuberance"[8] to warn of the possible overvaluation of the market during the dot-com bubble wiped out billions of dollars in equities from markets around the world in a matter of hours. In June of 2005 his mere description of the US housing market as "frothy" announced the beginning of the end of the longest period of affluence in the history of the West. It is said that toward the end of his last term, after his regular meetings with the heads of regional reserve banks, undercover financial reporters would follow him into coffee shops hoping for the slightest sign of policy direction. If the chairman ordered coffee, the interpretation of this act was that markets were overheating and higher interest rates were on their way. If he opted for tea the interpretation would be that he intended to keep interest rates low and the whole world could sleep a bit easier.

This is what modern day power came to look like. Thousands of lives are made or destroyed based on one man's choice of beverage. Billions are lost at the recital of a carefully crafted speech. If only Genghis Khan or Alexander the Great knew that this would be the natural progression in the evolution of humanity, they surely would have done things differently. The fight for the hearts and minds of the world's population moved from the gruesome and bloody battlefield to the sublime and innocuous market place. The conquest of nations was no longer accomplished through military might but through soft skills that are steeped in intricate knowledge of subject matters ranging from how to build the wealth of a nation and taming of dreaded business cycles to how to advance global trade.

This was a systemic shift in world culture, which requires closer examination of the thinkers who symbolized its values. Humanity was being steered away from poverty that causes war and famine into the open arms of prosperity, which is the cornerstone for peace, independence, and self-reliance. This was considered the final frontier where we conquer all our past shortcomings as a human race and can finally redeem ourselves. Everyone and every nation wanted a piece of this action and they all looked to the West to lead them to the new Promised Land. More specifically they looked to the United States because its economy has consistently shown the most resilience in creating and utilizing innovation and succeeded more than any other advanced nation in elevating the standards of living of its people. Now in charge of the money that fueled this economic miracle was the overly pragmatic Dr. Greenspan.

From the perspective of the theories of memenomics Dr. Greenspan's policies have had the most profound effect on human emergence since the dawn of the Industrial Age. The collapse of communism and the heavy burden of socialist ideologies made capitalism the de facto champion of humanity's cause to evolve to higher levels of existence. At no time in modern history have so many cultural groupings moved up the prosperity ladder as had occurred during his reign as the most important central banker in the world. This resulting upward shift in global economics has spun off many changes in global values and will continue to have profound long-term political and economic effects.

ENVIRONMENT SHAPING IDEOLOGY

With the global financial markets nearing the edge of collapse in 2008, the very nature of capitalism, when viewed by its most influential champion, had been dealt a crushing blow. For this reason, a closer examination of the forces and the belief systems that shaped the ideology of the most powerful man in capitalism is worthy of closer examination. Since memenomics views economic evolution from a perspective that integrates individual and cultural levels of development, it is essential that every person of significance is looked upon through a prism economists rarely consider in their field of study: the value-systems approach that uncovers the forces that motivate behaviors which shape individual ideologies and influence cultures. A wider explanation of the emerging field of value systems will follow in the next chapter. However, it is important to lay the ground for a paradigm shift about the premise of the theoretical framework of memenomics, and it is this: in the final analysis of any economic crisis it is the values and the belief systems of policy makers and individuals in power that must be understood in light of where the stages of cultural development are. This is essential in order to unblock the underlying causes of the crisis and design for sustainable economic policies.

To understand how a person thinks, we must understand both the individual and the cultural dynamics that shaped that person's way of thinking. To understand how one person can influence culture at such a profound level, a closer examination of the memetic structures within that culture needs to take place. While the debate among anthropologists goes on about which influence comes first, as the main forces that shaped Dr. Greenspan's life and career are chronicled we see that the two forces are woven into an intricate dance. How and why these belief systems emerge in individuals and culture is the focus of the studies of value-systems. When reframing our modern-day economic history through the prism of value systems, we come to the realization that the things that Dr. Greenspan advocated were all steps along the way toward a higher expression of socio-economic values, a trajectory that reflects economic evolution. At the time of his rise to power, his thinking was the best the system had to offer as it was transitioning out of an outdated mode of expression into a new and exciting phase of economic development.

So, how were Dr. Greenspan's individual values and belief systems shaped? In his autobiographical book *The Age of Turbulence* several mentors stand out in Dr. Greenspan's life as the most significant people who would shape his way of thinking. Not much attention has been given to the role or the ideologies that these people represented in Dr. Greenspan's success, but together they represent a powerful platform from which his ideas gained global prominence. With the benefit of hindsight, we're able to see that the beliefs of these mentors and the values they were advocating would be come to shape economic culture in decades to come. The first person to have a profound influence on Dr. Greenspan's beliefs was his own father. Herbert Greenspan was a stockbroker on Wall Street in the 1930s when his worldview began to shape the son's future in many ways. The Greenspans were divorced when their son was two years old. "Growing up without a dad left a big hole in my life," says Dr. Greenspan.[9] He recalls that his happiest childhood moments were the ones he spent visiting his father on Wall Street and accompanying him on business trips. In 1935 when the son was nine years old, the father authored a book entitled *"Recovery Ahead"* and dedicated it to his son. According to Dr. Greenspan the book accurately predicted the end of the Great Depression. It bore the following inscription:

> *To my son Alan: May this my initial effort with constant thought of you branch out into an endless chain of similar efforts so that at your maturity you may look back and endeavor to interpret the reasoning behind these logical forecasts and begin a like work of your own.—Your Dad.*[10]

Years of research in the field of developmental psychology support the claim that crucial areas in the brain that are responsible for planning, reasoning, social judgment, and ethical decision-making are developed during middle childhood. By the age of nine it can be assumed that these ideas of his father formed the foundation of Dr. Alan Greenspan's thinking and helped to inform his logical reasoning about the movements in stock markets.

The second person to influence Greenspan's thinking was the father of capitalism himself, Adam Smith. Like many great admirers of the moral philosophy of self-reliance and the virtues of capitalism, it is known that Alan Greenspan idolized the teachings of Adam Smith. With the birth of the Industrial Age and the Enlightenment philosophers came a new way of thinking about individual responsibility and how it can play a role in free markets. Greenspan repeatedly quoted Adam Smith on the virtues of self-interest, but left out many of the moral hazards that Smith warned of in such pursuit. Much of Smith's teachings in one of his earlier works provided the new moral base for the early stages of the Industrial Revolution and the Enlightenment philosophy. As capitalism evolved over two and half centuries, Smith never anticipated that complex market forces would cause the replacement of moral sentiments about the virtues of independence and self-reliance, that are good for individual economic progress, with the pursuit of self-interest. Advocates of laissez-faire capitalism like Greenspan would paint only a partial image of what the moral philosopher and the father of capitalism intended in the pursuit of creating wealth.

Harvard Economist Joseph Schumpeter was another influential thinker who profoundly shaped Dr. Greenspan's belief system during adulthood. Much of our economic policies that enabled tens of thousands of companies to close manufacturing facilities and move overseas were based on some of Schumpeter's economic theories. Dr. Greenspan described him as someone who provided a "profound appreciation of the central dynamic of capitalism."[11] Schumpeter's 1942 book *Capitalism, Socialism and Democracy* makes the case for the reinvention and re-coining of the Marxist term "Creative Destruction" through the prism of the Anglo-Saxon economic model.

The premise of Schumpeter's theory is that in a free market economy, entrepreneurs with technical know-how will always introduce innovation that is disruptive to the existing economic model, but which will improve productivity and that in itself will sustain economic growth.[12] As capitalist values evolved Creative Destruction evolved to become synonymous with innovation and progress. The motto for capitalism in following years became "innovate or die." It became the banner under which many industries maintained their competitive edge as the term made its way into every corporate board room and business school that took its teachings seriously. As we will learn, the value systems that create innovation and most innovative thought processes and ideas, including those about economic theory, are born out of a utopian ideal that starts with a noble purpose. It is when the exploitative element of our culture reinterprets the intended use of that innovation through a different prism of values that it turns into a weapon against its creators.

During Greenspan's reign at the Fed, Creative Destruction became the primary justification for the disappearance of the manufacturing base in the United States. Innovation in technology replaced the American worker with a machine, yet neither the government nor the Fed had a declared commitment to create new jobs to replace the ones that were lost due to this phenomenon. Innovation came to symbolize the inevitable march of progress that drove up productivity with increasing lower human input.

Arthur F. Burns was another influential figure that shaped Dr. Greenspan's belief system. He describes him as one of two people who've had the greatest impact on his life. Professor Burns was Dr. Greenspan's adviser when he was in graduate school at Columbia and Burns preceded him to the highest positions economists can attain in government. He was the head of the Council of Economic Advisors for President Eisenhower and later became the Chairman of the Fed for Presidents Nixon, Ford, and Carter. He is a person of interest because of his groundbreaking work on business cycles, which in later years was further developed by Dr. Greenspan and became an indispensable tool in setting policies at the Fed. Taming the business cycle is the greatest heroic act an economist can achieve.

Periods of economic prosperity uninterrupted by recessions are every business owner's dream. As we will see, Fed policies that accommodated this dream under Dr. Greenspan were just postponing the inevitable and creating a debt-based culture that gave the impression of an always-up business cycle, but made innovation less relevant in the long term. How accurate is a measure of business activity if that activity is debt-based and with much less equity than Burns' original work envisioned? By reframing economic issues through the prism of value systems we will repeatedly see how economic concepts must account for the different values and belief systems in individuals, corporations, and entire cultures in order to design sustainable economic policies.

According to Dr. Greenspan's autobiography, none of the people mentioned so far had as much influence on his thinking as did Ayn Rand, the founder of her philosophy of Objectivism. He describes her as someone who brought him out of his shell as a closed-up mathematician in his twenties into a world of enlightened self-interest.[13] Rand was a Russian émigré who despised communism and everything that had to do with central planning. A lover of intellectual discourse, she formed a school of followers in the 1950s and 1960s in New York City, of which Dr. Greenspan was a frequent visitor. No other mentor in his public life was as prominent as Rand. In the Oval Office, when he was sworn in by President Ford as Chairman of the Council of Economic Advisors, Dr. Greenspan was flanked by two important women in his life, the one who gave him birth and the one who birthed her ideologies through him that in years to come would shape the world in unimaginable ways. They remained close friends until the day she died.

THE LONG SHADOW OF OBJECTIVISM

Ayn Rand summarized her Objectivism philosophy as follows:

1. **Reality** exists as an objective absolute—facts are facts, independent of man's feelings, wishes, hopes, or fears.

2. **Reason** (the faculty which identifies and integrates the material provided by man's senses) is man's only means of perceiving reality, his only source of knowledge, his only guide to action, and his basic means of survival.

3. **Man**—every man—is an end in himself, not the means to the ends of others. He must exist for his own sake, neither sacrificing himself to others nor sacrificing others to himself. The pursuit of his own rational self-interest and of his own happiness is the highest moral purpose of his life.

4. **The ideal political-economic system** is *laissez-faire* capitalism. It is a system where men deal with one another, not as victims and executioners, nor as masters and slaves, but as *traders*, by free, voluntary exchange to mutual benefit. It is a system where no man may obtain any values from others by resorting to physical force, and *no man may initiate the use of physical force against others*. The government acts only as a policeman that protects man's rights; it uses physical force only in retaliation and only against those who initiate its use, such as criminals or foreign invaders. In a system of full capitalism, there should be (but, historically, has not yet been) a complete separation of state and economics, in the same way and for the same reasons as the separation of state and church.[14]

Much debate still goes on about the very nature of a philosophy that places individual self-interest over all else and champions laissez-faire capitalism as the highest form of social order. We can look at the extent to which its teachings were translated into ideologies that informed Fed policies under Dr. Greenspan's leadership. For example, Objectivists view any interference by government into its citizens' lives, including the imposition of taxes, as immoral. How much of these views were subtly woven into policy decisions that affected the collective values and behaviors on a large scale? When emphasis is placed on the freedom of the individual in a laissez-faire marketplace and that individual lacks the capacities to be fully responsible as prescribed for by the ideology, what stops that individual from exploiting others with less knowledge of that marketplace, and, in the absolute sense, where do the exploited go to act in their own best interest?

If the highest form of human consciousness is to observe reality as absolute and objective, the achievement of this very observation is limited to that individual's level of cognition his or her faculties can bare. Reason, as described by Rand, is man's only way of perceiving reality, but do people with different capacities and from different cultures around the world process reason in the same way, through the same channels of rationality and points of reference that are unique to the American experience, and for the same reasons that Rand aspires to in her teachings? This philosophy, as it applied strictly to varying belief systems, had the potential to repress as many lives as did other philosophies and governing systems that championed either communism or socialism. Although Objectivism satisfied Dr. Greenspan's intellectual curiosities, very few people holding power either in government or in industry in the United States and around the world could fully understand its teachings. Because of its very nature towards unfettered freedom to pursue self-interest, no one and no culture could control the outcome of a world when in the maddening pursuit of self-interest. These very ideals of Objectivism in the hands of non-philosophers can easily turn to weapons that create havoc and set back the progress of human emergence for decades to come.

THE HERO WHO SAVED AMERICA

Rand's most successful novel is entitled *Atlas Shrugged*, and it has direct relevance to how Dr. Greenspan might have perceived Rand's presence by his side at the White House when he was sworn by President Ford as chief economist. The novel was published in 1957 and has seen considerable resurgence in its popularity since the onset of the recession of 2008. In it Rand tells the story of a US economy crumbling under the weight of crushing government interventions and regulations. As conditions get worse, Washington, blaming greed and the free market, responds with more controls that only deepen the crisis. The depiction portrays a society ruled by oppressive government bureaucrats and a culture that embraces crippling mediocrity and egalitarianism, which Rand associates with socialist ideals. In the novel the industrialists of America are represented through the collective metaphorical archetype of Atlas, the Greek god who's holding up the sky. The hero of the story, John Galt, convinces Atlas to "shrug," by refusing to make available the productive genius of America to its parasitic government. As industrialists heed Galt's call, they strike and disappear, one after the other. An observer named Dagny Taggart starts the arduous search to answer the question "who is John Galt?" With the collapse of the nation and its government all but certain, Galt emerges as the hero who reconstructs a society that celebrates individual achievement and enlightened self-interest, delivering a long speech seventy pages in length, which served to explain the novel's theme and Rand's philosophy of Objectivism.

Conditions in the United States in 1974 weren't much different than those during Galt's days. Inflation, the biggest threat to capitalism, was running at an all-time high of 11 percent, labor unions were choking any meaningful industrial output, and the US stock market was in sharp decline due to the Arab oil embargo and had lost almost 50 percent of its value in two years.[15] The income tax surcharge, which was imposed on the taxpayer to finance the Vietnam War, had taken its toll. Add to these inauspicious circumstances the specter of the Watergate scandal and one of the darkest shadows in modern US history was cast on Washington. The American people were desperately seeking change. All their anger and frustration turned to a tainted presidency and Nixon became the focus of a mob that had no other place to turn. Nixon's resignation was seen as a turning point for the nation and its economy, but the seeds for real change in economic policy were being planted behind the scenes. President Ford needed a hero who would restore credibility to the American economy, and at the urging of his mentor Arthur F. Burns, who was the Fed Chairman at the time, Alan Greenspan accepted the nomination to the position of chairman of the Council of Economic Advisors.

This was the beginning of what would become a monumental shift in economic policy setting. Greenspan's private consulting firm had for years been pioneering state-of-the- art econometric models for the private sector. Now it was time to bring these models along with the Greenspan ideology to a morally bankrupt and out of control government that was at the edge of collapse and was looking to reinvent itself. This was the beginning of a cycle that championed the values of strategic enterprise, the first bookend to an era that was like no other.

The reappearance of John Galt symbolized the return of a hero and so did Alan Greenspan's appearance in Washington. Life followed art in perfect form; Dagny Taggart witnessed the return of unfettered capitalism in Galt just as Ayn Rand did standing next to the man who would place her ideologies into practice at the highest levels. In earlier years, when a *New York Times* book reviewer criticized *Atlas Shrugged* as a book written out of hate, Greenspan defended Rand and the premise of the book with the following rebuttal: "*Atlas Shrugged* is a celebration of life and happiness. Justice is unrelenting. Creative individuals and undeviating purpose and rationality achieve joy and fulfillment. Parasites who persistently avoid either purpose or reason perish as they should." [16]

At the swearing-in ceremony in the Ford Whitehouse the presence of Rand by Dr. Greenspan's side was tacit, but the symbolism of this act spoke louder than words of explanation for her presence for those familiar with her views. John Galt has taken the reins of an economy that has been stuck in antiquated politics and was now being brought into a new and pioneering era of "facilitator of prosperity" through enlightened self-interest and an ideology that believed a government rule of capitalism was immoral. Greenspan's only absence from top power positions was during the Carter Administration. That absence only strengthened the need for his return as the man who would be the true savior of capitalism. Carter believed in policies that were vastly different than the ones that Ford and Greenspan believed. In an effort to control inflation, Carter tightened the money supply and raised interest rates to over 21 percent, which turned his economic policies into complete failure. A disgruntled America voted in Ronald Reagan, who in his inaugural speech summoned Rand's views by proclaiming "government is not the solution to our problem; government is the problem . . . " The alignment of ideologies had finally been completed and America was on her way to the longest era of prosperity in its history.

The Greenspan ideology represented a philosophy that became the bookend to a phase of a value system that symbolized both the Enlightenment philosophies and the consciousness levels of the Industrial Age in the United States and around the world. Most economists agreed that something had to be done about the heavy-handedness of government regulation in the 1970s. The value system representing industry evolves much faster than our laws do. By the time the Reagan Administration took power, this value system was close to being paralyzed by outdated regulations, and a new policy that limited the role of government was exactly what the US economy needed. Since the first Reagan Administration the US economy has gone through some of the most profound changes in its history. The 1980s witnessed the loss of manufacturing and the rise of the post-industrial professional class, which paved the way to what logically became the next phase of progress. By the 1990s an increasingly higher percentage of our economic output was being determined by the highly venerated field of "financial innovation" about which the Fed Chairman had considerable knowledge.

As Financial Facilitator-in-Chief Dr. Greenspan understood the role money played in keeping economies moving. Capital markets are the lifelines of economic activity just like oxygen is to the very survival of all life forms. Financial innovation started gaining popularity as it was being touted by the few people who understood it as the tool that will save all those who were left behind—from poor farmers to poor undeveloped countries. Creation of derivatives and other complex financial instruments replaced the goal of creation of jobs that contribute to productive and measurable economic activity. Year after year Dr. Greenspan appeared on Capitol Hill and quelled any fear the American people had about the need to regulate this new and innovative banking system. Congress, not wanting to put sticks in the wheel of a roaring economy, always accepted the Maestro's complex explanations without ever fully understanding their meaning. But, as often is the case with innovation, as it matures the exploitive element of our society uses the technology for purposes other than the ones it was initially created for.

After Wall Street took charge of the global financial markets, the Fed Chairman was becoming helpless about navigating a ship that had become unruly in the rough seas of uncharted territory. During the first decade of the new millennium, the understanding of the term "enlightened self-interest" disappeared from the conscious awareness of anyone seeking the riches of capitalism. Instant gratification became the new banner for prosperity and its appetite was insatiable. The very ship of global capitalism was bankrolling a ravenous beast without any regard to future consequences of its actions. As the Fed Chairman's last term drew to a close, this ship had veered on to a disturbing course and was headed for sure disaster.

THE FINAL CURTAIN

The happy ending of *Atlas Shrugged* was not to be replicated in American history. John Galt had inspired the industrialist of America to create a utopian society that rose from the ashes of one burdened by a pillaging government. The industrialists of America rose to the occasion to rebuild an economy weighed down by disastrous economic policies and the social unrest of the 1970s. Reagan announced the beginning of this new era of prosperity by firing over 11,000 striking federal employees and continuing on with the ideology that outsourced Main Street jobs away from the American worker. As the pursuit of this utopian dream evolved over the years, availability of cheap money substituted for the need to create jobs and in the process removed much of the accountability that held together the ethos of America's Industrial Age society. As it all came crashing down in the fall of 2008, the United States Congress wanted to hear from the man who for decades had dissuaded their fears about America's new direction.

On October 23, 2008, the world was waiting for an important speech from the greatest wordsmith of our time. By then Dr. Greenspan had been out of office for two years. He was back in the private sector advising hedge funds on how to make billions by betting on the failure of the financial models he encouraged during his last decade at the Fed. This would be like no other testimony he has ever given. There would be no room for a single misplaced word. The supremacy of reason must be expressed at all times. Objective rationality of the human intellect must be maintained with every phrase. He knew he must reach into the highest levels of his consciousness to provide extraordinary answers in front of a Congress that was facing the wrath of its constituencies who had lost most, if not all, their net worth.

Congress never pried much into the maestro's testimony before, but this time things were different. He had based his entire career on a philosophy of no government interference, but now it was that very same government that was tasked with preventing the entire global economy from unmitigated collapse and disaster. Although his mentors had long been gone, their thinking had formed ideological institutions that took on a life of their own in government and in industry all over the world. If John Galt had covered this stage of laissez-faire capitalism in his speech, the maestro would surely have had a hint of what to say. But like all of our heroes the maestro was fearless. He knew he was the best orator to step foot on Capitol Hill in recent history. His creative genius must have roamed around the use of words to describe the current financial crisis, such as "rare" and a "once in a hundred-year event." Yes, now he was on to something he could say. Objectivism had yet again enabled him to project the thin layer of reason and objective rationalism into a world of extreme chaos and complexity. Perfectly logical references to past speeches could fill days if not weeks of testimony and debate that would defray any blame on past policy decisions. Those were the same decisions that for decades encouraged America's departure from its glorious industrial past to venture into a less certain future of the post-industrial testing grounds of financial innovation.

One must wonder during his many weeks of reflection before this day if the maestro ever thought of graciously accepting any of the blame for what was happening. Surely such inquiry would have opened him up to a far deeper layer of understanding human nature than the linear simplistic view seen through the lenses of intellectual discourse and accompanied by a plethora of metrics. Surely by now he would have known that enlightened self-interest was greatly misinterpreted by the varying value systems around the world. To think in these terms would have required a clear departure from existing logical patterns of thought and the maestro was not ready for that.

As he testified, the innocuous logic of his prepared statement, like all the ones before it, was impregnable. It included phrases about the market condition like a "once-in-a-century event" and "a severe correction" and a whole array of adjectives that would have made his friend Ayn Rand very proud. However, this time his remarks would not get him the praise he was accustomed to from years past. At the time of the recital of his speech the maestro had not realized that he had fallen out of favor with the crowd that loved him the most. Many Americans had not seen the value of their assets disappear so quickly and so deeply in decades, and they were angry. This was an election year and this disaster needed to be blamed on someone.

Just as in 1974 when the country was looking for answers to its misery and targeted Nixon as the scapegoat, several Congressmen on that October day were desperately looking for their next Nixon on whom to blame the collapsing economy and save face with the voters. The maestro's speech was perfectly logical, but logic would not be his ally on that day. At the end of the speech, Congressman Henry Waxman of California asked the maestro if he accepted any responsibility for any part of the impending economic disaster. Accusations of this magnitude had never before been leveled at Dr. Greenspan during his career. This was not a specific policy question nor was it a part of a scripted Q&A session. Acceptance of blame would have disastrous consequences for the very pillars of capitalism. Acknowledgement of fault in whole or in part would confirm the speculation around the world of the fall of America as an economic superpower.

As hard as he tried to keep his composure with Congressman Waxman's prodding, emotions seeped into his rational mind and with earnestness in his voice never seen before in public, Dr. Greenspan retorted with the following liberating response: "Those of us who have looked to the self-interest of lending institutions to protect shareholder's equity—myself especially—are in a state of shocked disbelief." As the relentless questioning turned to his views on free market ideologies he replied: "I have found a flaw. I don't know how significant or permanent it is. But I have been very distressed by that fact." At this juncture the Congressman knew there would be no room offered for intellectual hyperbolae as he pressed for a further simplification of the answer. "In other words, you found that your view of the world, your ideology, was not right, it was not working," Waxman countered. "Absolutely, precisely," the former chairman replied. "You know, that's precisely the reason I was shocked, because I have been going for 40 years or more with very considerable evidence that it was working exceptionally well."[17]

With these acquiescent words, the curtain closed on the most pragmatic leader of laissez-faire capitalism and on an era that has fascinated many individuals and every government around the world. October 23, 2008, was the symbolic end of a belief system that has informed the values of a global economy and will be the subject of much discourse in upcoming chapters. Capitalism had reached its greatest heights in the West. It had lifted the lives of millions out of poverty the world over. Now a flaw in its latest incarnation—financial innovation—had led to its unmitigated collapse. By unburdening himself with the truth, Dr. Greenspan had left all advanced economies around the world rudderless in the long and painful search for answers that might never come.

One of the harshest criticisms of the maestro came in a 2010 book by author Frederick Sheehan, in which he described in detail how government policies during Greenspan's tenure have shifted the distribution of wealth from Main Street to Wall Street. Below is Sheehan's summary of Greenspan's time at the Fed:

> Alan Greenspan's 18-year stint as head of the Federal Reserve Bank witnessed some of the most massive upward redistributions of wealth in our nation's history. It's now clear that his policies contributed greatly to the transformation of Wall Street from an engine that financed American business to a business-destroying machine—and that Greenspan abetted the hollowing out of the U.S. economy by giving Wall Street and Washington everything they could possibly want.[18]

The choice to chronicle Dr. Greenspan's policies and ideologies is without any intention of harm or malice, but to explain our circumstances, as well as to pay tribute to the courage that he had shown in taking capitalism through uncharted waters. It can be seen through the prism of value systems with the Age of Enlightenment that started with the dawn of the Industrial Age and scientific discovery and was an expression of just one system of human emergence. Dr. Greenspan was the last prominent son of that system that has gotten the entire Western world asking if there's something better that lies beyond individual success and prosperity. The economic problems we're witnessing in the world today are the prerequisite birth pangs of that new system that will include parts of those values, but they will no longer run our lives.

Once the values of this next system are fully manifested we will look back at our current expression of values with encompassing maturity and a healthy sense of self-effacement. Many political and economic policies from our culture will be reexamined through the prism of ^vMEMEs in order to give the reader a fuller picture of how values emerge and why. Much of the Fed's policies today under the leadership of Ben Bernanke remain subject to heavy criticism, but only when his actions are reframed through the understanding of how memenomic cycles work and how complex systems rise and fall, does one get a better picture of what is next. While Bernanke continues to preside over the slow decay of the current expression of capitalism, Greenspan, in the history of human emergence, will undoubtedly be recognized as a pioneering figure in Central Banking and monetary policy. Like many Americans before him, he has a true spirit of a pioneer without which the free enterprise system would have remained benign and uninteresting.

The Value-System Paradigm of the Economy

Classic economic theory, based as it is on an inadequate theory of human motivation, could be revolutionized by accepting the reality of higher human needs, including the impulse to self-actualization and the love for the highest values.[19]

—ABRAHAM MASLOW

The field of economics is as old as modern humanity itself. Historically, economic thought has always played an important role in determining political views of a culture. From Greco-Roman days up until the fall of the iron curtain the debate was always about which views and philosophies best serve the lives of human beings. As the Cold War started to wind down, Marxist views on economic policy were dealt an ideological setback as the economies of Russia and Eastern Europe collapsed with the fall of communism. Political economic thinking became the clear champion of capitalism, and the economists who were proficient in the applications of capitalism became indispensable in spreading its tools and values globally. Everything that championed the virtues of free markets, from large corporations, banks, and think tanks to former communist governments looking to privatize their arcane infrastructure, all held the professions of economics in high regard. For decades this discipline successfully quantified everything that kept the global economy moving, from the seemingly insurmountable task of determining global resource allocation down to forecasting consumer spending. Economists in the employment of the IMF and World Bank could tell the poorest countries in the world precisely what they needed to do in order to move their economies in the right direction. Vast arrays of mathematical models were created by practitioners in this discipline to forecast anything and everything that had to do with creating prosperity.

Over the years, and through trial and error, these economic models were perfected to within very narrow ranges of acceptance. These models ranged from the sophisticated and arduous analysis that determines the unemployment figures to very complex algorithms that forecast the relationship between interest rates and consumer spending. As the profession moved from the ubiquitous and subjective area of social science to the realm of statistical and mathematical data gathering, it attracted the scientific mindset that cared more about perfecting the empirical data than promoting the overall social welfare. If variables like food and energy prices were too wild to tame, they were simply dropped from the CPI calculation.[20] This was done in the interest of preserving the elegance of mathematical models and making them more predictable. No one in this profession liked uncertainty. If they couldn't quantify a variable and tame it in order to fit it into a given forecast and preserve its accuracy, that variable was simply dropped. The more accurate and specialized economic forecasting became the more it got caught up in theoretical silos of academia and private and public advisory.

As trends shifted more in this direction, the assumptions at the consumer level always remained the same. Although substantial indicators of consumer spending were dropped from their models, economists never questioned their presumptions that consumers will always act in a responsible manner regardless of what pressures they were subjected to. The need to study consumer behavior was not necessary since spending was automatically limited by the level of credit available to the consumer by the banks. In the recessionary aftermath of financial crisis, the failure of these presumptions is forcing the field of economics to undergo one of the most profound changes since the dawn of the Industrial Age. The very nature of capitalism as a philosophy was shaken to its core. It took a crisis of historic proportions to bring a very powerful and elite group of thinkers down from their ivory towers to go on a journey of self-discovery and soul searching. The insights they're uncovering are turning out to be very simple; in an economy where consumer spending represents 70 percent of total output, closer attention should have been paid to the consumer.

Behavioral economics is one branch of economic studies that has quickly gained popularity since the financial crisis of 2008. Yale University's Robert Schiller, who accurately predicted the tech bubble in 2000, and more recently the housing bubble, is one of the most prominent economists in this area of specialty. The field became popular by adopting the insights and methods of psychology. Behavioral economics focuses on how and why humans fail to act as the rational, enlightened, self-interested beings.[21] In other words, it is the study of why consumers stray from the highest ideals of self-enlightenment that Adam Smith and Ayn Rand spoke of. Most economists work with models that assume consumers make rational decisions based on standardized input such as income, capacity for short-term and long-term debt, and general changes in consumption habits. This new paradigm shift studies why we spend impulsively for instant gratification while not thinking of the future, how we succumb to peer pressure to keep up with the Joneses, and why we overestimate our abilities and minimize the odds of bad things happening. This is the study of a set of behaviors that led to the subprime crisis.

But without looking at a more comprehensive view of the higher-order value systems and the mindsets that created loose credit policies, and how these interacted with other value systems, this will be just another linear endeavor that will be relegated to the dust bins at the dawn of the next recession. The 2008 financial crisis clearly demonstrated that participants in free markets do not all subscribe to the same standard of "enlightened self-interest." Ideologies born out of pure philosophical discourse do little to address the different motivations that people have and how they pursue their own self-interest through the prism of value systems and those of the culture they're doing business in.

The approach to understanding the failures of capitalism from the perspective of memenomics is different from any other approach because it takes into consideration the hierarchical nature of human development, and it attempts to reframe economic issues through a value-systems framework that has been over sixty years in the making. What is unique about this approach is that it focuses as much on the psychology of an evolving culture as it does on the psychology of the individual and takes into account the ever-changing nature of both the environment and the human. If Adam Smith and Ayn Rand were alive today, they would have seen the complete and utter invalidation of their work after their prodigal son tried to implement their views in a world that looked nothing like the one of their respective eras. If economists were less attached to the elegance of their mathematical models, and more concerned with the evolving psychology of both the culture and the individual as seen through the eyes of this emerging science, things would have turned out much differently.

A BRIEF HISTORY OF THE EMERGING SCIENCE OF VALUE SYSTEMS

The late developmental psychologist and Professor Emeritus at Union College, Clare W. Graves, first laid down the foundation of this new and revolutionary paradigm. His framework, which took a lifetime of research, is called the *Levels of Human Existence.* Graves was a contemporary of Abraham Maslow, who was one of the first psychologists to lay claim to theories of a hierarchical nature of human development in his theory of the "hierarchy of needs." Graves set out to verify his colleague's work by shaping a more unifying theory of human psychology. After he interviewed over a thousand of Maslow's students over the years, it became apparent to him that at the surface the *needs* in Maslow's model appear to relate to what Graves called "levels." Graves was convinced that the model didn't adequately express the dynamics of human nature, the process of emerging systems, or the open-endedness of the psychological development of a mature human being, which he concluded characterizes our species' development.[22] Much like what is needed today, Graves was a visionary thinker of his time who, instead of getting caught up in finding variations on existing psychological models and theories, set out in search of the reasons behind the shifting views of human nature. The answers to why so many things went wrong to bring the global economy to the edge of collapse in 2008 with an aftermath of continued recession, start looking vastly different once they're viewed through the richer hierarchical lens of Grave's perspective. Below is his own summary of the framework of how he perceived human nature:

> Briefly, what I am proposing is that the psychology of the mature human being is an unfolding, emergent, oscillating spiraling process marked by progressive subordination of older, lower-order systems to newer, higher-order systems as an individual's existential problems change. Each successive stage, wave, or level of existence is a state through which people pass on their way to other states of being. When the human is centralized in one state of existence, he or she has a psychology, which is particular to that stage. His or her feelings, motivations, ethics and values, biochemistry, degree of neurological activation, learning system, believe systems, conception of mental health, ideas as to what mental illness is and how it should be treated, conception of and preference for management, education, economics, and political theory and practice are all appropriate to that state.[23]

Of importance to the field of economics, and specifically memenomics, is that what Graves's research created was the very first model that not only looked at understanding the behaviors and the motivations of consumers, producers, and economic policymakers. He also proposed that all these forces shaping the marketplace, whether individuals, groups, or cultures, should be looked at from a more integral view that takes into account the biology (brain capacities), psychology (how do people think), and sociology (where do people live), and examine them within a context of an ever-evolving dynamic culture. Graves placed these dimensions into eight known hierarchical levels of existence called value systems that these human groupings can belong to. This formed the very first comprehensive psychological map of the human experience, which became known as the bio-psycho-social model on which much of today's integral philosophy is based.

Don Beck and Christopher Cowan were the two most instrumental individuals in bringing Grave's academic work to worldwide audiences. As a result of many years of working closely with him, they put his vast research to real life applications that confirmed his findings and further augmented it with their own research. Beck and Cowan put much of Graves's comprehensive work into their own theory called "Spiral Dynamics" and co-authored a groundbreaking book *Spiral Dynamics: Mastering Values, Leadership, and Change*. In following years, Beck continued to evolve Graves's work by collaborating with integral philosopher Ken Wilber on creating *Spiral Dynamics, Integral* that added the four quadrants theme of the integral philosophy framework to the model, resulting in the AQAL model (All Quadrants, All Levels), which has defined much of Wilber's work since. On the theoretical end, both Beck and Cowan continue to verify the vast amount of research Graves left behind through different applications and methodologies.

Beck compares Graves's concept of *psychological mapping* to the Human Genome Project. Since his earlier work with Graves, he has become the acknowledged leader in applying the principles of this emerging science of value systems to global hot spots. Over a ten-year period he played a major role in designing South Africa's transition from Apartheid. He co-authored a 1991 book entitled *The Crucible: Forging South Africa's Future* that lays out the importance of understanding the macro memetics of cultures in order to design effective political and economic policies.

In more recent years Beck's work has influenced decision makers in Europe, South America, and the Middle East, including 10 Downing Street and the reshaping of the Icelandic government after the financial crisis, and empowering the leaders of Palestine to build a viable, self-reliant, and peaceful state. For the first time psychology on the large scale is beginning to replace arcane and linear ways of looking at what motivates groups and whole cultures. It is this paradigm shift of seeing the world through the stratified lenses of value systems as presented by the Beck/Graves framework that defines the principles of memenomics.

Today, Beck is well into his 70s and is working on yet another evolution of the theory currently called *The Master Code*. This influential research into the nature of human values continues to unfold through many third-generation Gravesians who've been trained all throughout the world. Today there are over fifteen Centers for Human Emergence that dot the globe from Chile to the Middle East and Russia and they all use the Graves/Beck methodologies to advance the understanding of human nature.

SPIRAL DYNAMICS: THE THEORY THAT EXPLAINS
THE LEVELS OF EXISTENCE

Spiral Dynamics is a developmental model that provides a new way of framing and understanding the forces of human interactions and behaviors. It describes stages of development and works on the individual, organization, and culture.[24] Beck and Cowan took Graves's eight levels of human existence and fashioned them into eight value systems called ᵛMEMEs. As described in the introduction of the book, the word "meme," which rhymes with gene, was first coined by British scientist and evolutionary biologist Richard Dawkins. He described it as a unit of cultural information that is capable of self-replication and uses the human mind as a host. It could be compared to social, cultural, and psychological DNA that contains behavioral traits passed from one generation to the next. The Beatles were a meme. The Tea Party is a meme. *The Daily Show* with Jon Stewart is a meme. Oprah Winfrey is a meme and so is the Occupy Movement. To a lesser-known extent, Wall Street is a meme, and so is the banking sector. Memes form general groupings of larger meme categories that are unique to every culture. These general meme categories, such as music, philosophy, religion, architecture, literature, economics, language, psychology, and so on, are bonds that glue together social systems. In value systems studies, they are called ᵛMEME attractors or General Category Memes (ᴳMEMES). When they come together in a cohesive package of thought, they form ᵛMEMEs, or value-system memes that come to define individuals and cultures.[25]

ᵛMEMEs, or value-systems memes begin to shape how individuals, organizations, and cultures think. Both Spiral Dynamics and the Graves framework have identified several levels of value systems. Graves called them levels of existence while Spiral Dynamics called them ᵛMEMEs. Within the scope of Spiral Dynamics, the Graves framework, and the memenomics framework, the term "value systems" refers to values as a set of assumptions about the world that indicate what is important. For example, they determine how time is spent, or—more relevant to this discussion—what money, wealth, and affluence mean to the different level ᵛMEMEs. On a cultural level, these values systems have a great impact on what is important to a society, how resources are allocated and distributed, and how decisions are made. In this context, values and value systems determine almost every aspect of life.

Because humans and human societies are adaptable, new memes evolve as biological, psychological, and social conditions change, allowing for the emergence of new value systems. The evolutionary aspect of this theory lies in the emphasis that it places on the changes in "life conditions." This is what makes the Spiral Dynamics and the Graves framework approach for change

^GMEME: THE ^VMEME ATTRACTOR

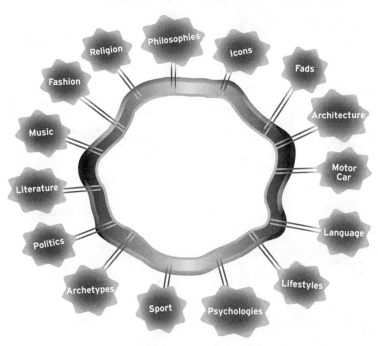

*Each ^VMEME is an organizing principle, center of gravity, geometric fractal, self-replicating force, and magnetic field that attracts content-rich little ^GMEMEs.

Adapted from *Spiral Dynamics* by Beck and Cowan and used here with permission

unique, adaptable, and transformational by nature. By taking into account the ever-changing nature of human needs and values and placing that into a design scheme for solutions, one can create a sustainable-change model that anticipates change as it happens. Most change models today address surface manifestations and behaviors and pay little attention to real and structural change that a system needs. In most cases these changes are the fine-tuning of a healthy system. The change inches the system forward without rocking the boat. As we have seen in the current political debate, culture is in a completely different stage of development today, and issues need to be considered at a far deeper level than we're used to. By examining changes in "life conditions," spiral dynamics as well as the memenomics framework penetrate through five layers of value systems in order to provide answers that inform a lasting and sustainable change.

THE SPIRAL OF DEVELOPMENT

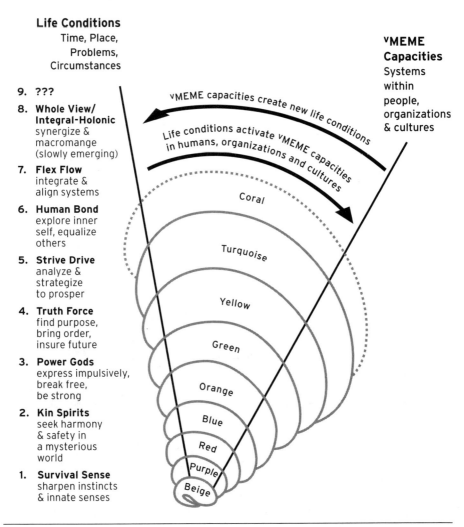

Life Conditions
Time, Place, Problems, Circumstances

ᵛMEME Capacities
Systems within people, organizations & cultures

9. ???
8. **Whole View/ Integral-Holonic**
   synergize & macromange (slowly emerging)
7. **Flex Flow**
   integrate & align systems
6. **Human Bond**
   explore inner self, equalize others
5. **Strive Drive**
   analyze & strategize to prosper
4. **Truth Force**
   find purpose, bring order, insure future
3. **Power Gods**
   express impulsively, break free, be strong
2. **Kin Spirits**
   seek harmony & safety in a mysterious world
1. **Survival Sense**
   sharpen instincts & innate senses

ᵛMEME capacities create new life conditions

Life conditions activate ᵛMEME capacities in humans, organizations and cultures

Coral

Turquoise

Yellow

Green

Orange

Blue

Red

Purple

Beige

Adapted from *Spiral Dynamics* by Beck and Cowan and used here with permission

Based on Graves's research and as further reinforced by Beck and Cowan's real-life applications, the eight known ᵛMEMEs fall into two alternating types. One type is individualistic and expressive, where individuals break away from the group, creatively break new ground, and take actions that are considered individualistic and expressive. The other type, which alternates with the individualistic and expressive value systems, is group-oriented and sacrificial.[26] Actions of this type are based on group needs where individuals are asked to sacrifice for the good of the group. With the passage of time, existential problems arise within each value system that can no longer be solved at the current level. This is true with both the individualistic and the group type. The excess pressure and energy created by the value system's inability to solve its problems eventually leads to the emergence of the next level, spiraling upwards and alternating between each type. Both humans and cultures tend to resonate to one type over the other. Since no stages can be skipped, a system with preference for one type makes its way through the alternating type at a faster pace. Capitalism by its very nature is an individualistic ᵛMEMEs system, while a concept like socialism is a collective ᵛMEMEs system.

Even with this brief description of the emerging science of value systems so far, one can begin to see how most of the solutions that our government came up with to save our economy have done little to put us back on the road to a sustainable recovery. Because of the progressive nature of human values, tools from an old value system become obsolete in the face of rapid change without policy makers ever knowing the consequences of their continued use. The myriad of solutions that were proven successful in the past only create dissonance and polarization in the present, as the government's bailout did after the financial crisis. Many experts in the United States believe that an economic collapse is still possible, and there is a common belief among the general population that prosperity will not return to pre-crisis levels for decades. The dysfunction and the division that we are seeing across wide swathes of our culture today seem to be irreconcilable. We are at that stage where the tools to fix our problems can no longer come from the same value system that created them. According to the theory of spiral dynamics, the dissonance the United States is going through today—as painful as it is—is a natural evolutionary process that will propel us out of the current expression of our values system and lay down the foundation for a new and higher-order system from which we can find solutions that will make our current problems a thing of the past.

THE EIGHT LEVELS OF EXISTENCE

In their 1996 book *Spiral Dynamics*, Beck and Cowan assign a color to each value system according to its numbered level in the flow within the spiral. The color chosen to correspond to the system or level number has no particular meaning or historic relevance other than to distinguish the placement of each value system within the levels of human development. The colors and numbered levels for each ᵛMEME are used interchangeably in the discussion of each particular value system. The ᵛMEMEs form a spiral with increasing cultural and human complexity. Each group of six levels form a tier. At this point in time the theoretical framework has identified eight known levels of existence. The "first tier" contains the first six that Graves called the "subsistence levels," and there are only two identified levels of human existence in the "second tier," which he called "the levels of being."[27]

To extend their thinking, it can be seen that within each level a description of the economic system that existed when that ᵛMEME first emerged and dominated the culture can be provided. Since the world continues to emerge at different stages and at different levels, emerging cultures borrow from other value systems to help them achieve their dreams of economic prosperity. For that reason, present day examples of dominant vMEMEs will be given in order to paint a fuller picture of the contemporary manifestation of value systems that make up a memetic profile of an economy of a particular country or region.

THE DOUBLE-HELIX NATURE OF THE FRAMEWORK

Although it might not seem so to the casual observer today, in the midst of the economic dysfunction that Western cultures are going through, humanity is in a search for higher values. According to the Graves/Spiral Dynamics framework, this has always been the pattern in cultural emergence and always will be. The driving force behind these assumptions is the "double helix" nature of the framework uncovered by years of research on the interactions between what Beck calls our internal states and our external worlds. The two sides of the double helix model are described as follows:

1. **Humans possess the capacities to create ᵛMEMEs:**
   Humans possess within themselves the capacity to exist at different levels of psychological development that reflect different perspectives on what the world is like and the different complexities that exist in it.[28] This is what Graves referred to as the different levels of our neurological equipment that, when activated can create a "new brain system" capable of handling the complexities that life throws our way. I've heard Beck refer to this unique neurological phenomenon as a software system with latent upgrades just waiting to be turned on. There are three conditions that determine the level of manifestation of these new brain systems: The brain's capacity to house the number of these systems, a set of instructions that are likely encoded in our DNA, and the net effects of the nature vs.

nurture dynamic that trigger brain capacities in response to environmental challenges.

2. **Life Conditions awaken ᵛMEMEs:** The importance of *life conditions* in this model cannot be understated. It is what provides the framework with the continuous adaptability aspect that defines the very nature of human and cultural evolution. It is the interaction between our internal states and our external worlds that needs to be understood in order to provide robust solutions to the problems that face the world today. There are four important aspects to *life conditions* that determine the ᵛMemetic patterns of cultural emergence: Time, Place, Problems, and Circumstances.[29]

   a. **Time:** This is the location along the overall line of human development. In any given Western community today, one finds different people whose thinking is rooted in very different eras living alongside each other. Different people in their lives develop their own bundle of ᵛMEMEs designed to fit the Time of the era they live in. While in the West, we view the 1940s completely differently from the 1960s; the times in traditional cultures have remained extraordinarily unchanged for generations. Time plays a crucial role in defining *life conditions* in the historic analysis of the different economic cycle we've been through. It is economic policies that become increasingly misaligned with the Times that people live in that have been the primary cause of failure of many economic systems.

   b. **Place:** This is the geographical location and physical conditions under which individuals and groups live. Where we live has direct impact on the levels of capacities within the brain that can be activated. External stimulation affects an urban dweller in a far different way than it does a suburban dweller and is still vastly different from the dweller of the rain forest or desert. Place effects the air we breath, the food we eat, and the architecture of the dwellings we design to work in and inhabit.

   c. **Problems:** These are the human challenges presented in terms of needs, priorities, concerns, and requirements for a particular individual, group or culture that are common at every level of existence. Much of Maslow's hierarchy of needs framework addresses these aspects of life conditions, which involve survival, safety, belonging, and so on. It was Graves who uncovered that when problems overwhelm the existing coping mechanisms they trigger new systems in the brain that can more accurately perceive the problem and deal with it appropriately.[30]

d. **Circumstances:** These are the cultural placements within hierarchies of power, status, and influence. One's socio-economic class, level of education, race, gender, and family lineage play a crucial role in defining this element of *life conditions*. It acts like a set of blinders that prevent an individual centered in a given ᵛMEME from seeing the rest of the levels that exist in reality. Understanding this last aspect of *life conditions* allows for a value systems expert to design tools that naturally help people in certain Circumstances to transcend the values created by those blinders and allow the system to emerge.

ᵛMEME "DNA" SPIRAL

A PSYCHOLOGICAL MAP

Adapted from *Spiral Dynamics* by Beck and Cowan and used here with permission

The interaction between human capacities and life conditions create the most important aspects that define the emergent nature of this framework. They describe the mechanisms that define the movement from one value system to the next. *Life conditions* play an important role in upcoming chapters in designing the economic system of the future, which makes the *Memenomics* framework different than any other approach to economics. Still, within each value system there are many characteristics that impact how, when, and why cultures emerge that give each culture its unique ᵛMemetic contours.

CHARACTERISTICS COMMON TO ALL VALUE SYSTEMS

There are many characteristics that are common to all known levels. The following are the most relevant to our discussion about the economy and to the three most important levels that shape the dynamics of capitalism and the interactions of the consumer, the producer, and the policy-maker at the individual, organizational, and societal levels.

- ᵛMEMEs affect individuals as well as societies. An individual develops through the various value systems in his or her own life as *life conditions* change. The number of levels expressed in an individual depends on the biological, psychological, and social conditions he or she faces as his or her life progresses.[31] Forces affecting *life conditions* at the individual and societal levels play an integral part in determining why and how economic policies at any ᵛMemetic level succeed, stagnate, or fail.

- Different value systems can coexist at the same time in a person or a society.[32] Yet each will have a center of gravity or fault position. For example, an individual might act from one level when he or she is with family and from a completely different level when at work. In the same way, people, groups, or whole societies operating from one or another ᵛMEME can co-exist. No single value system exists on its own; it's the values-system's stack, or the *spiral* that determines the totality of what's important for an individual or a culture.

- Each value system can exhibit both healthy or unhealthy expressions.[33] In the communal systems the unhealthy expression is also referred to as a false expression. For example, one could argue that Google's business practices are a healthy expression of the fifth-level system (individualistic), while Wall Street's business practices of late are an unhealthy expression of that same fifth-level system. Democracy in the West might appear to be the healthy form of expression of the order-driven fourth level system (communal), while other forms of governance like Iran's theocracy might be considered a false or unhealthy expression of the same fourth-level system.

- When determining the capacity for change in an individual, organization, or culture, each level can be described as being under one of three conditions: open, arrested, or closed.[34] Identifying the historic presence of these conditions in the economy will give the reader a better understanding of how the expression of different ᵛMEMEs coalesce to form what I call "Memenomic Cycles" and how policy makers can act more effectively once the change states of our economy are understood through this new prism.

- As a person or a culture moves up to a higher-level order system, they transcend and include all the lower level value systems.[35] The ones that transcend and include tend to experience a healthier existence on the spiral than the ones who reject the lower values. Just like rings on a tree. The outermost ring only shows the most recent growth pattern while all the rings before it remain essential for the healthy function of the tree. In value-systems the highest level represents the outer ring, but must include all the lower levels within it for healthy existence.

- When a person or culture solves the problems of existence within their value system, they immediately create the problems that will trigger the emergence of the next value system. Faced with higher complexity, humans deal with the dissonance that leads to insights. This activates higher capacities in the brain and develops coping mechanisms and new tools specific to the new level of development that eventually spread within the culture.

- Cultures cannot skip a developmental stage. This is true still in the age of technology and the knowledge economy. Law and Order must precede Prosperity and Science. In the age of globalization the developing world might move faster than previous cultures through these phases, at their own pace, with their own unique indigenous content. The ones that skip a stage run the risk of collapse when the culture experiences stress.

Understanding the most important characteristics common to all value systems helps in painting a fuller picture of what *Memenomics* is all about.

The role that money plays in the evolution of humanity and in the modern history of our economy, and where we stand as far as the role of money today and how we can design a sustainable economic system for the future, all become simpler to understand and follow once seen through the prism of value systems. As a background to this discussion, the following is a description of each of the eight value systems that form the spiral.

THE FIRST-TIER SYSTEMS

BEIGE: the First-Level System

In the Beige level of value systems all energy is directed toward survival through innate sensory abilities and instinctual reactions. At this level, humans form loosely organized and herd-like survival bands with little structure.[36] This is the first emergence of humans from their animal nature. Food, water, warmth, sex, and safety are the primary focus of attention. This value-system level is uncommon today, but is seen in newborns, the senile elderly, late-stage Alzheimer's disease, and mentally-ill street people. Beige is an individualistic system where the motto is express self now to survive. At this level there is no attention available for anything but survival. The movie *Quest for Fire* provides a good example of the Beige value system. No *economic system* or any sort of barter or trade is noteworthy in this ᵛMEME. As food becomes scarcer and the habitat for this first level of existence no longer supports survival bands, Beige gives way to the second-level system.

PURPLE: the Second-Level System

This is the value system level of Kin Spirits and the tribe.[37] Thinking is magical and is a response to a mysterious and threatening world. Nature is powerful and must be feared and we must band together to survive. Although the emphasis is still on survival, unlike the Beige system, survival is achieved through the banding together of the tribe. It takes an entire hunting party to kill the beast in order for the tribe to eat and survive. The Purple level system is a sacrificial group-oriented system, in which people sacrifice individual needs for the tribe, the elders, and the ancient ways. Pleasing the gods and spirits, maintaining the tribal traditions, and keeping the tribe's home warm and safe become the highest priority. In this value system there is no room for individual thinking or action. In the Purple level there must be sacrifice for, and allegiance shown to, the chief, the elders, and the clan; the group preserves sacred objects, places, events, and memories; the group observes the traditional rites of passage, the seasonal cycles, and the tribal customs.

There are many places in the world where Purple is the predominant value system, including Africa many parts of Asia and South and Central America, and on tribal Native American land in the United States. The Middle East, in spite of the sudden appearance of oil wealth over the last one hundred years, remains predominantly in the Purple value system. Many aspects of Purple value systems are found in first world societies as well. Beliefs in guardian angels, blood oaths, and good luck charms, family rituals or superstitions, are all signs of the Purple ᵛMEME. Fraternities and sororities, fraternal lodges, teams in professional sports, and certain corporate tribes are all manifestations of Purple. Much of religious thinking, regardless of faith or denomination, is Purple, especially in third world countries. Labor unions carry heavy Purple undertones.

Decision making in this second-level system is based on custom and tradition and is made by a council of elders, often relying on mystical information supplied by a shaman. The average tribal member is uninvolved in much of the decision-making process. Attempts to introduce democratic thought into tribal groups do not work since the idea of individual decision-making does not exist in the Purple ᵛMEME. Wealth is divided in a communal manner, regardless of who may have actually created it. A good example of this practice is how native Indian tribes distribute gambling revenues from their casinos among tribe members. In oil rich countries of the Middle East, tribes believe that god placed the oil under their feet and therefore should be shared.

THE PURPLE SECOND-LEVEL ᵛMEME'S LEADERSHIP STRUCTURE

Tribe/Clan

▲ Tribal Leader/Clan Chief (usually the oldest and wisest)
▲ Small Tribal Leader/traditionally responsible for safety, rituals, medicine, etc.)
● Tribal Member/Clan Member

Adapted from *Spiral Dynamics* by Beck and Cowan and used here with permission

The nature of thinking in this second-level system is fearful and mystical. Tribe members must behave in the traditional ways, with no room for individual action or thinking. The taboos must be obeyed and tribal leaders must be honored with absolute obedience and conformity, with a reverence for seniority and ancestors. Education is paternalistic and relies heavily on rituals and routines. Learners are passive, and individual creativity is not possible. The family is one of extended kinships marked by strict role relationships. Rules and traditions are designed to protect kin bloodlines. Ritualistic rites of passage are an important aspect of each stage of life.

Land and territory have sacred meaning to this value system and tribes will fight bloody battles to regain and protect ancestral land. Since there's no individual thinking in Purple, a leader who has ascended to the next value system can easily control the group. Many dictators past and present had most of their subjects in the Purple ᵛMEME. With the passage of time and as *life conditions* change, younger and stronger members of the tribe start to develop individual thinking. This emerges when there is diminishing fear of nature, a weakening of tribal bonds, if the traditional offerings and rituals fail to fend off evil spirits or bring the desired benefits, or if the tribal order for some reason begins to collapse. The tools of tribal existence no longer serve the *life conditions* and that's when a culture moves to the next level of existence.

A Purple economic system historically existed for thousands of years before the Industrial Revolution. Localized, tribal, and primarily agricultural, this ᵛMEME defined the simplest of any form of trade or barter system. Subsistence was the order of day if not the century. Life was lived from one harvest season to the next and at the mercy of nature and the gods. Tribes remained in the same geographic location for centuries cultivating their ancestral land. A grandfather's and a grandson's income varied very little. Technological advancement was to fashion a better hand tool to till the ground or a better harness for the oxen. Occasionally tribes exchanged food or grain with other tribes as an early sign of the emergence of trade. While *life conditions* have changed considerably in most of the world, this second-level economic system still exists in many subsistent parts of the world, such as Africa, South and Central America, the Middle East, and many remote parts of emerging countries around the world.

Contemporary manifestation of Purple in one of today's advanced economies forms the bottom part of the economic meme stack, the first level on the memenomic spiral. These are the foreign laborers that are seen all over the globe, from the Indian and Pakistani construction worker hanging on a scaffold on the 95th floor of a Dubai skyscraper to the Mexican or Guatemalan farmhand in the fields of Bakersfield, California, packing strawberries in the hot sun. They live in close quarters with many members of their extended families and friends. They fear authority and much of the outside world because it all remains foreign to them. This self-imposed *closed system* begins to open up as some members start to trust the outside world and as their children start to interact with the complexity of the world around them.

RED: the Third-Level System

Red is an expressive individualistic level and represents the first emergence of real and effective individual action and individual ego. This is the value system of impulsive action and is often described as that of Power Gods. Red is interested in power and domination and enforces power over self, others, and nature through exploitative independent action.[38] The Red motto is "express the self now and impulsively, and the hell with others." Red grabs what it wants through personal power, with no guilt and no thought of others. Perhaps the biggest problem facing the world today is how to manage the transition of Purple by having it go quickly through Red while on the way to the next value system to avoid the heavy cost of Red's exploitation. Good examples of this are the West's current efforts in helping the governments of Iraq and Afghanistan escape the grip of Red power lords like the Taliban and the various militias that sprang up in Iraq after the fall of Saddam Hussein.

To a person in Red, the world is a jungle full of threats and predators. An individual in Red wants to break free from domination or constraint. He wants to stand tall, receive attention from others, demand respect, and call the shots. He or she acts without conscience, enjoying life to the fullest without guilt or remorse. Red individuals operate totally in the "now," with no sense of future consequences or any desire or ability to either delay gratification or make personal sacrifices. Examples of Red include the terrible twos, rebellious teenagers, the frontier mentality, feudal kingdoms, soldiers of fortune, rap musicians, prison culture, dictators, and gang leaders. The mob culture as represented in the television series *The Sopranos* is a good depiction of a Red ᵛMEME in modern Western culture.

In the Red ᵛMEME decisions are made by the most powerful person and are based on what creates the most respect or what feels good in the moment. The leader must supply immediate gratification to his followers. All information flows downward, from the leader, and little if any information flows upward. A typical Red-dominant leader, such as Robert Mugabe or Saddam Hussein, typically does not want the views of his followers. Participatory democracy is not possible in Red. While it may use the appearance of equal participatory process, Red will corrupt the vote. The most powerful gets the spoils and decides how they are distributed, if they are distributed

THE RED THIRD-LEVEL ᵛMEME'S
LEADERSHIP STRUCTURE

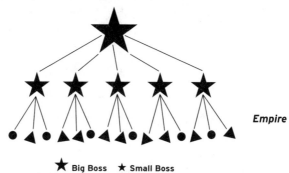

Empire

★ Big Boss ★ Small Boss
▲ Small Tribal Leader/traditionally responsible for safety, rituals, medicine, etc.)
● Tribal Member/Clan Member

Adapted from *Spiral Dynamics* by Beck and Cowan and used here with permission

at all. Education is based on tests of worthiness and tough-love tactics. The community is one in which predators are in control, outsiders are in danger, fiefdoms are formed, and turf wars are constantly being fought. Red includes exploitation of women, children, and the weak, and total reliance on the power principle.

In terms of societal structures, Red is the level of the empire, examples of which include the Sumerian Dynasty, the Babylonian Dynasty, the Persian Empire, and the Roman Empire. Julius Caesar had the healthy expression of Red, emerging from the Purple Roman Republic and operating as a transition agent to the next higher-order value system for the Roman Empire (though many Purple and Red elements remained for centuries).

Red ranges in functionality from the vicious to the heroic, and Red can contain healthy aspects. Healthy individuals at the Red level are resourceful and powerful. This ᵛMEME takes society out of Purple and creates the first individualists and proactive humans. Julius Caesar and Alexander the Great were Red. They united tribes and cultures to move up to the next level. A modern day expression of a healthy Red leader is the Ruler of Dubai who's undertaking one of the bravest experiments of human emergence in history by attempting to move an entire culture up the emergence ladder several stages in what seems to be a blink of an eye.

Unhealthy Red is selfish, predatory, and violent, and it refuses to recognize the limits of individualistic expression. Red also has an unrealistic view of its own abilities and knowledge, and an unrealistic sense of invulnerability, as commonly seen in dictators such as Saddam Hussein or Robert Mugabe. This stage however, is a necessary phase. We all go through it as teenagers, to emerge into the next system hopefully before we drive our parents crazy. Tribal societies in places like the Middle East and Africa must move through Red to get to the next stage where democracy and typical civilized social institutions are possible. The approach as to how to facilitate this transition is one of the biggest challenges facing the world today.

A Red economic system historically existed during the era of empires when exploitation defined economic rule. Resources belonged to the strongest pillager. The weak masses were easily exploited for their labor and were put to use to satisfy the urges of the emperor. It was Red Pharaohs using Purple slave labor that built the pyramids of Giza. It was ships of Red merchants from colonial powers that conquered new lands and exploited their natural resources. Historically this system was represented by wars that were fought between Red empires for the control and exploitation of resources of new or disputed territory. This was also the economic system where Red land barons either owned slaves or hired inexpensive labor to make fruitful use of the land for little or no wages paid in return.

A contemporary manifestation of a Red economic system today is Russia after the collapse of Soviet Communism. A few oligarchs that were members of the communist party before the collapse now control of the country's resources. Today Dubai, under the leadership of its ruler, provides for a good example of a healthy Red economy. Although many lessons still await Dubai, at least its economic emergence is not being achieved through tyrannical or exploitive means of humans in the lower Purple system. Red economic activity in advanced Western economies makes up the second level in a meme stack and is primarily known for its exploitive, if not its altogether illegal, activities within a complex economy. A wider discussion of how Red activities grew and contributed to the financial crisis of 2008 will take place in upcoming chapters.

Red in a predominantly Purple culture that's rich with natural resources and can accumulate massive amounts of wealth, but may not have the strength to defend it. The need for law and order becomes apparent. Red can transition to the next ^{V}MEME when there is a questioning of personal power and a need for structured discipline. A healthy Red leader is generally an open system thinker and would recognize when a culture is ready for the next stage. In most cases, however, Red leaders desperately hold on to power and must be removed by force in order for the next system to emerge.

BLUE: the Fourth-Level System

The Blue level of value systems is the beginning of what most people think of as civilization. The Blue ᵛMEME is often described as that of the "Truth Force" because it is organized around an absolute belief in one right way and obedience to its authority.[39] Examples of Blue Truth Force ideas and groups include the Catholic Church, Islamic Sharia, The Jewish Noachide Code, God, Country and Apple Pie; The Communist Party; the Marine Corps. The Boys and Girls Club, and the Boy Scouts are another example. The basic theme of Blue is that life has meaning, direction, and purpose, with predetermined outcomes. If the True Meaning is found and followed, everything will be okay. Blue is a sacrificial system, where individuality is sacrificed to the transcendent Cause, Truth, or Righteous Pathway. In Blue, the order enforces a code of conduct based on eternal, absolute principles. Regulatory structures within governments at various levels fall into the Blue ᵛMEME; the local police department, the local zoning board, the Securities Exchange Commission, the FDIC, and the Office of Thrift Supervision are all examples of government Blue, and so are the FBI and the IRS.

Blue believes that righteous living produces stability now and guarantees future rewards, that impulsivity is controlled through guilt, that everybody has his or her proper place, and that laws, regulations, and discipline build character and moral fiber. Blue society is highly stratified with each person having his role, and upward mobility is slow or non-existent. Blue is about law and order, a reaction to the lawlessness of Red. Because right and wrong are guiding forces, the spoils in Blue go to the righteous. Whatever the organizing truth, in Blue there is only one right way, and that right way is enforced with laws, punishments, and guilt. On the other hand, adherence to the Truth is rewarded with guaranteed retirement and the hope of a better future or afterlife.

Education is seen as truth handed down from authority and is accomplished in traditional and hierarchical stair steps. It often takes the form of moralistic lessons reinforced with punishment for errors. Teaching is strict, punitive, and black and white. The motto is: Spare the rod and spoil the child. The family is the seat of truth and values, teaching moral values and codes of conduct. The community ideals are peace and quiet, law and order, and compliance to rules. The best citizen is a law-abiding citizen who knows his place.

Though the theme of Blue is the One True Way, the exact nature of this truth can vary widely. The Cold War, for instance, was a struggle between two different Blue truths, the American Way and the Communist Way, and the conflict between the West and Islam is one of two opposing Blue Truth Forces. These can be as divergent as the Christian Right, Islamic fundamentalism, Communism, the Catholic Church, or "left-wing" causes. An Advanced culture like the West might view Islamic fundamentalism as a false Blue, while for the less advanced culture practicing it, this might be the only Truth Force it knows. In Blue, there are no shades of gray. Everything is Right or Wrong. Because it is so easy to be on the wrong side of the truth in a black and white world, Blue deals with an almost perpetual guilt burden.

Blue is a sacrificial system that supplants individuality for communal acceptance. Its motto is to "sacrifice self as authority dictates to obtain later." This is a move from the *now* awareness and instant gratification of Red to an awareness of future consequences. In Blue, the reward is often so delayed that it sometimes only comes in Heaven, as with fundamentalist Christianity and Islam. Blue comes into being to deal with the excesses of Red, and those in this level are good at it. Law and Order and punishment are major aspects of Blue. Rather than managing Red and guide it through to the next level, the Blue strategy is to educate, reform, and shape Red with either the design of a "good authority" apparatus or, if necessary, to use more punitive measures. In one sense this works, in that it surrounds Red and contains it, but it does not accomplish the transition to Blue that irrevocably ends the Red problems. The challenge the Third World faces is that most of its value-system stack is made up of Red and Purple, along with a weakened Blue system. Before it can pass to a ᵛMEME stack that is similar to the First World, it must pass through a prolonged period of basic, but robust Blue, one that runs the trains on time, provides safety and security to society, and imposes a form of justice and stability.

The Blue organizational structure is a passive hierarchy, as in the Catholic Church or the military, with rigid rules for structure and rank and a strict adherence to the organizational chart. The person with positional power makes decisions, and power accrues to the position, not to the individual. The system, rather than the individual, is of prime importance, and the system, not the individual, is promoted, preserved, and maintained. Communication is downward, but also horizontal—unlike in Red, where there was no horizontal communication within an organization. Blue strongly supports the seniority system, one of delayed gratification where everyone has his or her place. This creates a stratified society with little upward mobility and many bureaucracies. Generally the only way to move up in the organizational chart is for someone to die or retire.

The healthy aspects of Blue include control of Red violence and the creation of a more stable society based on the rule of law. In Blue there is an emphasis on fairness, equity, and uniform treatment. In Blue there is an equal

THE BLUE FOURTH-LEVEL ᵛMEME'S
LEADERSHIP STRUCTURE

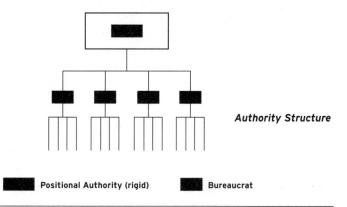

Authority Structure

Positional Authority (rigid)   Bureaucrat

Adapted from *Spiral Dynamics* by Beck and Cowan and used here with permission

application of laws, the motto being: A country of laws, not of men. Blue also has created great progress over Purple and Red societies in eliminating human suffering. One of the unhealthy aspects of Blue is its punitive and inflexible nature, seeing everything in black and white. Blue gave us the Salem Witch Trials, the Spanish Inquisition and McCarthyism. It gave us fundamentalist religions, racism, and totalitarian Communism.

Blue inflexibility will keep out new capacities and innovations needed to detect fraud, especially when it's perpetrated from a higher value system. A good current example of this is the SEC's inability to detect the twenty-year scam perpetrated by Bernard Madoff, even after whistle-blowers stepped forward with details about how laws were being broken. Blue inflexibility can have a very negative and fault-finding outlook while at the same time missing the bigger picture. Most Truth Force points of view provide automatic defense of prejudices. Blue wars are fought to promote or defend true beliefs and ideology. In many ways, this makes Blue-inspired wars more vicious and destructive than Purple or Red wars. Wars for territory seek to preserve the wealth of the territory being conquered, which often includes the people and their ability to work for their new masters. When a Red approach is violent, it is also often based on principles of honor, and Red warriors often show great respect for their opponents. Blue warriors, on the other hand, generally demonize their opponents and are quite willing to wipe them out.

A Blue economic system is one predominated by central planning and production. There's no room for individuality and innovation. A financial system could be well developed, but its purpose is to serve the one true way as determined by its leaders. This was the economic model romanticized by the communist ideology and quickly proved to be susceptible to corruption and obsolescence if policy makers were out of touch with the needs of the people. Although this fourth-level economic system could be labeled as a closed-system, it is essential to have in the emergence of a culture to the next stage or when a culture is threatened. During WWII, United States productive industrial output was placed at the service of one true Blue purpose, and that was to win the war. China's centrally planned economy, though subject to much criticism by the West, is playing a significant role in giving China a powerful presence on the global economic stage. Much like other sectors of a culture, a nation has to go through a Blue stage of economic policy in order to consolidate gains made along the road of emergence. Economic policies aimed at building a nation's infrastructure such as highways, airports, the railroad, and seaports are the truest form of healthy Blue economic policies.

Blue can transition to the next, higher-value system when society has been stabilized through the spread of Blue institutions. When there is a hunger for autonomy, and little purpose found in the Truth Force, or if guilt becomes too paralyzing, a culture can be ready for transition. If the Truth no longer guarantees order, and the future is in doubt, skepticism and new options appear. Stronger members of society, regardless of their position in the social hierarchy, begin to say: Why wait for material abundance? I am smart enough and have enough drive to create rewards for myself now. This leads to the emergence to the fifth value-system level, which once again is an individualistic, expressive system.

ORANGE: the Fifth-Level System

The fifth level, Orange, is called "Strive Drive." Orange appears when conditions change in such a way that Blue methods of dealing with existential conditions no longer work as effectively, and when the idea of group sacrifice for the Truth Force loses its luster.[40] At this point the stronger and more enterprising members of the group begin to realize that they are being held back by adhering to the rules and procedures of the group, and that they could create better results through individual action. Orange believes in better living through technology. It wants to uncover the secrets of the universe through science, technology, and medical discoveries. It wants to create an efficient trade system with enlightened self-interest at its core. The changeability of technology and innovation is the hallmark of this ^{V}MEME. The main idea behind Orange is that we can shape, influence, promote progress, and make things better through the use of the scientific methods, quantification, trial and error, and the search for the best solutions.

The spread of Orange ideas started with the Enlightenment Movement and the dawn of the Industrial Age. Orange gave us Adam Smith and Capitalism as well classical music and Mozart and Mm. Currie and the X-Ray. Scientific discoveries are a significant hallmark of this value system that has brought the quality of human life to unprecedented heights in a very short period of time and through these discoveries popularized the idea that a human being can control his or her own destiny.

In this value system, progress is the natural order of things. The goal is to constantly innovate by learning nature's secrets and seeking the best solutions to the problems of better living. Orange also seeks to manipulate the world's resources in the most efficient and effective manner in order to spread the good life. Orange is optimistic, risk-taking, and self-reliant, and believes that those with such qualities deserve their success. To Orange, a society prospers through science, technology, competitiveness, and execution of good strategies. Orange seeks to create material abundance for everyone, and those who contribute the most garner the greatest share of the spoils. The basic rule is to *act in your own self-interest by playing the game to win*, to express self in a calculated way to get the result you want.

Orange believes there is a job to be done, money to be made, products to be created and sold, and a world to be tamed. Don Beck cautions that although Orange uses materialism to keep score, materialism is not its core principle. It is innovative Orange entrepreneurs who built the modern technological society with its medical miracles, worldwide transportation systems, labor-saving devices, instantaneous communication, and other material progress. On the healthy side, Orange will compete, but within the bounds of fair play. One of the ways Orange differs from Red is in creating tremendous material rewards and progress based on the latest science and technology. Orange does not act rashly, but weighs the various options to create the best possible outcome, using the minimum resources to get the maximum benefit.

Orange is the value system of material prosperity through merit. In fact, upward mobility is expected and admired to a greater degree than "old" money, which was more admired by the Blue system. Status comes not from being from the right family, but from success in this life. While Blue often looks to the past, Orange looks to the now and to the future.

The Orange organizational structure is an active hierarchy, where authority or positional power can be delegated. Communication can be up, down, or horizontal. Power, while still related to position as in the Blue system, can be much more easily attained through moving up the hierarchy and by demonstrating the ability to successfully creating desired results. Orange decision-making is based on bottom-line results. Options are tested to see what works best. Achieving the desired outcome is of prime importance,

THE ORANGE FIFTH-LEVEL ᵛMEME'S
LEADERSHIP STRUCTURE

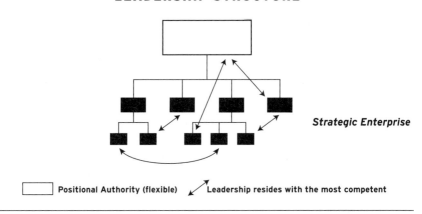

Strategic Enterprise

☐ Positional Authority (flexible)   ↗ Leadership resides with the most competent

Adapted from *Spiral Dynamics* by Beck and Cowan and used here with permission

sometimes at the expense of the people involved, or the environment. Experts are the most important people, especially those with scientific or entrepreneurial expertise. The successful receive the spoils in an Orange world.

The family is child-centered, with the expectation that each generation could and should do better than the last. Expectations are high, image is important, and upward mobility is encouraged and expected. The community caters to and admires the more prosperous, proudly displays its affluence, seeks material things as a measure of success, and honors competition. Success is measured by material abundance; *He who dies with the most toys wins.*

An Orange economic system is symbolized by the capitalist ideology in the West where individual property rights and the private ownership of resources provide the basics of its foundation. This fifth-level value system will occupy much of the discussion here about economic systems and the theories of memenomics. Wall Street and the banking system have a formidable expression here. The industrialists in Ayn Rand's *Atlas Shrugged* and economists like Dr. Greenspan who shaped the ideologies of the most powerful policy makers of the last century reside in this ᵛMEME. An *Orange economic system* has a robust private sector that seeks to reinvent itself through innovation and often does so with the help of a cast of collaborators from investment bankers and scientists all the way down to the consumer who seems to have an insatiable appetite for anything and everything that is produced. Most institutions in this fifth-level economic system are geared to accommodate the advancement of a better life, but for those who have the meritocracy to participate in it. The ones that do seem to advance by strategically manipulating resources and bending the rules that were set up by a lower fourth-level system that has little capacity to detect what is called white-collar crime.

Some of the unhealthy expressions of Orange are that it can place too much emphasis on the end result at the expense of the people involved and the possible cost to the environment. Orange can rationalize exploitation in the service of goal achievement. This attitude created such brilliant ideas as planned obsolescence born out of the initial ideologies of thinkers like Schumpeter. The uses of many hazardous and non-biodegradable materials are other rationales that Orange uses in its quest for efficiency. Orange-level thinking considers that more money or more technology is the solution to every problem as compared to the other value systems where Blue thinks the answer to every problem is more law and order and more rules, and Red thinks the solution to every problem is more power and aggression. Though Orange will work a long-range plan and delay gratification, there is also a strong desire for here-and-now results. As we will see in later discussions on what went wrong with the economy, Orange in its unhealthy expression can take advantage of a week Blue system and act much like Red. Unlike Red, whose actions are blatant and in your face, when it comes to law and order, to an unhealthy Orange it's an inconvenience or nuisance that has to be strategically manipulated and overcome.

Like all other value systems, Orange has a healthy and an unhealthy expression, and it is the unhealthy expression of a very thin, sub-sector, of this ᵛMEME that brought the world's financial markets to the edge of collapse. During the financial crisis, the remaining accomplishments of Orange seemed to have disappeared in the presence of such systemic threat, but it's in the value system's nature for its varying sectors and subsectors to spawn their own seeds of destruction on their endless quest for better innovation and higher efficiency.

Somewhere along the journey through Orange, some members begin to ask, "Is this all there is to life?" The attainment of significant material abundance makes for easy living, but something is missing. Questions start being asked about the existential or spiritual elements of life that are beyond the quantifiable and material world of Orange. Individuals and culture can transition to the next value system when there is a growing need for existential significance, contribution to society, and a desire for internal rather than merely external fulfillment. The world has been "conquered" through technology and competition, but this "good life" is somehow unfulfilling. In the pursuit of achieving all of our Orange goals, a certain cost was paid in terms of the human element. The consequences of not caring for the environment have begun to come to light, and the absence of the spiritual element has become more apparent.

GREEN: the Sixth-Level System

The Green value system, which is the last in the first tier of levels, appears in the search for inner peace and human connection. The human bond becomes the highest value. The well being of all the people, not just those who are willing to risk and compete, becomes the highest priority. Green's motto is "sacrifice self now for the needs of the group."[41] Like all the sacrificial levels that came before it, Green wants to sacrifice self, but this time it does not want to postpone its gratification; it wants to obtain it now, which is an adaptation from Orange. But unlike Orange, Green wants to obtain things now for both the self *and* others. Green responds to the lack of internal fulfillment of Orange by seeking peace within the inner self and through exploring the more caring and spiritual dimensions of humanity. To the Green ᵛMEME feelings, sensitivity, and caring supersede results and will not be sacrificed for results. Attention turns away from material goods and greater productivity to the inner dimension of feelings. When outer-directed, the ideal Green social organization is the network, governed by consensus decision-making. Green assumes that each person's input has equal value. Though well intentioned, this is often shown to be untrue, and much time can be wasted on hearing everyone out. The Green motto is "Egalitarianism and Humanitarianism."

This value system believes that resources should be shared equally and that decisions should be reached through consensus, rather than through the desires of the chief and elders, as in Purple, by the most powerful, as in Red, by strict rules of the Truth Force, as in Blue, or by experts and entrepreneurs, as in Orange. The role of Green is to renew humanity's spirituality, to bring harmony, and to focus on the enrichment of human development. Green can be seen in the music of John Lennon, in Doctors Without Borders, Greenpeace, the Sierra Club, Canadian Health Care, the ACLU, sensitivity training, Jimmy Carter, and PETA.

Green is organized around community and feelings. Important values include inner peace, equality and inclusiveness, the relativity of all moral positions, group harmony, the exploration of feelings, shared experience, and cooperation rather than competition. Green thinking is behind "political correctness," socially-aware investing, victims' rights, and social safety nets. In terms of its ability to create results, Green is diametrically the opposite of Orange in its approach. Where Orange is capable of sacrificing the human

THE GREEN SIXTH-LEVEL ᵛMEME'S
LEADERSHIP STRUCTURE

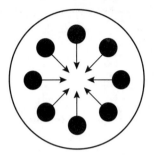

Social Network

● **People, organizations and cultures are groupings of equals
coming together to deepen the human bond**

Adapted from *Spiral Dynamics* by Beck and Cowan and used here with permission

element to get a desired result, Green will sacrifice the desired result to preserve group consensus and the human element. This results in an emphasis on feelings and harmony, certainly a positive development, but often at the expense of productivity and actually accomplishing something.

Under a classical Green economic system, policies and institutions are geared towards "equal economic opportunity for all." Although ownership of resources is private, it is heavily taxed and regulated, and as a result it exercises considerably more restraint than the fifth-level economic system in being a good corporate citizen. Awareness of the environment, and the health of the planet, as well as the worker, is woven into every private and public sector decision. Allocation of capital for an advanced fiber optics research center is as important as setting aside funding programs for empowering businesses in poor urban areas. Government spending on social programs is the hallmark of this sixth-level economic system. The European Union is a good example of a system that champions Green economic policies as evidenced by their bloated social welfare programs. Green ᵛMEME corporate practices have helped bring equality in pay to the worker, but that same system has taxed those corporations at such a high rate that innovation is often stifled. This system can unfairly burden a whole culture and bring it to the brink of financial disaster. Many conservative economists in the United States argue that it was Congressman Barney Frank's Green value-system views that everyone in America should own a home that eventually brought about the subprime crisis.

A more contemporary manifestation of a Green economic system is the knowledge economy today in its earliest appearance in *life conditions.* Rooted in the World Wide Web's undeclared mandate to democratize access to information, the knowledge economy is redefining the values of the sixth-level system as they mature. These emerging values that are giving impetus for a more functional economy in the future will be the subject of much discussion in the third part of the book.

Despite its concern for the human element, Green has many unhealthy or false expressions. Once consensus is reached, everyone must comply, and there is no room for individual expression or individual action. In fact, Green leaders often do not care what the majority wants. Green leaders may manipulate the group to gain consensus for their idea and then disregard what the group wants after that. Or, they may decide the group just isn't "conscious enough" if they don't see the politically-correct point of view. One of the big problems of Green is its reliance on consensus decision-making. The main problem with this method is that the energy required to reach consensus takes much too much time. The process of coming to consensus often really amounts to wearing down those who disagree rather than actually changing their minds. As a result, little if anything of substance is ever actually accomplished. Green is well known for being overly permissive, especially with Red, and has trouble effectively dealing with the harsher realities of life. In wanting Red to be "part of the circle," and looking at Red through the filter of their own values, Green believes that if we were only nicer to Red they would stop being so aggressive, selfish, and cruel. Red, of course, doesn't want to be part of the circle, sees this attitude as insane, and is happy to take advantage of it.

On the positive side, Green has done the world a service by exposing Orange damage to the environment, and by bringing holistic and spiritual thinking and concern for the human element back onto the stage. Emphasizing humanistic rather than material goals, valuing inner peace and the spiritual dimension, and seeing humanity as a universal family, are all positive contributions. But in seeing all experiences, all opinions, and all points of view as equal, Green produces a false sense of utopianism, which inherently creates complacency that leads to decay. In a complex global society where egalitarian Green can't see Red, and where Red has access to nuclear weapons, annihilation of the human race becomes a distinct possibility under its form of governance. Graves believed that this sixth-level system would be the shortest-lasting of the values systems, and also one of the most dangerous.

Green transitions to the next level of existence when some of its members begin to realize that in spite of all their work over several decades, not much has really changed. The warm, human aspirations of Green begin to wear thin as the realities of complex social problems and the limited ability of the Green approach to actually solve them becomes apparent. As a result, many Greens become frustrated and become alienated from the group approach. They decide that more could be accomplished if they worked on their own to create the necessary global changes. The lack of solutions through group effort gives way to individual initiative again and the amazing upward journey on the spiral continues at a much higher level of complexity and within a whole new second-tier system.

THE SECOND-TIER SYSTEMS

YELLOW: the Seventh-Level System

This is the level that Clare W. Graves describes in his groundbreaking article in the April 1974 edition of *The Futurist* as the point at which humanity takes a "momentous leap." This is the first level of human existence in the second tier and the first *Being* level. This is where we begin to understand where we've been and what we might come to be. Yellow is called "Flex Flow"; it is interested in functionality.[42] This is an individualistic and expressive ᵛMEME, taking many of the healthy expressions of Green, Orange, Blue, Red, and Purple and integrating them into a more effective system. Yellow has a big-picture view and creates a systemic approach to problem solving and has the ability to handle many different variables. Because of humanity's inability to solve problems through first-tier ᵛMEMEs, Yellow sees the world as a complex system in danger of collapse and explores the different ways in which to act responsibly. It recognizes the different evolutionary stages and works to unblock the hurdles standing in the way of a healthy systemic flow for all of humanity with the understanding that chaos and change are a natural part of the process.

Yellow intuitively sees how all first-tier ᵛMEMEs can work together, unlike Blue, which only sees everything in right or wrong terms, or Green, which sees the greater complexity in the world but has no effective method of getting anything done. In this ᵛMEME there is an emphasis on information, competency, and knowledge. The person with the most knowledge leads and makes the decisions, and as the situation changes, leadership changes. Good leadership is based on the ability to handle complexity. In the quest to create real solutions, knowledge and competency supersede rank, power, and status. At the same time, the need to hear all points of view gives way to a practical desire to listen to those with knowledge and expertise. Yellow decision-making is highly principled and is centered on knowledge and data that is derived from the paradigm that there's an existential urgency to

THE YELLOW SEVENTH-LEVEL ᵛMEME'S
LEADERSHIP STRUCTURE
Integrative/Functional/Natural/Knowledge-Centered/Highly Principled

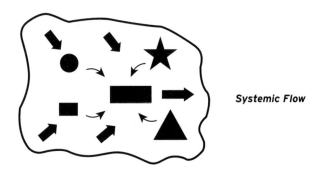

Systemic Flow

Adapted from *Spiral Dynamics* by Beck and Cowan and used here with permission

manage the chaos of human existence. Intelligence in this ᵛMEME has the innate ability to filter out data that is tainted or heavily influenced by any of the lower ᵛMEMEs.

Yellow is an expressive value system, where the motto is "express self, but not at the expense of others or the earth." In Yellow, the competent receive the spoils, and the competent are those who understand complexity, are self-directed, and have the flexibility to base their approach on existential conditions, taking each situation as it is and recognizing that those conditions are continually shifting and changing. Yellow does more with less, and uses appropriate technologies to get the job done with less waste and fewer ecological problems. Since power flows to the most competent in each situation, it is less concentrated. Different people are in charge in different situations, with the most competent in control of what they know best.

Yellow has many of the healthy expressions of Orange: a desire and ability to shape, influence, and promote progress to make things better, to use the rationality of the scientific method, and to search for the best solutions to problems. Yellow also has many of the healthy expressions of Green; attention to the human element and the effects of human activity on the environment, less emphasis on status and materialism, and a greater emphasis on the spiritual element. Yellow cannot build much of its functional flows without a healthy and viable Blue system that has the capacity to stop the unhealthy practices of all the lower ᵛMEMEs before they can collapse the system. This was apparent in 2008 where the Blue that regulated the banking industry all but disappeared, allowing the banking sub-sector in Orange to bring the world to the edge of collapse. A detailed discussion of how these factors influenced the entire ᵛMEME stack will the subject of upcoming chapters.

A *Yellow economic system* is one of intuitive intelligence and functionality. It is the tools of this value system that will be used to create The Platform for Functional Capitalism. Economic policies set from this seventh-level system have no biases toward any other policies or practices set from any systems of the first tier, known as the subsistence tier. Since Yellow is interested in functionality and Natural Flow, it takes best practices from all the lower ᵛMEMEs and creates a stratified approach towards solving the world's economic problems. In advanced economies that face systemic risks from unhealthy Orange practices, whether it's the financial sector or the environmental degradation brought about by the Industrial Age, Yellow designs policies for a system that will naturally regenerate Orange innovation before it becomes unhealthy and prevents the fall of Orange into the hands of the exploitive elements of lower ᵛMEMEs. According to Don Beck, Yellow stitches together a world that has been split open by the varying unhealthy practices of the first tier. From an economic policy perspective this ᵛMEME must design what is naturally appropriate for a culture in order for it to emerge economically.

Today's complex global economy can no longer be modeled on the teachings of any of the existing subsectors within the Orange ᵛMEME nor can they be modeled on the principles and ideologies of one school of thought or another. Keynesian economics seems to be the answer right now to the laissez-faire Reaganomics of the past three decades, but from a Yellow perspective this is nothing more than trading horses between one ideology of the Blue ᵛMEME for another from the Orange ᵛMEME. Sustainability for the long-term health of the planet is not the ultimate objective of either policy. Unlike unhealthy Western Orange practices that exploit the resources of third-world countries, Yellow looks at the cultural content of each lower ᵛMEME in these countries and designs economic policies that take on the form of an indigenous ecosystem reflecting that culture's ᵛMemetic values.

In demanding functionality in a world that is aligned to first-tier ideologies, Yellow can become impatient with incompetency or narrow thinking and therefore become unhealthy. It can also become impatient with how the Internet has made the world a flat place, since it perceives networking as ill-informed people coming together to share their ignorance without being an effective catalyst for change. Yellow does not like a lot of communication and Green-oriented group meetings, but instead wants to work outside of a group context. It prefers being left alone to solve the problems once they're defined.

As Yellow thinking begins to spread and conditions change, it becomes apparent that individual approaches to global problems are less effective. At this point Yellow begins to transition to the eighth and last known value system when there is an acceptance of the need for coordinated action to effectively deal with world problems.

TURQUIOSE: the Eighth-Level System

Since there's very little of the Yellow ᵛMEME present today, Turquoise is practically non-existent; therefore information about this ᵛMEME is largely conjecture. Turquoise is a sacrificial system in which the motto is "sacrifice self and others as needed for global survival." Turquoise shares Yellow's global view and its ability to think systemically. Turquoise emerges as some Yellow individuals step forward to be global leaders rather than continuing to work individually. In this ᵛMEME, physics and metaphysics are used together to explore the problems of life and being by combining the physical with the metaphysical, the objective with the subjective. To Turquoise, the world is a single, dynamic organism with its own collective mind, and the self is at the same time distinct and also a blended part of a larger, compassionate whole.[43] Everything connects to everything else, and holistic, intuitive thinking and cooperative actions are to be expected.

Turquoise deals with complexity easily and sees patterns and consequences not apparent to the subsistence ᵛMEMEs in the first tier. In doing so, Turquoise discovers the connections and principles that underlie the entire living process. Green often thinks it's operating from Turquoise, but there are some key differences. Turquoise realizes that there may be difficult choices and that some may have to be sacrificed to ensure global survival. Green's inclusiveness and its belief that everything and everyone is of equal value keeps Green from making such difficult choices; Green does not want to sacrifice anyone because everyone is equally valuable. Turquoise, however, is willing to make such choices, if necessary. Turquoise, like Yellow and Orange, is interested in results. Unlike Orange, however, Turquoise is able to keep in mind the synergy of all life and to see the consequences of its actions in a way that creates a safe and orderly world.

It's difficult to speculate what a *Turquoise economic system* would be like because it will look like nothing we have ever seen. Systemic Yellow thinking is just beginning to emerge around the world and it will take several decades if not centuries before the Yellow economic system can fully manifest itself to create enough problems that propel the global culture into Turquoise. Based on the description of this eighth-level system by Graves and Spiral Dynamics theory, one can speculate that economic conditions might look something like this: groups that are taxing the precious resources of the planet, whether it is

THE TURQUOISE EIGHTH-LEVEL 'MEME'S LEADERSHIP STRUCTURE
Synergistic/Conscious/Interconnected/Globally Aware

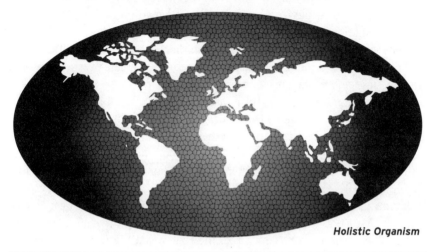

Holistic Organism

Adapted from *Spiral Dynamics* by Beck and Cowan and used here with permission

Wall Street, the poor, OPEC, Russian Oligarchs, or Chinese Central Planners, will simply not exist in a Turquoise system. Waste and inefficiency is eliminated through a process more akin to natural selection and confirmed by a committee of highly-evolved world leaders. There will be elements of Marxism that will distribute resources equally combined with the best elements of capitalism that will empower innovation and research and development with the overall goal of guarding our precious global resources and regenerating nature.

A full merit-system of exchange that recognizes the totality and efficiency of serving the biosphere will replace all monetary forms of exchange. Every productive member of society, from the landscaper to the healer and the non-monetary banker, will perform his or her job knowing he or she is a highly specialized, efficient, and indispensable member of an ecosystem that naturally reciprocates in providing for all his or her needs. The emerging science of bio-mimicry and its construct of an economic ecosystem provides an early glimpse of what a future under Turquoise would look like. Without a doubt, this is a distributed intelligence that is intuitively prudent. If boundaries still exist by the time Turquoise appears, nations with natural resources will place priority on their efficient distribution to keep the ecosystem functioning over their need to build the wealth of a nation. Intelligence of all types will be distributed to the highest degree possible. Global villages that use the highest, best, and newest forms of technology with the smallest environmental footprint will become the norm. Commodities and futures markets will disappear. Efficiencies in markets of all types will be naturally built in as a reflection of the *life conditions* of the value system that recognizes the seriousness of what it is to be alive.

This last known ᵛMEME can have an unhealthy expression as well. It can become lost in metaphysical issues and become detached from reality. Visions and ideas become difficult to translate into actions to create practical solution for pressing global challenges. It can look down on those who think more simply and cannot grasp the Turquoise approach. Like all sacrificial, group-oriented ᵛMEMEs, Turquoise can be heavy-handed and arrogant when others don't get with the program. The definitive characteristics of this ᵛMEME are beyond our knowledge at this time. Any specific timeframe on its emergence and the specific nature of its content remains purely Utopian and therefore highly speculative at this point. Evidence from the scientific community today points to increased environmental degradation caused by the first-tier subsistence ᵛMEMEs, which lays out a horrifying scenario that humanity may not be able to survive long enough for the Yellow ᵛMEME to fully perform its functions in order for humanity to emerge into the Turquoise ᵛMEME.

At the time the *Spiral Dynamics* book was published, there was speculation about the existence of a ninth-level system, CORAL, that is shown on the diagram of the original spiral. The debate about the existence of this level has created a philosophical difference between the integral philosophy community and the Gravesian school. While followers of integral philosophy believe that this system is manifesting itself, Gravesians contend that in order for a new value system to emerge, problems of existence from the previous system must be solved. This is the "life conditions" aspect of the Gravesian framework. What is discussed here about the emergence of the seventh-level Yellow and eighth-level Turquoise is from Beck's decades of experiential observations and practice. When I asked Beck to address the casual reference to Coral by the integral philosophy community, he acknowledged that there are few individuals around the world with "Coral thinking." Coral life conditions would not be manifested until a time when culture is ready to exit Turquoise, a phenomenon that remains speculative and far into the future.

SUBSISTENCE ᵛMEMES IN CHARGE OF ECONOMIC POLICIES

Seeing economic policy through the prism of the eight levels of existence provides the reader with a good sense of how exploitive the individualistic ᵛMEMEs have been in the pursuit of economic prosperity and how utterly

WHAT INVESTMENT AND MONEY MEAN TO THE DIFFERENT VALUE-SYSTEMS

ᵛMEME	INVESTMENT PHILOSOPHY/ VIEW OF CURRENCY	INVESTS IN
Second-Level System: Purple ᵛMEME	Investment world is scary and troublesome. Barely make enough to feed and shelter family. Must always help the extended family. The whole clan chips in for essential rituals. Survival of clan is priority above all else. Cash is key to keeping family together.	Cash under the mattress, if any left. Entire extended family saves for years to buy a car or a truck or primary residence to house many generations.
Third-Level System: Red ᵛMEME	Short term, high-risk with little or no money of their own invested in the venture. Create lots of noise about non-existing value to resell ASAP for the highest price and profit. Cash is king. Amass as much status icons as possible.	Underground activities. 100%+ financing deals. Little understood schemes that promise extremely high returns. The biggest house. The biggest car. No savings.
Fourth-Level System: Blue ᵛMEME	Long term, safe, conservative. Always save for a rainy day. Providing for family comes first. Employer, social security, and savings provide for good retirement. Trust the system that their golden years will be taken care of.	Savings, CDs, 401K, blue-chip stocks, conservative mutual funds with low but consistent returns. Pay off primary residence before retirement.
Fifth-Level System: Orange ᵛMEME	(HEALTHY) Constantly creating and investing in NEW INNOVATION. Always seeking undervalued assets through hard research. Creating value by bring-ing products from ideas to the marketplace and investing long term in ventures that do the same.	Strategically balanced portfolio. (short, mid-, and long-term) Stocks, bonds, real estate, start-up ventures. Google, Yahoo, Green Chip Companies.
Unhealthy Fifth-Level System	(UNHEALTHY) Exploit and manipulate EXISTING INNOVATION to maximize profit until (a) The system collapses, or (b) Stopped by BLUE, or (c) Healthy ORANGE produces a better, more marketable product.	Highly leveraged financial instruments. Commodities and Futures contracts. Sophisticated but little understood commercial paper. (DERIVATIVES)
Sixth-Level System: Green ᵛMEME	Invest in socially conscious enterprise. Less ROI (Return on Investment) and more ROC (Return on Consciousness). Shares the abundance through democratizing of resources.	Green and renewable technologies, micro-lending, Google and social networks, socially responsible funds.
Seventh-Level System: Yellow ᵛMEME	Invests to encourage the poor to do better. Turns away from high-risk and no equity in deals. Appreciates long-term stable investments. Limits investment in non-innovative technologies/products. Invests in innovative enterprise. Encourages conscious enterprise and practices that are sustainable.	Google, GE, 401K, micro-lending, start-up ventures. Green and renewable technologies. Believes in stratified and distributed economic systems. Disruptive innovation.

ineffective the collective ᵛMEMEs have been in bringing about long-term change in human behavior. Most of today's world economies have a cultural ᵛMEME stack with its heaviest expression in the third, fourth, and fifth levels. Much of *life conditions* in oil-rich nations of the Middle East are centered in a Purple-Red culture that borrows memes and expressions of the Western Orange system to further cement their own presence in Purple-Red with luxury, and rarely ever makes the provisional plans to sustain a presence in Orange. China with its Blue central planning approach to capitalism also borrows from the Western Orange system, and builds entire cities that remain vacant for years due to the absence of individualistic Orange metrics that would have predicted the supply and demand for housing. The United States has followed Japan in its struggle with the current expression of Orange in its finance subsector, but both nations still supply their obsolete banking systems with liquidity and wonder why their economies are not experiencing meaningful growth.

The EU has embraced the Green ᵛMEME in its generous social welfare programs at unsustainable levels of expenditure that tax economic activity. This unique brand of Green that has emerged out of post-colonial and post-war guilt leaves little room for investment in exploring new technologies. Yet its leaders continue to bail out insolvent members. These meme stacks around the world have different cultural content, but they are all approaches from the first-tier subsistence systems. It's only when these current systems collapse or when visionary leaders rise above their first-tier values that they realize that economic policies set from first tier are inherently ineffective in dealing with the complexity of human emergence. We may not fully know the tools we need to create second-tier economic policies yet, but what we do know is that first-tier policies have placed our planet in peril, and the need for a more systemic approach beckons world leaders at this crucial time in history.

THREE

The MEMEnomics
Theoretical Framework

Memenomics is defined as the study of the long-term effects of economic policy on culture as seen through the prism of value systems. When I first set out to define the elements for this concept, I wanted to find an easy way for the reader to be able to reframe modern economic history through the unique lenses of ᵛMEMEs. This task seemed to be monumental at first, especially when there is very little research that employs this unique approach. By placing economics into the evolutionary framework of value systems, the resulting research had to reflect the historic accuracy first before it could be used as a model to predict future economic emergence. The inextricable relationship between economics and cultural progress had to be supported through a historic reframing of facts through this unique prism. I started my work by researching the field of evolutionary economics, hoping to find patterns leading to higher expressions of cultural values. What I discovered instead was an area of study that barely nudges the field forward. Evolutionary economics has adopted concepts based on evolutionary game theory and evolutionary psychology that claim that economic change comes naturalistically and not as a result of technological changes that are aimed at improving the human condition.[44]

The field of evolutionary economics is rich with data on human behavior and complex systems, and although it is a change in the right direction, it remains a part of mainstream economics that is beholden to measures informed and designed by the system that has created the problem in the first place. It is when economics widens its scope to study both individual evolutionary psychology and psychology on a large scale, that it becomes a model that offers sustainable economic solutions that fit the unique ᵛMemetic contours of every culture. Without having a unifying theory that answers the question of how and why people and cultures behave in certain ways, the evolution of the field of economics will be limited to a more sophisticated expression of the fifth-level system. Nevertheless, the fact that the field is venturing away from traditional areas of cold empirical metrics means it is becoming an open system that can embrace concepts such as *Natural Design*, which provides answers to much of the naturalistic causes of systems evolution and is a part of the Spiral Dynamics framework for large-scale change. It is the adoption of this "naturalistic evolution" of economics through the prism of value systems that defines the basic elements of the memenomic history of economics. This wide view of how different value systems interact from the local level all the way through policy setting levels will provide a clearer picture on how economic activity is interpreted and whether that activity is exploitive and temporary or sustainable and evolutionary.

MEMENOMIC CYCLES

Aside from the endless empirical measure of economic performance that one reads in the daily newspaper, such as unemployment, the CPI, GDP, consumer sentiment, and so on, modern economics also focuses on cycles. There are hundreds of cycles that are studied, from global macroeconomic ones to industry-specific ones. Cycles range in duration anywhere from two years to ten, and they are all designed to inform consumers, producers, and policy makers about how to adjust their strategies to enhance growth for the next quarter, the next fiscal year, or for the rest of one's political term. Memenomic cycles have very little to do with daily or quarterly movements of markets or the effects of political speeches. Since memenomics studies the long-term effect the economy has on culture and cultural emergence, it doesn't limit itself to the narrow and efficient metrics of the fifth-level Orange systems that have little regard for factors that lay outside the focus of their cycles. By focusing on both economics and cultural emergence, memenomics attempts to predict long-term patterns and upcoming changes through a unique prism before they happen. My research has uncovered certain cyclical patterns that are closer in duration to a sociological era or an ideology. A single cycle is based on how long a certain belief system informs the dominant narrative of *life conditions*. It spans many decades from beginning to end, and as it declines, its remnants become a lower expression in the next system.

To establish the outer parameters of my research in this area, as a starting point I used what Graves and the Spiral Dynamics theory describe as a ᵛMEME "Life Cycle." It hypothesizes that each value system carries the seeds of its birth, death, and residue from the previous system and goes through three distinct phases in its lifetime: Entering, Peak, and Exiting.[45] Theoretically, the three phases serve as a measure of where the emerging ᵛMEME is in relationship to *life conditions*; is it ahead, in sync, or behind? If it's ahead of *life conditions*, the new system is still being defined. If it is in sync, its balanced and its values will grow to define the culture. If it's behind it will be identified with misalignment, fragmentation, and, in worst cases, toxicity and collapse. The challenge I faced in conducting my research was that aside from Grave's bio-psycho-social academic research and Beck's applications in specific global hotspots, no one has attempted to redefine macroeconomic theory through the parameters of value systems.

Throughout the many months of research I conducted, I observed several patterns that kept emerging that might have escaped the notice of many historians and economists. These became undeniable to me and to anyone who is familiar with the sequence of value systems evolution that were outlined earlier and will be discussed more in detail. One of the main challenges I faced was the fact that individual ᵛMEMEs don't exist in a vacuum by themselves. They interact with each other within a complex hierarchy of values with different memetic content that can influence the outcome of my research. Before proceeding I identified certain elements to look for in order to detect patterns of change within the whole hierarchy.

As I continued to develop my methodology I began to detect healthy and unhealthy expressions of a ᵛMEME. For example, one of the patterns that emerged was during times when the fourth-level system is diminished, unhealthy practices from both the third- and fifth-level systems dominate the economic landscape, leading to recessions, or in more severe cases to the decline of a system. Knowing a system's potential for change by identifying whether it's an open, closed, or arrested system, created yet another research tool for me that is not currently a part of econometric consciousness. I also detected unique patterns of ᵛMEME interaction when a system becomes toxic but its values continue to spread. As my research expanded, I found other value system patterns that were common in bringing an end to a system. These patterns represent the gross misunderstanding that economists and politician have of the role that money plays in the emergence of culture. I have also discovered that technology plays a big role in defining the character of every era, as far as how and when the era emerges and the impact it has on the varying stages within a specific cycle. Many other patterns kept emerging that made me reexamine the ᵛMEME Life Cycle model, and I found it necessary to expand it in order to accommodate for the complexity of economics and culture. The result is a much denser cycle with several more distinct stages of development that are articulated through real historic experiences.

The basic construct of a memenomic cycle has seven phases of change. Together these phases will reframe the history of the US economy through an evolutionary memenomic narrative. By using this unique approach I was able to identify three distinct cycles that the US economy has been through

THE FOUR MEMENOMIC CYCLES

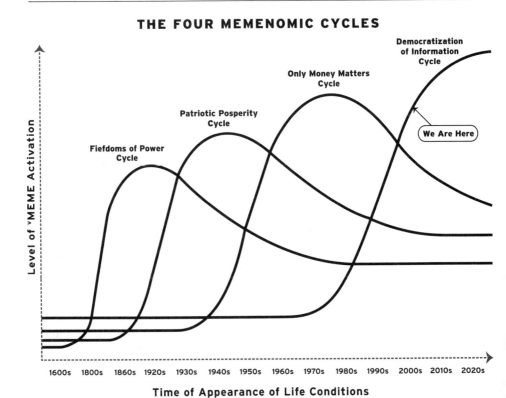

since the Civil War and how today we stand on the cusp of a fourth cycle. Although each of these cycles represented a dominant value system during its time, analysis is necessary for the other value systems that were present and how they were affected by the different phases of every cycle. What follows is an outline of the phases of each cycle, what they are, and how they are applied in reframing the past and the future of economics through this unique approach.

PHASE I: INQUIRY The inquiry phase of a memenomic cycle is similar to an incubation or gestation period in life cycles of animals and plants. This is a time period that must pass before things come into form. This is when the initial elements of the new memenomic cycle begin to appear in the minds of futurists and oracles. Much of it remains hidden from view just like a dormant seed under the winter snow. It is nourished by the inevitable forward march of progress brought on by being in an open system. It carries within it the DNA of past cycles, but must evolve to a new and more advanced form of expression in order to be the fittest of all competing ideas. Evolution at this stage is a lot like Darwin's natural selection where ideas instead of living creatures fight for survival to be able to have a chance at being a part of what defines the next system. The longer the dominant cycle is in sync with *life conditions*, the longer the new cycle remains in the dormant inquiry stage. It continues to develop antibodies that it will need to fight off attacks from the current system when that system starts to decline.

Historically the inquiry phase was a set of embryonic ideas that gestate for years or even decades in the minds of visionaries before becoming the shared values of the mainstream. This is the stage when Adam Smith cultivated his thinking on the virtues of capitalism before they jelled into the declaration of moral sentiments and the wealth of nations. This is where John Maynard Keynes added to his thinking over years before it came to define the crucial role governments can play in a capitalist system and became the model that rebuilt the world after World War II.

A more recently example is Alan Greenspan's consulting practice, where for years he developed ground-breaking econometric models for the manufacturing industry before being noticed by his professor and predecessor at the Fed. In the last few decades, academia has played a far greater role in being an incubator for ideas that inform the next cycle. The healthy Orange and Green environments of research based universities like the Chicago School of Economics gave us Milton Freidman and the Monetarist ideology. Today, Stanford University is a hot bed and a birthplace of ideas that shape the knowledge economy. As culture moves forward with the help of social networks and the knowledge economy, the gestation period of this phase has many more minds shaping it and gets vetted at a much faster rate than any time before in human history.

PHASE II: IDENTIFICATION In biological life cycles this phase is recognized as birth and early years. This is when the ideas that survived the gestation period come to define the next cycle in waiting: a first look at the phenotype of the next system. The identification stage is much like seeing a newborn for the first time when one learns the color of its hair and eyes and other markings that won the battle to identify that person for life. The unique identifications in a memenomics cycle are not just from visionary economic ideas. They come from a collective of visionaries from every segment of culture. It is the jelling of futuristic mindsets from economics, sociology, technology, and science that contribute to identifying the whole new system while having been through the vetting process in the inquiry phase that shaped the new identity. Still, this phase remains invisible to the mainstream. Its approaches continue to be regarded as fringe by the powerbrokers that believe that the dominant current system will last forever. The distinct characteristic of this phase is the confirmation that fringe thinking might not be limited to one area of culture but represents the systemic emergence of new thinking among the most intelligent members of the human species across the board.

PHASE III: INTRODUCTION This is the phase when the new system moves from the visionary-fringe through to the testing phase and on to becoming a trailblazing innovation as it goes through more refinement and articulation. Initially the premise for the new ideals is defended within the elite environments that created them. This is where the values of the new system gain institutional acceptance. This phase is similar to a web-based company that uses a beta test of its technology by its employees in order to work out the bugs before it's offered for general use. Instead of employees within a company, this beta phase is conducted across all sectors of culture that are early adopters of the emerging system. Theories and concepts for the new system gain more prominence as they are proven and consequently spread through university classrooms and other learning environments. As business models and scientific experiments undertaken by early adopters of the new system make it past the trial phase, the acceptance of the new system widens. This phase reaches its pinnacle as the dominant system begins to decline and wider segments of culture begin to associate it with alternative cutting edge values.

PHASE IV: GROWTH This is the phase where the values of the new system spread widely and come in sync with *life conditions*. This is also when the system enters an open state. It is no longer in the visionary phases, since the majority of people now elect politicians who can bring its values to full fruition. In the two most prominent cycles of the past, political figures representing the entry into the growth phase were Franklin D. Roosevelt and Ronald Reagan. There's a renewed sense of optimism as chaos from the decline phase of the previous system gives way to an emerging order that is hopeful and optimistic. Ronald Reagan's television ad "morning in America again" indelibly captured the mood of this phase. This is a paradigm shift where the new direction and its future hold far more explanatory powers than any previous systems before it. Although remnants of past systems are present, everything about this phase is being experienced for the first time. New memes informed by the values of the new system are generated in business, technology, academia, architecture, the media and other areas and become socially standardized as they attract greater attention, larger market share, and increased revenues.

PHASES OF A MEMENOMIC CYCLE

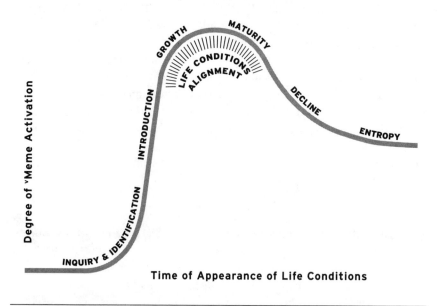

At this stage, the majority of the culture identifies with the values of the system and believes in its future. As optimism begets prosperity, the new system reposes into a prolonged period of stability. It becomes the primary generator of new jobs. This is where the fifth-level system is at its healthiest expression. Innovation moves fast as it tries to keep pace with the increasing demands of the new *life conditions.* New opportunities for economic development appear in places that previously didn't exist or were simply overlooked. The system hums along through many election cycles only needing minor adjustments because all institutions are in tune with the needs of their citizens, and all needs arising from the system are matched with the skills and intelligences of the people. All life seems to be at balance. This phase is identified with the greatest periods of economic expansion like the 1950s that established America's middle class as the most power consumer group in the world.

PHASE V: MATURITY This is the phase where the innovative drive of the system reaches its half-life. This is also when the system shifts from an open state and enters an arrested state. Creating new technologies and cultural memes becomes harder as the system approaches a saturation point.

The excitement that came from the climb into the system subsides as culture realizes it has reached the peak and there are no further heights to climb. The economy settles into a calcified state where it uses existing technologies, policies, and business strategies for the sole purpose of insuring its long-term presence in the system and guarding against future losses. Societies settle into a monotonous routine where preserving the order of the current system is the primary motivation. Minor tweaks to the system in this phase don't result in technological breakthroughs. They are designed as not to rock the boat and maintain a course towards long-term stability.

At this phase of the cycle, success that was achieved in the growth phase gives birth to a whole new set of problems, which inform the visionaries of the new system that is still in the inquiry and identification phase. Leaders and managers at this phase still believe that solutions from within the system are still on the cutting edge and continue to use them, and this provides less effective solutions. The further we move into this phase the lower the marginal utility of these tools become. This was clearly demonstrated during the second memenomic cycle when the values of the era were aligned with patriotic prosperity and the government continued to implement tax increases well into the 1960s, expecting that *life conditions* have remained in sync with "big brother knows best." In the third memenomic cycle we will see how some of the Clinton Administration policies during this phase believed that *life conditions* were still in sync with an environment that favored deregulation and proceeded with deregulating the banking industry, which hastened the system's entry into the next phase.

PHASE VI: DECLINE   This phase is when the powerbrokers in the system begin to panic about the future and start exploiting the values provided by the system to avoid collapse. At this phase of the cycle the system becomes a closed system. Minor tweaks no longer achieve the results they did in the previous two phases. New management training and educational programs only nudge the system forward in the smallest marginal way. Efficiency measures and lower costs resulting in lower prices barely move levels of consumption forward. After being on a complacency trajectory since the maturity phase, innovation specific to this system reaches its lowest levels. This is the time when the focus of powerbrokers within the system shifts away from innovation towards mass production, allowing the system to fall further into complaisance and begin to target mass consumption as its primary goal. Products are repackaged with minor enhancements and reintroduced to markets with the expectation that consumers will react to them with the same excitement as before. The automobile industry believes that the same vehicle with a different color and leather seats makes for an entirely different year model.

By now, the system is defined by mass consumption and all its resources are placed in the service of achieving that goal. As normal consumption slows down, the system invents new and unorthodox ways to keep itself in balance. In patterns similar in all three cycles the powerbrokers within each system work on expanding the purchasing power of the consumer without adding much to real productive output. In the first cycle, this phase was identified as the "roaring twenties" when bankers flooded the streets with cash and gave money to whoever asked for it regardless of their ability to repay. During that era institutions in charge of the money set new lending targets that are far beyond their normal circles of qualified individuals and businesses. During this phase lenders wrongly speculate that everyone, regardless of what value system they belong to, will always act in their own best interest as seen through the value systems of the bankers. This is the phase when blatant consumerism hollows out personal wealth as it reaches every corner of society regardless of income levels. This is also when money begins to decouple from its historic relationship to productive output. In the second cycle, this phase brought on the collapse of the Bretton Woods financial framework as spending and consumption in the United States could no longer be constrained by antiquated values that were not in sync with a peace time, consumer-based economy. The variation in comparison between the first and third cycle on one side, and the second cycle during this phase will become clearer by understanding how money is reframed through the prism of memenomics.

In the third cycle this phase represented the millennial years when tapping into equity from an average home represented multiple times the spending power of a paycheck. As problems arise during this phase the predominant solution is to supply more money to the consumer and more capital to banks and financial markets and hope for the best. Although minor tweaks to the system worked in the previous two phases, this is an entirely different type of tweaking. Instead of nudging the system forward towards a known end point, a policy of *money for nothing* creates a false sense of economic security based on speculative borrowing. Reliance on the financial sector and on high levels of consumption beyond normal means places the system at an inflection point and begins the end stage of the decline phase. Without technological innovation playing a leading role in moving culture forward, financial innovation will derail the system in very short order. As we'll see, money has always been a representative of productive output, an agent of the fourth-level system that has historically provided far greater order for society than any other incentive. Once money stops being a representative of productivity it will inevitably pervert the very nature of exchange-for-value, and it creates bubble economies that rupture and create systemic toxicity forcing the most complex of systems into a final phase of decay.

PHASE VII: ENTROPY This is the final phase of a memenomic cycle when the ideology of the dominant system becomes bankrupted and goes through orderly disintegration. The system's values in this phase have become out of sync with *life conditions.* A severe correction in stock markets and a sudden drop in employment that lasts for years almost always announce entry into this phase. This is also known as a period of economic contraction where we must pay for years of misaligned spending and misallocation of capital resources. We know we have entered this phase when solutions from within the system, regardless of magnitude, fail to nudge it forward. The primary goal of powerbrokers here is to prop up the value of assets as close as possible to levels before the end of the decline phase and the bursting of bubbles in order to avoid systemic collapse. In the absence of other viable sectors that grow the economy, these actions only serve to spread the toxicity and hasten the system towards its endpoint.

By the time the tools from the system become obsolete, economic growth stagnates. High long-term unemployment and poverty become the norm. Billions, even trillions, in stimulus money don't add to the employment roles. Hopelessness and anger among the masses spreads and demonstrations against ineffective politicians and powerbrokers within the system grow by the day. The brightest thinking from within the system becomes worthless in the face of increased desperation. As the system lingers for a few years under this type of pressure, its values collapse and transform into informational units that join similar units from past cycles. These become a part of the toolbox for the visionaries of the next system, allowing the system to ascend into the introduction phase of the emerging system and beyond.

At the end of the first cycle, this phase represented the Great Depression and its prolonged aftermath, which has many memenomic similarities to what we are going through today. It is important to point that this phase—at least in advanced economies like the United States, Western Europe, and Japan-rarely results in the collapse of the entire economy. This has become more so especially as we move forward in history with more economic layers and value-systems complexity. The more a system believes in the virtues of research and development and scientific inquiry the less likely the possibility of collapse. My research has shown that almost simultaneously with the onset of this phase, the new system accelerates through its introduction phase from being on the fringe to entering the mainstream. The faster a new system goes through the introduction phase, the less severe the effects of the dominant system going through its entropy phase will be. Strategies and observations on how to shorten the last phase of a system while accommodating the emergence of the new system will be discussed in the last part of this book.

THE TECH-LC GAP

One of the most crucial catalysts for emergence under this methodology is the role that technology plays during the different phases of a memenomic cycle. Technology is present in its highest raw form during the *inquiry* and *introduction* phases. This is when the focus is entirely on research and development and on the science and not on markets. Mad scientists in white lab coats working on things that we'll never understand will be an appropriate metaphor to describe this phase. Along with the cycle's movement into the *introduction* phase, technology moves from R&D to early cutting edge adoption by visionary technological innovators. It plays its greatest role in a memenomic cycle during the *growth* phase as it empowers most economic advancements and accommodates all the tweaks to keep the system in sync with *life conditions*. As we enter the maturity phase and we shift from innovation to mass production and consumption, we force technology to decouple from *life conditions*. Maximizing the benefits of existing technologies becomes a necessity for the success of the business model during this phase. As it moves forward the gap between *life conditions* and technology continue to widen. As we enter the *decline* and *entropy* phases, technology has moved so far ahead of *life conditions* that a retraining of the labor force becomes necessary. As we reach the final stages of *entropy*, the gap between technology and *life conditions* is at its widest, and the economy has to suffer through many years of re-education and realignment as a far more sophisticated form of technology appears in the new cycle. This pattern was clearly noticeable during the Great Depression as automated farming equipment replaced tens of thousands of farm workers during the decline and entropy phase of a system that had no capacity to retrain workers. Similar patterns from the two subsequent cycles will be expanded on in upcoming chapters.

AESTHETIC VS. SYSTEMIC CHANGE

In this brief description of the phases of a memenomic cycle one can see the stages during which change is possible. Change becomes increasingly difficult as the system moves from open to arrested to closed states. By the time it enters decline and entropy, change becomes almost impossible. In talking about the varying degrees of change, I often hear Beck ask the question: change FROM what TO what? In other words is the change we're seeking one of a translational nature within the same system that keeps it aligned with *life conditions* or is it one of a transformational nature that requires systems thinking that evolves it into a higher level of existence. In modern economic history there have been very few thinkers who were able to help a system evolve into the next memenomic cycle without having people suffer through severe corrections and long periods of recession.

On the other hand, there have been many translational leaders who claimed success for economic prosperity when they had very little to do with placing the economy on a long-term trajectory towards success. During the growth phase of a cycle, as long as the fundamentals of an economy are healthy, minor tweaking to the system almost always results in success. In memenomic cycles, this is known as *aesthetic change*. An example of this type of change is when an economy is at full employment and suddenly the rate nudges up from 4.2 percent to 4.9 percent. The Federal Reserve lowers interest rates by .25 percent and unemployment falls back to original levels six month later. Small *aesthetic change* achieves the end result and the system moves forward. During the growth phase these changes could come from technological, economic, or political shifts, but they always achieve high net results with minor degrees of variation. During the maturity phase these tweaks become less effective as structural problems begin to appear but remain insignificant. By necessity these tweaks become bigger just to achieve the same results under the *growth* phase.

By the time we move into the *decline* phase the size of every tweak becomes even greater. It is no longer unemployment in the 5 percent range needing a .25 percent interest rate reduction. It might be closer to 7 percent and the Fed reduces rates by .75 percent without achieving the corresponding reduction in unemployment. The same philosophy of employing *aesthetic change* methods with increasingly higher quantities of the same remedy continue into the entropy phase till they become completely ineffective or even toxic. This is when *systemic change* becomes the only option and the values of the current system must be retired in favor of values that are informed by the new system, which carries with it the DNA of all past systems. Throughout my research it became apparent to me that the more a system becomes closed the less effective *aesthetic change* is and the greater the *systemic change* needs to be when it collapses.

Since complete collapse is not a part of economic reality, structural changes must be addressed in real time while the new system is emerging. This is when the entire memestack must be examined. Failures in the fourth-level value system in that cycle must be assessed and redesigned to withstand similar vulnerabilities in the future. New institutions might need to be created while others that have become ineffective must be dissolved. Certain practices within the fifth-level system might need to be banned or severely restricted in order not to create the threat of systemic risk in the future. These are changes that need to take place at an institutional level and must address structural vulnerabilities before a new system can leave the first two phases and enter the growth phase. This is the time when tools from second-tier values are most needed. A seventh-level system's perspective that takes into consideration the values of the emerging system, combines them with the lessons learned from the current system and all past systems, and places them on a functional trajectory to serve a new common goal. The three memenomic cycles will be examined in more detail in upcoming chapters where many more of the historic nuances will be reframed through the language of value systems and placed into a real model of evolutionary economics based on memenomics. In general these three cycles represent the economic transition of the United States from a culture centered in the Red value system all the way to where we are today, on the cusp of the Green value system.

Before that can be done the role of money in human emergence must be examined and reframed through this unique value-systems approach that gives for most an entirely new view about money. It will be important to first understand the historic role this essential agent has played in economic emergence and offer advice on how to evolve its role without causing global economic collapse while still empowering a functional form of financial innovation.

FOUR

The Role of Money
in Human Emergence

The best way to destroy the capitalist system is to debauch the currency.[46]
—VLADIMIR LENIN

It is important to detail the three memenomic cycles the United States economy has been through since the start of the Civil War and Reconstruction. Special emphasis will be placed on the many factors that have aligned to create the perfect storm, which culminated in the financial crisis of 2008 and entered the United States into the entropy phase of the third cycle. Although the United States seems to be slowly recovering, the shocks from the structural faults that were decades in the making have permanently exposed the speculative and risky nature of the current expression of capitalism. In Chapter one I briefly chronicled the evolution of capitalism through the eyes of policy makers as it became identified primarily through financial innovation. Up until the time when the US dollar was taken off the gold standard in 1971, the finance function in an economy, whether it was lending activities or raising capital, was a measure of current and future productive output of our economy.

In the last four decades, money has gone through a monumental shift that has violated that historic role; it has become a part of productive output itself. It is this dramatic shift in the role of finance, a classic case of the tail that wagged the dog in the functioning of an economy, that must be understood from a value-systems perspective in order for capitalism to correct its course and emerge to higher levels of healthy expressions. To better understand the damage that continues to be caused by having a finance-based economy I will briefly chronicle the historic role money played in human emergence. Observation of the history of economic development through the prism of value systems differs from those observations of a traditional historian of economics. The goal is to show that the function of money was naturally and historically identified with the Blue fourth-level system with a limited but highly regimented role in the Orange fifth-level system. This meant that Orange financial innovation had to remain a function of Blue productive output in order for the system to remain healthy. The deviation from those historically proven standards and the false belief by policy makers at the top that financial innovation can move the functional role of money and place it squarely in the hands of the Orange ᵛMEME, have been the primary causes of the financial collapse. Memenomic cycles have consistently proven that an economy enters the decline and entropy phases when money is removed from its historic Blue role. This is where we are today, overlooking the role money served for thousands of years and not having learned the lessons of history.

MONEY AND THE TRIBAL ORDER

Throughout human history money has played a crucial role in helping humanity emerge into more sophisticated forms of expression. Human beings have been involved in various modes of exchange of goods for many centuries. Before Adam Smith defined modern economics, simple bartering or gifting was a form of exchange that had been in use from the time humans banded together to form tribes in order to survive. From a value-systems perspective, the rewards received from an exchange of one item of consumption for another represented the earliest appearances of the Truth Force ᵛMEME or the fourth-level Blue system. Although in its earliest appearances, *life conditions* were primarily tribal, and nations with rules and laws or modern religions that define the current fourth-level system were many centuries in the future, the tribes engaged in frequent exchange. This was ascribed to the higher meaning of the activity as it provided them with creature comforts they couldn't attain on their own. The two most prominent social contracts that represented the thin layer of the order system in tribal times were marriage and exchange or barter.

The earliest known manifestation of an ancient barter system was in Mesopotamia. The Shekel, which is the official currency of the state of Israel today, was named after a bushel of grain that was a standardized unit of exchange more than 8000 years ago.[47] Since grain did not suffer from the same spoilage factors as other foods for barter, it was stored in a common depository, and it became the first official form of exchange when accounts were kept on how much grain belonged to whom. As *life conditions* moved forward and tribes developed the capacity to save more of what they produced, modes of exchange started to multiply. Bartering evolved to a variety of goods, including items such as artifacts, jewelry, and precious metals, which eventually lead to the use of coins as a widely accepted form of exchange of value.

Ancient bartering was in essence the invisible force, along with tribal chiefs and holy men, that provided for the early existence of tribal order. But unlike the other symbols of order within this early second-level Purple system, bartering or gifting provided for peaceful coexistence with other tribes. For the first time, tribes traveled to other tribes not to pillage, steal, or kill, but to perform peaceful exchange. As tribes came to trust their trading partners, trade grew to more sophisticated levels and the number of trading partners increased. In the process, barriers that defined protected tribal living for centuries started to slowly disappear, and larger tribes began to form in bigger villages and ancient cities. During this course of tribal evolution, money in the form of commodity exchange formed the most widely agreed upon social contract and constituted what were the broadest acceptable symbols of hard work, prosperity, and social status.

THE EMPEROR'S COIN

As humanity continued to evolve and it entered the empire-driven third-level system, money took on a more important role. Emperors needed to impose power over their subjects and at the same time allow for a system of exchange that paid wages and permitted basic trade to function. This was made easier when rulers created their own money and passed laws that punished anyone who did not accept coin money as a legal form of tender. As this practice became more common, in the feudal third-level system it replaced previous forms of barter, but was still being identified as a vehicle that expressed a fourth-level order system simply based on the nature of its function. As the role of money evolved within this system, the Babylonians and their neighboring city-states took it to its next form of expression. They created the earliest system of economics as we think of it today, in terms of establishing rules on debt, legal contracts, and laws relating to business practices and private property.[48] Many other dynasties took their turns over the centuries to modify the type of commodity that would represent the impenetrable function that money provided in keeping workers paid, trade moving, and peace among the masses. From the early days of the Sumerian Dynasty to the Ottoman and British Empires, the more complex and widely spread the use of a monetary system became, the more laws were created that guided its uses and punished its misuse.

As this feudal third level system continued to evolve so did the mode of exchange. By the time the Industrial Age and the era of nation-states began, precious metals like gold and silver became the preferred currency of the British Empire. In the late 1600s, with their colonies spanning the globe, the British single-handedly made gold the compulsory mean of exchange the world over.[49] With its influence so widely spread, it became easier for the Colonial British empire, from which to create a banking system backed by the economic strength of the empire from which evolved the notion of currency backed by the gold standard.

THE GOLD OF NATIONS

During the age of empires, commercial banks played the biggest role in advancing commerce and determining monetary systems and modes of exchange without much interference from anyone. As empires started to dissolve, and *life conditions* allowed for nation-states to emerge, the critical function of money in everyday life was further defined by the appearance of national banks. Through acts of national governments the use of paper money backed by gold became wide spread, and after many trials and errors and runs on banks, it gained the full trust and confidence of the public. From a value-systems perspective, this was a defining stage of the fourth-level Blue system where finance played some of its most crucial roles in modern human emergence. The prosperity of a nation became deeply intertwined with how well developed its monetary system was. Development of infrastructure and institutions that would have not attracted the interest of the merchant class took place under a Blue governmental system that guaranteed their implementation by guarantying the currency.

As attention turned to nation building, the banking sector turned its attention to the development of a modern banking system that created much of the distributed wealth we see today. Once *life conditions* were identified with the safety and security of the rule of law in banking, debt financing for trade expansion and the creation of stock markets came into being to symbolize this new era of prosperity. Modern banking was being built on a more defined Blue structure that was initially identified and followed by ancient dynasties centuries before. The psychological motivation that compelled human beings to work hard, exchange wages for goods and services, save money, and borrow and repay when needed, became the foundation from which the West was propelled into the Age of Enlightenment and signaled the beginning of the Industrial Revolution.

Life conditions in the West at the dawn of the Industrial Revolution were still in the nation-forming stage of the fourth-level Blue system. Trade, however, was being redefined through the eyes of the Enlightenment Movement and was set to take a monumental leap forward into what would become the foundation of capitalism as we know it today.

Adam Smith, the Scottish moral philosopher, started laying down new grounds related to the sentiment of exchange and trade by contributing to the new Blue code of the British Empire and examining the moral thinking of his time. Smith first introduced the *Theory of Sympathy*, which puts forth the notion that conscience arises from social relationships, and is the source of mankind's ability to form moral judgments. During the act of observing others, people become aware of themselves and the morality of their own behavior in spite of their natural inclinations towards self-interest.[50] A few years after this new Blue code of the Enlightenment Era that tied human nature to moral restraint, Smith authored his groundbreaking book *The Wealth of Nations* in which the argument for the spread of self-interest becomes the new meme that defined the systemic spread of wealth. Smith refers to an *invisible hand*, which performs this role in helping humanity emerge in this manner:

> As every individual, therefore, endeavours as much as he can both to employ his capital in the support of domestick industry, and so to direct that industry that its produce may be of the greatest value; every individual necessarily labours to render the annual revenue of the society as great as he can. He generally, indeed, neither intends to promote the public interest, nor knows how much he is promoting it. By preferring the support of domestiek to that of foreign industry, he intends only his own security; and by directing that industry in such a manner as its produce may be of the greatest value, he intends only his own gain, and he is in this, as in many other eases, led by an invisible hand to promote an end which was no part of his intention. Nor is it always the worse for the society that it was no part of it. By pursuing his own interest he frequently promotes that of the society more effectually than when he really intends to promote it. I have never known much good done by those who affected to trade for the publick good.[51]

Life conditions during Adam Smith's era were primed for a paradigm shift in human emergence. The empowerment of the individual came about in the most natural way, and a new definition of nation building was taking root. Except this time the effort wasn't being brought about by an act of government. Man, just by simply performing the craft he knew best, created an invisible hand that spread good deeds to building the wealth of a collective culture. These early stages of the fifth-level Orange system established the self-empowerment of the Strategic Enterprise ᵛMEME and forever placed Adam Smith into the history books as the father of economics and capitalism.

As this enlightened capitalist philosophy spread through Europe and the United States, further development of monetary controls within each country was needed to accommodate the spread of wealth and protect against the abuses of predatory and monopolistic practices. The Bank of England turned its attention from financing wars to the development of its industrial infrastructure. Modern day institutions that supported the evolution of capitalism, such as stock markets and central banks, started to appear all throughout the Western World. For most of the eighteenth and nineteenth century economic theories competed for the heart and minds of the industrial worker as the merchant class that had become identified as capitalists competed with socialist schools of thought, such as that of Karl Marx, over fair wages and worker abuses. Up until the end of World War I these institutions that helped spread capitalism through its early expressions of the Industrial Era, were backed by the gold standard. The role of money in human emergence was further recognized for the critical fourth-level Blue function it played in developing humanity and advancing its cause through an endless quest for higher forms of expression.

RISE OF THE DOLLAR

At the end of World War I an era began which saw the slow erosion of the fourth-level Blue system in the role that money played in human emergence. The stable and consistent use of paper money and financial instruments created a natural departure from the gold standard. This precious commodity only came into demand at times of war and economic uncertainty when the survival of the predominant fourth-level Blue system was being threatened. Trading nations had the long established understanding that although they subscribed to the gold standard, there would not be a demand for redemption of 100 percent of the money in gold. Paper money in the mid-nineteenth century started to stand on its own merit as a medium of exchange as long as its acceptance remained widespread and protected by the rule of law. During periods of stability and economic prosperity very few questioned the validity of paper money and whether it was backed by the gold standard or not. Paper had taken on the function of the exchange for value that for centuries had been backed by one form of commodity or another. By the beginning of World War I the complexity of finance could no longer be defined by an arbitrary system that relied on the availability of a certain precious metal and kept the boundless potential of economic activity and global trade limited to how much gold a nation had in storage. Just as it did in adopting the gold standard many centuries before, England took the lead in abandoning it, and soon many other nations followed.

The evolution of money up until the beginning of the twentieth century has consistently shown its functionality as a direct representative of productive output. Whether it was wages for work performed or financial rewards as a result of strategic planning and investment, the rewards were commensurate with quality and the quantity of human productive input. As *life conditions* in the West continued to move into the Strategic Enterprise ᵛMEME, global powers looked to redefine the nature of the guarantee aspect of money. In essence nations looked to replace the tangible market value of gold and other commodities with the intangible market value of the power and credibility of the currency's issuing government. From a value-systems perspective this was a necessary step to move money away from its historical false fourth-level Blue system attachment to gold to a new, yet undefined, Blue-Orange expression. If gold was a true expression of the wealth of a nation, then only those nations rich in gold deposits would have economic superiority. This was the presumption that made the world go round until the last century of the industrial era.

As scientific discoveries further shifted economic power to industrial countries gold became less and less important and the notion of paper money backed only by the faith of its issuing government gained more prominence. This is the phase known as fiat money, the word derived from the Latin "let it be done." This was a meritorious system of determining the true worth of an economy. Productive output of industry had a direct correlation to the presumptive value of the currency. From a value-systems perspective this new Blue expression of currency had boundless possibilities for expanding economic power and trade and was the truest representation of the fifth-level Orange system, as long as a Blue structure remained in place that held the value of the currency to a direct relationship of total economic output and accounted for adjustments in balance of payments and trade. Unlike its previous and simple uses in previous centuries, the use of fiat money in a modern industrial era during the twentieth century represented a wholly different platform for economic expansion.

After the end of World War II the West entered into an economic alliance that would hasten the end of the gold standard and bring about the global acceptance of the US Dollar as the most stable world currency. The Bretton Woods system was set up to define the new role of money and through it the US dollar became the world's reserve currency. To the victor belonged the spoils, and to the United States belonged the unprecedented opportunity to set itself up as the undisputed champion of the Strategic Enterprise ᵛMEME. As the United States rebuilt Europe and Japan, trade agreements were enacted that further cemented the function of the US Dollar as the new fourth-level Blue system to which this new world-order subscribed. The United States had set its currency as the world reserve currency, and although it guaranteed its redemption in gold for decades, no Western nations sought such redemption. The new role of this paper money served to make the United States an economic superpower and at the same time accommodated the distribution of wealth at a systemic level with its trade partners.

This experiment in the worldwide use of this new quasi-fiat fourth-level Blue system was put to its first test in the 1970s. The challenges from the modern dynamics of an advanced industrial economy were intertwined with complex trade agreements that started to test the limits of the new powers of the US Dollar under the constraints of Bretton Woods. Deficit spending of the post WWII reconstruction effort, the overseas flight of the dollar, the cost of the Cold War and later the Vietnam War, presented insurmountable challenges to the long-term viability of the dollar as the world's reserve currency.[52] Since a member nation under Bretton Woods could not finance spending by printing more of its currency. The United States, after three short decades, abandoned the principles of this system and any remaining ties to the gold standard. Although the US dollar has been a fiat currency since 1971, the fact that the US economy remains the largest in the world has kept the dollar as the unofficial reserve currency of the global economy till this day.

INFLATION: THE FIRST HISTORIC THREAT TO THE MONETARY ORDER ᵛMEME

The financial needs of the increasing complexities of *life conditions* in the 1970s and beyond could no longer come from a stringent and antiquated system with limited functionality. The shift away from the dollar as defined by the Bretton Woods framework symbolized an upward movement to an advanced expression of the fourth-level Blue system that had rejected the gold standard. A government with a diligent eye on the money supply and its cost were the controls that were initially thought of as the new fourth level system mechanism that will keep the function of money in check and as close as possible to the role it had under the gold standard but with a greater degree of flexibility. Backed solely by the perceived value of the corresponding economic activity, this new merit system symbolized the birth of the very first modern fiat currency with unprecedented global reach.

The fundamentals of this new system, along with the prevailing *life conditions,* are worthy of further examination, as they would eventually pave the way to the current expression of capitalism in the West. As is often the case with the emergence of a new system born out of the dysfunction of a prior system, the initial phase of a fiat dollar was quite tumultuous. With government spending out of control for decades, abandonment of the gold standard put market forces immediately into play. With levers and parameters that had not yet been tested the results sent shocks through every corner of the US economy. This act was paramount to a debtor unanimously declaring that he or she no longer wished to play under the same rules under which the extension of debt took place. This was the US government, the largest representative of the fourth-level Blue system, declaring to its citizenry that it no longer wished to honor its debt obligations based on centuries old rules. Without the Blue role that gold represented, the US dollar was in a free-fall and inflation emerged as the biggest threat the capitalist system.

In years past, upward pressure on prices was tempered by the notion that long-term inflation was determined by the growth rate of the supply of gold relative to total productive output.[53] Much of the power and control structure that was held to a definitive set of rules under the gold standard was now given to interpretation by free market economists, most of whom were top advisors to policy makers and presidents. From a value-systems perspective this was the shift that freed monetary policy from an *arrested* fourth-level Blue system, one that was encumbered by tradition and limitation, to a new and *open* expression of what was still the fourth-level system, but was now being informed by market forces, which changed the dynamics of its expression.

As the United States faced competition from foreign manufacturer and experienced the effects of the oil crisis on the consumer, the blame for the failure to contain inflation was directed towards policy makers who were being accused of taking the economy off the gold standard irresponsibly and prematurely. The faith of the US Government in the backing of the fiat dollar continued to be put through strenuous tests and increasing challenges throughout the 1970s and early 1980s. Although this phase of monetary evolution caused much social upheaval, a return to the limited functionality under the gold standard would have made matters worse as *life conditions* were getting more complex and needed more advanced ways to deal with a rapidly diversifying economy. Money continued to evolve in search of a new and stable fourth level Blue role that would define the road ahead and the new expression of capitalism.

It had been a few decades since Keynesian economics gave the world the Bretton Woods framework and now it was time to replace it. FDR's New Deal policies that created much of America's middle class and improved the lives of so many had become outdated and burdensome to the very economic class they helped create. Policy makers' focus on the micro-economic dynamics surrounding price controls and Fed policies emanating from that view failed miserably in taming inflation and putting America back on the path to economic growth. These failures became directly associated with an ever increasing governmental role that was incompetent and out of touch with the citizenry. The heavy handed intervention of government was hampering individual freedom and burdening the tax payer much like the premise of Ayn Rand's *Atlas Shrugged*. Perception of the failure of government programs was spreading to new levels and their ineffectiveness became ingrained in the mind of the American voter. Along with the growing call to end the Vietnam War came the cry for government to get out of the pockets of Americans and American business. Calls for a long and sustained program for deregulation were growing louder by the day. Although many of the earlier attempts at deregulation came during the Nixon, Ford, and Carter years, *life conditions* had not reached the tipping point until a better picture emerged of what a new deregulated US economy looked like during the first Reagan Administration.

Inflation, as it relates to the role of money from a value-systems perspective, was the first shot fired across the bow to tell the consumer that paper money no longer held its end of the bargain in being an accurate representative of productive output. The faith in its Fourth-level Blue role was beginning to erode. The year that best demonstrates this was 1980 when the CPI was gauged at 14 percent and actual worker pay decreased by 0.3 percent for the year.[54] In less than a decade, one of the oldest social contracts in human emergence met the most complex *life conditions* under a modern economy, and that economy failed to deliver on its obligation to maintain the value of money as an accurate representation of hard work. By 1980 it was becoming very clear that the limited role policymakers, economists, and the Fed played in focusing on the micro-economic aspects of price controls was becoming obsolete. Within a few short years fiat money had shown policy makers that different thinking was needed to accommodate the ever-increasing complexity of an economy that no longer had the safe harbor of the gold standard. A wide ranging view with a central command over economic policy was needed as the Reagan Administration turned its attention to implementing its economic reforms which would come to define capitalism through a whole new role for monetary policy.

THE NEW FED, DEBAUCHER OF CURRENCY

Not much memetic analysis of the role of the Federal Reserve Bank has been given in this chapter until now. Since Congress passed the Federal Reserve Act of 1913 into law, which brought the central bank into its modern day existence, its primary role has been consistent with a fourth-level Blue system. Since its creation and until the 1970s the US central bank was responsible for controlling the supply of money to insure the availability of capital for a growing economy. Its preamble called for a regulatory purpose more than any other and that was to establish effective supervision of banking in the United States.[55] This task became considerably more difficult with the dollar becoming a fiat currency and with the pressures from the prevailing *life conditions* of the 1970s. As one administration after the other failed to establish monetary stability and tame inflation, lawmakers started looking at different ways to empower the Fed to play a greater role in stabilizing the economy. In 1977 Congress passed the Federal Reserve Reform Act, which charged the central bank and its oversight committee with many new areas of responsibilities, such as insuring maximum productivity, promoting the goals of maximum employment, and insuring stable prices and moderate long-term interest rates.[56] This was a newly empowered institution that had brought the varying aspects of macro-economic debate under one roof and now had the power to direct economic policies with a mandate from the United States Congress.

Behind the scenes of the inflationary era of the 1970s and early 1980s, a new school of economic thought was emerging. The Chicago School, as it is commonly known, with economist Milton Freidman at the helm was preaching a new gospel for a whole new role for money. The destructive effects of inflation has given impetus for comprehensive deliberation on its causes and a new generation of economists were ready to tame this beast by methods far superior than price controls introduced in the past decade. This new macro-economic school of thought known as *monetarism* had the view that productive economic output is influenced greatly by the money supply. Friedman's influential thinking advocated a central bank policy aimed at keeping the supply and demand for money at equilibrium, as measured by growth in productivity and demand.[57]

This expanded definition of the role of money on the part of government was in keeping with the upward emergence of a complex capitalist society. The function of a central bank that supplies money in accordance with a targeted level of economic output was more in line with a culture's movement into an ever-increasing level of social emergence. Whoever had the power, authority, and influential thinking to alter the course of the next decade would become the hero who would be etched in the nation's psyche for many years to come. For Congress, what seemed to be a revolutionary idea at the time would become the standard way of thinking and was the beginning of altering the perceptions held for millennia of the role of money.

Life conditions in the early to mid 1980s were such that any innovative ideas that advocated the limited role of government were fully embraced. The Reagan Administration blamed all that had gone wrong with the economy on a bloated government. It introduced sweeping reforms from which a new platform was launched to redefine not only the role of money, but also the new and evolving nature of capitalism. Reagan's economic policies, which became known as "Reaganomics," called for reductions across the board in government regulation, spending, taxation, and controls over the money supply in order to tame inflation.[58] The new powers granted to the Fed in 1977 would not prove to be of much consequence until the Reagan reforms had fully begun. In 1982 the Chairman of the Fed, Paul Volker, took the first monumental but unpopular steps to tighten the money supply, and inflation dropped from 13.5 percent in 1980 to just 3.2 percent in 1983.[59] The beast has finally been tamed. This was the victory the advocates of the Fed's new powers needed to create the new platform from which monetary policy would become central to the US economy. This institution had moved from mundane regulatory beginnings of providing supervision of banks to having a powerful presence at the biggest table of capitalism, and was now part and parcel of the entire economic debate of the largest economy in the world.

This shift in power cannot be underestimated. The traditional innovative leadership of a free market economy that lay in the hands of various corporations and industry leaders was now being helped along by an accommodative monetary policy that had the mandate to insure the economy was running as close as possible to full productive capacity. It became entirely within the powers of the Fed to provide liquidity as it saw fit as long as inflation was tamed. If laws governing capital markets were barriers to liquidity before, the new Fed had innovative ways to deal with them on the behalf of industry and the consumer. If the chairman of the Fed had certain views or ideologies on how money or liquidity should be used or what its role ought to be, then the entire economy would either benefit or become greatly burdened by the implementation of these views. This new concentration of power in the hands of so few had the potential to become elitist and misguided as it would exclude many valued views on the economy that have traditionally come from the different economic sectors. But, since this was money, the common denominator that fueled all economic sectors equally, the Fed never considered itself elitist especially after it had just tamed runaway inflation with its newly acquired powers.

From a value-systems perspective this was a turning point that moved the central bank from a regulatory fourth-level Blue system role that was charged with enforcing specific policies to a quasi-fourth-to-fifth level system that had the potential for collusion with the unhealthy elements of the fifth-level Orange system. Money as a catalyst for emergence has just signaled humanity that it might not have to work as hard as it did before to reap the rewards of its labor. It could borrow without many restrictions and reap the rewards now. With Reaganomics in full swing, *Monetarism* and the new Fed had scored their largest victory and were now front and center in the economic debate. From the point Congress gave the Fed the powers to tame inflation, money became an instrument of innovation from which unlimited types of products can be created and utilized just as if it were another segment of the economy that had its own productive output. The memetic dance that started with an act of a fourth-level system by a desperate Congress in 1977 was now putting in place an infrastructure of a new meme more closely characterized by the financial innovation of Wall Street than the supervision of banks on Main Street.

As this succeeded, government agencies across the board, from the Treasury Department to the President's Board of Economic Advisors, threw out their antiquated belief in the fourth-level system to regulate commerce and fully embraced the expanded powers of the Fed. Most of these regulatory agencies were now staffed with similar value-systems decision makers anxious to deploy the promise of the new economy under its growing expression of financial innovation. These new powers would be used by the Fed to expand the US economy to heights that were never before attained and at the same time created a shift in the culture that became highly dependent on debt to finance its dreams and aspirations.

The role money played in the fourth-level Blue system up until this point in history had been determined by an unseen social contract that set forth the terms for rewards resulting directly from hard work and smart and strategic planning. Economic programs and policies throughout the twentieth century that helped create the American middle class introduced the meme of debt financing to the culture. Prior to the Fed becoming so central to our economy, consumer debt that financed partial purchases of goods and services still held borrowers to a position of accountability. Lenders demanded that borrowers have some of their own hard earned money into purchases of homes and consumer goods. Borrowers with too much debt or history of irresponsible spending were not extended the benefit of debt financing.

During these decades of wealth building, debt had evolved from its negative connotations of centuries past to becoming a partner meme that helped redefine money and its historic role. As long as this new mixture of debt and equity remained highly regulated, money would have continued its evolution into new and modern expressions of human emergence but

EFFECTS OF FEDERAL RESERVE POLICIES ON CULTURAL EMERGENCE

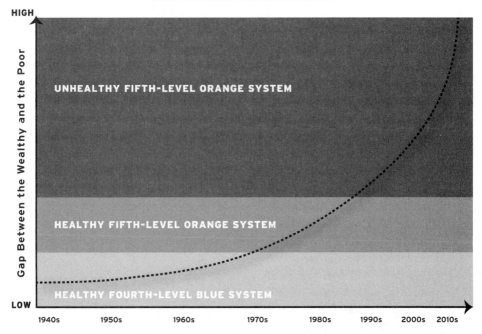

Exposing the fallacy of financial innovation with a fifth-level ʸMEME Federal Reserve that gradually decoupled from alignment with *life conditions* and shifted wealth away from the working and middle class.

would have remained firmly placed in its fourth-level Blue role. But that role did not remain for long. As often is the case with the appearance of a new meme once its potential uses are fully quantified, the exploitive element of culture took its shot at corrupting it. A new infrastructure in consumer and corporate finance started immediately to build around the Fed's newly expanded powers, which along with the birth of the Internet and technological advancement created one of the fastest and most profound paradigm shifts in the history of modern economics.

THE END OF MONEY AS WE KNOW IT

As we have seen so far from the brief memenomic history of money, it not only formed the highest common denominator for peaceful relations among tribes and countrymen. For tens of thousands of years it has been the catalyst of change and human advancement. Even before the appearance of any of

Abrahamic religions that offered humanity the notion of "Sacrifice Now for future gains." Humans had to control their impulses for immediate gratification to "save" for future rewards and in doing so, evolved into a higher level of bio-psycho-social complexity. This sense of postponing gratification allowed for a trade system of bartering that gave birth to money and eventually to the complex global financial system we have today. According to Graves, humanity's greatest challenge is the transition from this egocentric stage of compulsivity to a higher level of existence under law and order. [60]

Over the centuries the need to accumulate goods and capital became the catalyst that moved culture away from its earlier savage nature. Money became the symbol that represented the fourth-level Blue system and became a very important cornerstone for building the cultural codes that in part define who we are. The simple discipline required for the accumulation of savings became the means to separate compulsive acts for short-term gain from behavioral patterns directed toward long-term gains that lead to human progress. Simple things like payment of wages in return for hard work became the model that defined human interaction and the driving force behind better and more enlightened lives.

Through the prism of value systems, we see how money has historically had a dual role; first as a code of the fourth-level system and second as a catalyst that propels culture into higher value systems. As empires and nations fought destructive battles that further determined human emergence, in the end it was agreements among the feuding entities on resource allocation and monetary retribution that brought about peace. At the dawn of the Industrial Age that spread the Strategic Enterprise ^{V}MEME money played a crucial role in the development of nations and their infrastructure. With the development of monetary systems and capital markets, money continued its role as a representative of productive output to which humans in every corner of the world ascribed. It had brought humanity from its earlier tribal existence to its current level of sophistication and interdependence. This role more than any other has provided the motivation for humanity to pursue its quest for higher meaning in life, and until a more systemically accepted form of exchange spreads, money will continue to assume this role.

The role of money more relevant to the premise of memenomics is its role as the most accepted form of an invisible regulator meme among the masses. The function of money in the fourth-level Blue system is inherently intertwined with human nature and gives meaning to our current values and human existence. In a modern day capitalist system that is void of corruption, money plays a primary role in helping culture evolve to the next stage. But, what happens when that role is corrupted? What happens when a system that

HISTORIC ROLE OF MONEY IN HUMAN EMERGENCE

1. *Provide Blue Fourth Level Order in Whatever Historic Life Conditions Existed*

2. *Act as Catalyst (Open System) to Drive Culture into Next ᵛMeme*

PURPLE LIFE CONDITIONS~6000–2000 BC

Form:	Barter. Grain, Food, Gifting.
Blue Function:	Peaceful Coexistance among tribes.
Catalyst/Open System:	Tribes became bigger tribes. Formed earlier cities.

RED LIFE CONDITIONS~2000 BC–1700 AD

Form:	Emperor's coin.
Blue Function:	Widely accepted form of payment for slaves' labor, merchant's goods and war reparations.
Catalyst/Open System:	Ended wars between empires and established trade.

BLUE/ORANGE LIFE CONDITIONS~1700–1970s AD

Form:	National currencies backed by gold.
Blue Function:	Paid for basic societal functions, wages, trade.
Catalyst/Open System:	Allowed for globalization, single currencies, and abandonment of gold standard as an obsolete/false Blue System.

ORANGE/GREEN LIFE CONDITIONS~1970s–PRESENT

Form:	Fiat/paper money backed by the merit of country's economy.
Blue Function:	Became subjected to exploitation by unhealthy Orange. Still provide functions under Blue Life Conditions.
Catalyst/Open System:	Unleashed debate about "Green/Yellow" money.

is thousands of years in the making is taken over by a segment of an exploitive 'MEME that corrupts it to the core? What happens when consumer debt that has been a partner meme of money for decades decouples from that role and answers to a different master? What are the effects of a government that is supposed to be in charge of economic policy but chooses to ignore nagging structural problems and prints more money in an effort to postpone the inevitable? These are the questions that will define the modern day forces that corrupt money and hasten a memenomic system to a premature end.

PART TWO

---

*The History of the Values of
a Subsistence Economy*

FIVE

The First and Second MEMEnomic Cycles

The Fiefdoms of Power and the Patriotic Prosperity Memes

The test of our progress is not whether we add more to the abundance of those who have much; it is whether we provide enough for those who have too little.

—FRANKLIN D. ROOSEVELT
Second Inaugural Address
January 20, 1937

In order to provide a better picture of how the financial sector became the tail that wagged the dog and placed itself squarely in charge of productive output in the final phases of the cycle we are in today, we must first take an historic look at the institutions that built our economy and that represented the diversity of productive output through the prism of value systems before this change started to occur. No one doubts that America's greatest economic expansion took place between the time we entered WWII and the early 1970s. This was the era during which the United States established itself as the world economic superpower. This was the height of government involvement in two areas that are critical for creating a thriving economy: regulating industry and facilitating economic growth. But what happened during the few decades before that era is crucial in understanding the important role that a visionary fourth-level Blue system plays in defining the future of a nation and its economy.

THE FIEFDOMS OF POWER MEME

The decades that represent the first memenomic cycle identified through this framework is the era that spanned from post-Civil War Reconstruction through the dreadful days of the Great Depression. Economic history is still divided on how to identify this era. Depending on one's value systems, during the Gilded Age the powerful leaders of industry were either known as "robber barons," or as the great "captains of industry." The latter was a noble reference to those industrialists who defined the virtues of the great growth and progress of a modern industrial America that began at the end of the nineteenth century.

From a memenomics perspective, both of these assessments are correct as the time period captured both the healthy and the unhealthy expressions of the RED system. I have come to call this cycle the *Fiefdoms of Power.* These were the days when American industrialists redefined economic values over the landscape of a nation that was still being formed. As leaders sought to connect the country through the railroad, new thinking had to come to the forefront and by necessity had to transcend the rural Purple values of small farms and scattered and decentralized production facilities that defined the preceding era. Economic systems were, for the first time being defined on a large national scale, but without an infrastructure of laws that would prevent exploitive practices from taking place. Massive rail projects gave rise to speculative dealings in real estate and finance and built many other service related industries.

As the values of this meme aligned more with *life conditions* in the *growth* phase these industrialists populated the national landscape in other areas such as oil, steel, and construction. The system became identified with mass production aimed purely at making money for those few industrialists. Although worker pay was better than it was on the farm, large-scale exploitation, fraud, and corruption came to identify the values of the era as the system entered the maturity phase. This is when calls for Blue system measures and higher industrial ideals start to come from the embryonic stages of the next cycle. In a confirmation of Grave's claims that transition is the most difficult between the third- and fourth-level systems, the entropy phase of this cycle was the longest of all three as the emergence of the next cycle was repeatedly thwarted by the tight grip of the Red values of these industrialists. In history, the decline and entropy phases of this system were overlaid with a prolonged birth of the Blue system during a period called the Progressive Era. The main goal of this movement that lasted from the 1890s to the 1920s was the purification of government, elimination of corruption, and exposing political machines and bosses.[61] These goals will only succeed after the system collapsed during the Great Depression and the codes from the first cycle informed the design of the emerging cycle.

Prior to the onset of the Great Depression the 1920s looked much like the decade of the 2000s. Predominated by Republican Party rule with laissez-faire economic policies that favored the industrialists. The country witnessed the birth of many innovations but saw little regulation of financial markets. With money available for the asking, ideas for innovation whether feasible or not attracted tremendous investor interest. The dreams of becoming rich quickly overcame most rational objective thought and the availability of easy and cheap money spread the speculative and exploitive nature of this meme. By the end of the decade investor overconfidence in the stock market and in startup ventures lead to an asset bubble that eventually burst and caused the failure of many banks. This destroyed much of the individual wealth that existed, which would eventually lead to the Great Depression.[62] In patterns similar to the aftermath of the financial collapse of 2008, there was no specific, fail-safe solution or a single easy answer to get the United States out of the trap created by the destructive forces of unregulated capital flows in an era riddled with antitrust practices.

At the time there were moral ideas to restrain the act of printing money in the basement of the Federal Reserve Bank in order to provide a temporary fix to our problem. The Fed since its inception in 1913 was still an institution with untested abilities to provide effective policies for a national economy that was still being defined. It was the limited money supply and the overall shifts in demographics that were the greatest contributors to the Great Depression. Compared to the diversity of the US economy today, the Great Depression represented the collapse of most sectors of the economy that was driven by RED exploitive values of the time. There was no single sector representing economic growth that the government could empower or nudge forward to pull the rest of the country out of its economic misery.

This era also witnessed a tremendous shift in the employment base in the rural farming sector that had represented such a prominent meme in the past and had helped settle the country. By the 1920s the family farm was becoming less and less relevant to the labor force. Advancements in farming technology that started in the late 1800s continued to place pressure on the economic feasibility of the small family farm. This *technology-life conditions* gap continued to grow over the decades leading to the Great Depression. As we developed efficient distribution systems through the railroad, and higher-yield seed stock, a new breed of industrialists saw the potential profitability in large-scale farming. Crops and livestock became commoditized, thousand-acre farms run by a few Deere plows and automated reapers replaced hundreds of family farms that employed thousands of workers. Banks and Wall Street saw tremendous opportunity in this new farming model and flooded big agricultural corporation with capital that enabled them to buy even more land, eventually leading to the demise of the small family farm.

As is often the case with technological innovations that part ways with the *life conditions*, no plans to shelter or employ the displaced farmers were ever made. The memetic shifts caused by the advancements in technology on the farm became the most prominent example of how creative destruction initiates the pull for the advancement of a culture while *life conditions* are not ready for the complexity and the fallout from it. In the 1930s this technological pull rendered a substantial segment of the labor force useless. With the obsolescence of much of the heartland's farm workers and the crash of a highly speculative stock market, America was facing one of the most profound economic and social challenges in its modern history. Of the three cycles, the *fiefdoms of power*, the *patriotic prosperity*, and the *only money matters* era, the entropy phase of this first cycle was the longest and most painful as the United States looked for methods to leave chaotic value systems behind and prepared to usher in a cycle identified with the values of the fourth-level system of law and order.

FDR'S VISIONARY NEW DEAL

Government social programs such as unemployment insurance or welfare benefits that would have provided a safety net for individuals in financial stress simply did not exist at the time of the Great Depression. The United States had not faced such an ominous economic calamity before and both the Congress and the White House knew that extraordinary leadership with vision and a willingness to make great efforts had to go into re-defining a federal government with expanded powers. For the first time, the dysfunction of the previous system had provided the political, economic, and social impetus to creating robust institutions intended to redefine America. A new paradigm was in the making. Any new government agencies had to create a level playing field that would prevent the future reoccurrence of the predatory and opportunistic behavior that contributed to the Great Depression. Lawmakers saw it was necessary to provide a sense of security for the American worker should employment opportunities lag behind the fast- paced changes created by technological advancements. Crafting new laws that anticipated where technology was heading and how the business sector would react to it became the platform for shaping the future of America. Roosevelt had to take on the responsibility for creating a new economic paradigm that no nation had ever seen. Capitalism without regulation had been shown to have a corrosive moral compass, and in no uncertain terms had failed to sustain itself as a viable form of governing. The very pillars that upheld American values were in danger of collapsing, Exceptional leadership was essential in order to rescue it.

Life conditions leading up to the onset of the Great Depression had changed tremendously but without a corresponding change in a fourth-level Blue order system that would have spread among the institutions to sustain the change. Government leadership and commitment to create the new institutions and infrastructure had to insure against the failure and the shortcomings of past leadership and more importantly anticipate the challenges that would face the US economy in the future. Like highway engineers who anticipate future growth and proceed to design and build highways in anticipation of that growth, legislators went to work on enacting new laws to evolve the values of capitalism to new levels of fairness that would define its future.

The outcome was FDR's New Deal policies that were ambitious in their reach. Among the most striking things created by these policies was America's middle class, which to this day remains the largest consumer of goods and services and constitutes the greatest economic engine in the global economy. Without this visionary fourth-level system role that government played in establishing the institutions under the New Deal programs, very little of the distributed wealth we see today would have been possible. From a memenomics perspective, this represented the first serious attempt in US history with the spread of the fourth-level Blue order system to design methods to protect consumers. This was the *introduction* phase in this cycle on which a solid base was built to promote prosperity to every corner of America. For the first time we saw institutions like the Securities and Exchange Commission, the FDIC, and the FHA, which still play essential fourth-level roles in today's economy.

In the early days of FDR's New Deal most of our GDP, although still anemic, was determined by the output of our factories. The early expression of the fifth-level Orange system was still in such an adolescent state that economic life was a struggle between management and labor. There was a clear separation between the wealthy industrialists and the working poor and neither side trusted the other. The industrial workplace simply operated from two completely different mindsets. Management in general belonged at the time to an earlier closed expression of the fifth-level Orange Strategic Enterprise System. This bordered on an unhealthy expression of a third-level Red Feudal System that regarded the workers as a unit of production and didn't possess the consciousness level to recognize when it was engaging in worker exploitation. Similarly, in absence of fourth-level system laws, the workers and labor unions belonged to a second-level purple system of brotherhood that lived in fear of management. Labor disputes about work conditions and pay were drawn out and were often fruitless as government was ineffective in its encouragement to have both sides resolve their issues voluntarily.[63]

These prevailing *life conditions* during that period of America's Industrial Age underwent a tremendous transformation once the US entered World

War II. With the creation of the War Production Board, both labor and management had to set aside their differences to answer to a much higher calling and that was to win the war. This specially created government agency was charged with coordinating the nation's productive capabilities so that military priorities would be met. Plants that produced consumer products were filling many military orders. Automakers converted their factories and were building tanks and aircraft.[64] Patriotism, which always plays a significant part in a fourth level Blue system has acted as a catalyst that helped American manufacturing bolster its heroic role as the answer to the world's greatest existential threat. In the process the war effort expedited the emergence of labor's relationship with management, which became the platform from which the US established its economic superiority.

In memenomics, WWII served as a super-ordinate goal that allowed for the emergence of ᵛMEMEs to higher and healthier levels of expression. Once this goal, which called on all Americans to set aside their differences, was achieved the memetic landscape of America was forever transformed leaving little chance for a return to the way things were during the Great Depression. The call to set a super-ordinate goal is not always for patriotic reasons, and this is where the visionary aspects of the institutions created by New Deal policies play a prominent role. Banks that considered lending money to returning war veterans would not have done so without the assurance that their loans were guaranteed by the federal government. As we see with the emergence of American culture throughout the 1940s and 50s, government agencies created under FDR's New Deal acted as the catalysts that propelled institutions to ascribe to the values of a more inclusive society. The patterns of setting super-ordinate goals emerge naturally as a solution that serves a greater purpose. This is a healthier alternative to the limited scope of the traditional win-lose scenarios that dominate everything from political bickering and the setting of economic policy to corporate negotiations that only serve as temporary fix for the winner.

The process for setting the ideal super-ordinate goal is not designed from any of the first-tier subsistence value systems that currently dominate politics and business. It is designed from a place that Beck and Graves call the "being" second tier. Or to be more precise, from the first-level Yellow ᵛMEME of the second tier of informed intelligence, which sees the limits of the lower ᵛMEMEs and designs *functional* solutions that offer a third win. The first two of the wins transcend the bickering of the two parties in a negotiation and the third win is the long-term health of the planet. There will be a more detailed discussion in the second part of the book about how to identify super-ordinate goals in our economy today and use them to create wins for all the stakeholders involved.

It is worth noting at this early stage in the memenomic analysis of the history of our economy that it was the same bankers who were newcomers to the visionary fourth-level system set up by the New Deal ideology who ended up exploiting it to the point of near collapse by 2008. In spite of it being visionary when it was created, a second-tier functional ᵛMEME that places the health of the entire system above all else must inform a first-tier order ᵛMEME. As the historic analysis will prove, unless the regulatory structure of the fourth-level order system has characteristics that enable it to shift in response to the changing *life conditions*, bust and boom economic cycles will continue to threaten the attainment of prosperity for all and increasingly place us at the mercy of ill-timed cycles.

THE 1950S: BUILDING THE MIDDLE CLASS MEMES

After the end of WWII the United States continued to see robust levels of economic growth as the institutions that were set up by the New Deal facilitated economic expansion well into the 1950s and 60s. These were the years when we saw that the infrastructure that was put into place was beginning to define our new values. This was the phase of the cycle that was aligned with *life conditions* for such a prolonged period that it redefined America's capitalist values at their core. Returning GIs could apply to special government-sponsored programs to get loans to finance a college education or buy a new home. College enrollments more than doubled. Suburbia became a new meme that defined the expansion of America's middle class in the 1950s. The creation of Fannie Mae and Freddie Mac encouraged banks to underwrite mortgages, which facilitated the suburban sprawl of America's middle class away from crowded cities. Although the 1950s were known as the complacent era, it was a time during which America's fourth-level Blue system was being reinvented. The *Leave it to Beaver* television show was a meme that symbolized the core strengths around which the new American family was being defined. The television show presented four specific themes—education, marriage, occupation, and family—as essential requisites for a happy and productive life.[65] These became essential elements of the new fourth-level Blue system that fueled the peaceful expansion of the US economy.

During this decade the United States saw a surge in construction and industrial investment. Consumer credit reached levels that were previously unheard of. The economy was booming in every sector and it was due to a visionary regulatory structure put into place two decades before that had taken the time to anticipate and define the parameter for an emerging economy with a much greater level of complexity. Not only did FDR's New

Deal policies confidently predict the return to prosperity, they became the catalysts that defined the level playing field for both consumers and business. By the end of the decade of the 1950s America had been redefined economically. This era is often recognized as the decade that eliminated poverty for the great majority of Americans as per capita income had doubled, inflation was kept at just 1 percent, and unemployment dropped to just 4.1 percent.[66]

Economic prosperity was not the only factor shaping the new American meme. An average of three million people per year were added to the population during the postwar "Baby Boom." With rising incomes American consumerism took hold of a new values paradigm as we started spending on items that had been previously thought of as luxuries but by then had become necessities. An explosion of memes took a hold of our culture. Memes that defined the modern American dream, such as fashion clothing, televisions, washing machines, homes in the suburbs, Thunderbirds, and the American highway, all saw their birth in the 1950s.

In creating the first middle class, America was redefined at a deep memetic level as it related to the changing expression of capitalism. One of the most profound changes was how the American merchant class came to view the working class. A few decades before this, the businessman or factory owner perceived the worker as someone living in squalid, or at best modest, conditions who was to be kept from claiming a piece of the pie called the American Dream. By the 1950s cultural values had shifted so much that the same worker was being viewed as a potential consumer of the merchant's goods, and services, and would be partaking in the creation and consumption of an ever-increasing pie. American business became obsessed with the rise of the middle class, and an entire economy refocused itself on creating innovative ways to redefine upward mobility. With an economy focused on consumerism, less and less of our productive output was coming from traditional manufacturing. By the late 1950s the number of people working in white color jobs surpassed that of the ones working in blue color jobs.[67] America came to be redefined under the single umbrella of memes called "the American Dream" that still defines many elements of our lives till this day.

THE NEW FRONTIER AND THE GREAT SOCIETY

America's greatest economic expansion continued unabated during the 1960s, a decade during which the nation added more density and diversity to its fourth-level blue system of laws and institutions. Standing on a firm foundation of expanded peacetime prosperity President Kennedy urged Americans to meet the challenges of the "New Frontier" by shifting their thinking from how to passively benefit from the existing resources and institutions to playing a more active role in contributing to the country's innovative genius. In memenomics, under Kennedy the power that steered the passions of innovation and technology was unleashed into the field of science and space exploration. The challenges of Kennedy's New Frontier could be summed by his philosophy of "We do these things not because they're easy, but because they're hard." With this declaration the 1950's era of Americans sitting on their laurels was over, and the search for innovation and scientific discovery that would keep the American economy in sync with *life conditions* became a new platform.

Yet another super-ordinate goal that aligned the *growth* phase of the *patriotic prosperity era* with *life conditions* during the 1960s was the Cold War. Although government involvement in marshaling the resources of America's manufacturing sector during the Cold War was not a pervasive as it was under the powers of the War Board during WWII, the super-ordinate goal of triumphing over communism was very clear to both government and industry. The predominant meme of the Cold War expressed itself through advancements in technological innovations. The mid-1960s was the time in the cycle when the forces behind the economy begin to misalign with *life conditions* and the mandate of patriotism created for it by the New Deal ideology. While government mandated price controls under the War Board, it could not do the same with the manufacturers of the war machinery during this time known as the arms race era. The industry that was honored for its patriotic duty at the beginning of the cycle was becoming misaligned with the evolving *life conditions*. Known now as the military industrial complex, it exploited its monopolistic privileges in the pursuit of profits.

At the same time that Kennedy was empowering technological innovation to lead the United States in new scientific frontiers, he also looked to pursue new frontiers in fiscal policies as he sought to accelerate economic growth through a paradigm that challenged the conventional wisdom of the time. Keynesian economic thought had dominated government economic policy since the end of World War II and was believed to be responsible for much of the post-war prosperity. Like his post-war predecessors Kennedy embarked on an ambitious spending program that pressed for the creation of social programs to provide medical help for the elderly, aid for inner cities, and increased funds for education.[68] Contrary to past policy, however Kennedy sought to cut taxes. His belief was that if businesses and families had more money to spend, this in itself would generate the additional tax revenues to fund government programs.

This was the birth of trickle-down economics, which in later years defined Ronald Reagan's legacy. Looking through the prism of memenomics, the lowering of the tax burden, combined with the challenge to do the hard things, achieved the *aesthetic change* needed to prevent the system from moving into the maturity phase and kept it in line with *life conditions* that were expressing different content. By continuing to empower scientific discovery, the decade became iconic in establishing America's scientific superiority around the world, from setting the goals to land a man on the moon to the creation of Apranet, the predecessor to the Internet.

With lower taxes, a robust economic expansion, and the rising costs of the Cold War, inflation started to rear its ugly head. For the first time in decades rising prices presented a big threat to America's upward mobility, and the Kennedy White House took the challenge of taming the sources of inflationary pressures head on. Kennedy wanted to make an example out of what his administration perceived as the most blatant violations of anti-trust rules, the pervasively monopolistic practices of the steel industry. At the height of the Cold War big defense contractors building military ships for the Defense Department were the steel industry's largest customers. Looking out for the interest of the taxpayer who would incur the burden for the added cost of military expenditure, the Kennedy Administration accused the industry in public of price fixing. In what became his administration's defining moment the president declared war on the steel industry. He leveled the accusations of betrayal of public trust and backing away from their promise not to increase prices. This became known as the Steel Crisis when Kennedy did not back down from his position. He publically declared his intentions to put the full resources of his administration into exposing the industry's alleged illegal practices. Seeing the potential harm this could cause their image, the leading steel companies backed down and soon the crisis subsided.

This rare and brave display of governmental powers established Kennedy as a formidable fourth-level order system presence that could very effectively stand up to the corrupt and exploitative practices of an unhealthy fifth-level system. Although much debate still goes on about Kennedy's use of the raw power of the state in a free capitalist economy, the harm caused to the consumer in a highly diminished fourth the level system like the one we're in today makes Kennedy's actions heroic and visionary. The belief of memenomics is that in order for a thriving culture to achieve the prosperity promised under a free market economy, a vigilant fourth-level system has to make its presence known to a fifth-level system, but not be too invasive in order to keep it engaged in the healthy expressions of its values.

Whether the rest of the sectors of the orange 'MEME took note of Kennedy's vigilance or not, it is clear that the economy performed very well during the mandate of his policies for the remainder of the decade after his death. During his brief presidency, the US economy grew annually by an average of 5.5 percentage points.[69] Inflation for the same period was successfully kept around 1 percent.[70] The level of confidence Kennedy instilled in the government's ability to protect the consumer, combined with his capacity to inspire the culture to unleash its innovative potential, allowed the US economy to achieve unprecedented levels of peace-time industrial production. By the time we reached the late 1960s, the manufacturing sector grew at the rate of 15 percent and motor vehicle sales leapt by as much as 40 percent.[71] These accomplishments have not been repeated by any administration since then for such a sustained period of time.

The Kennedy White House provides a good example of what a dynamic fourth-level system can be. By the beginning of the decade the post-war prosperity that has been riding on the coat tails of the New Deal was beginning to fade. No longer would the same super-ordinate goal created by FDR, WWII, and the Great Depression have as much power as the memes that were being born anew. America's expansion to the suburbs and the pursuit of middle class prosperity has altered the debate and the search for a new paradigm had started. The inspiration drawn from Kennedy's New Frontier way of thinking and governing had proven to be an effective value-systems model for an economy that balanced the interest of business with that of the consumer and the taxpayer. It had challenged the wisdom of traditional economic policy and liberated monetary policy from its strict conformity of adhering to the relationship of money supply to interest rates and inflation. In the process it created a potentially sustainable model for economic policy, the full effects of which will never be known.

It could be argued that the high cost of a vigilant fourth-level system cost Kennedy his life. His assassination brought an end to a new paradigm that was in its infancy—a paradigm that had transformational potential to establish new characteristics of what an evolving government would look like. It also had the potential of transforming the values of US corporations and how they perceive their role in being responsible corporate citizens. As Lyndon B. Johnson took over the presidency, we entered the *maturity* phase of the *patriotic prosperity era* as many of the bitter fights that kept the Enterprise 'MEME on its toes and made the Kennedy leadership so appealing to Americans, gave way to our indulgence in the fruits of system's labor.

Johnson settled into making his presidency one that would cement Kennedy's legacy as the champion of civil rights. The Great Society became the benefactor of Kennedy's New Frontier that had not exhibited the full capacities and vision that Kennedy had to keep the system in sync with *life conditions*. LBJ's administration fought many bitter battles to bring Kennedy's dreams of having the demands of the civil rights movement become the law of the land. The rest of the decade saw an explosion of social programs that aimed to provide all Americans equal access to the American dream. Medicare and Medicaid became a reality. Many social programs that were created under the umbrella of the War on Poverty, such as the Food Stamps Act of 1964, the Community Action Program that was charged with helping the poor become self-sufficient, the Jobs Corps to help disadvantaged youth develop marketable skills, and the Head Start program that offered preschool education for poor children, all became the hallmark of Johnson's legacy. Throughout the decade Kennedy's tax cuts that went into effect in 1961 continued to add to the prosperity of the middle class as personal income continued to rise well into the late 1960s. In 1966 alone, disposable income rose by 15 percent [72] while tax revenues rose dramatically from $94 billion in 1961 to $150 billion in 1967.[73]

As this decade came to a conclusion, the creation of the greatest expansion of social programs since the New Deal had placed the country close to a complete transformation from where it had been socially and economically at the height of the Great Depression. The long-term goals for establishing the institutions and the opportunities that FDR spoke of in his vision of America four decades earlier have been taken up by every administration that succeeded him. The design and implementation of this fourth-level order system has come as close as possible to meeting its intended vision.

By the end of the 1960s America had reached the maturity phase of the patriotic prosperity cycle—in its cultural and economic progress. What has been noteworthy from a value-systems perspective all throughout these four decades is the preoccupation with winning wars, be it WWII, the Korean War, the Vietnam War, or the ever-present specter of the Cold War with Communism. Wars had become the ultimate super-ordinate goal that aligned all stakeholders in American culture on the patriotism motherboard. The financial costs of war and social programs had not played a big factor as a prosperous middle class continued to expand and establish itself as a formidable economic power.

By the end of the 1960s the paradigm of post-war prosperity and the optimism of believing tomorrow will always be a better day was slowly diminishing. The children of the post-war era who grew up in suburban middle class families had already created cracks in the ⱽMEMEs of this system as we entered the *decline* phase of the second cycle. The memes of "no war" and other forms of defiance of governmental powers became a part of the new *life conditions* heading into the 1970s. In the life cycle of an ideology, things were reaching maturation point. This was a time during which the cultural mores from the last five decades could no longer project their inspirational values into the future without facing social resistance. This was a time for the United States to take inventory of its meteoric social transformation and begin a long journey in search of a new paradigm that would define its future.

THE HEAVY COST OF VISIONARY MANDATES AND THE END OF AN ERA

Much like the years following the financial crisis of 2008, the decade of the 1970s was most characterized by a decade-long crisis of confidence. Many factors that were domestic and global, and economic and social, converged to make it a decade in which America started a long and arduous search for new social and economic models. This was the birth of the *inquiry* phase of the next cycle and the beginning of the end of a unique mix of value systems that carried the United States to new levels of prosperity and social emergence, while at the same time helping to rebuild the post-war industrialized world. Subtle changes in our economic alliances began to take place. Germany and the rest of Europe had been rebuilt under the Marshall Plan. Their economies have been retooled to target peacetime prosperity. The rebirth of Europe's industrial base with peaceful pursuits was making the Europeans less dependent on the post-war institutions that were a part of a global fourth-level order system of which the Americans were in charge.

The United States had given itself carte blanche in designing the Bretton Woods financial framework, and as a result the US Dollar was the de facto reserve currency of the world. This meant that if there were inflationary pressures on prices in the United States, and the government chose not to devalue the dollar, members of the Bretton Woods system had to inflate their currencies accordingly to maintain the exchange rates fixed to the dollar regardless of whether they were faced with the same inflationary pressures or not.[74] With such a mandate came the responsibility of looking out for the collective interest of everyone under the system, since the potential for abuse by unbalanced US monetary and fiscal policies would create cracks in the alliance. Many administrations beginning with FDR understood the importance of this fourth-level code, and at the first sign of inflation, interest rates were increased and money supply tightened to slow down economic expansion and head off inflationary pressures. In the 1960s these sensitive relationships between inflation, interest rates, money supply, and exchange rates were greatly ignored in favor of

Kennedy's initial testing of trickle-down economics that were soon curtailed after his death. With Johnson's inability to create the shift Kennedy sought, the vision defaulted to a monetary policy that was out of touch with *life conditions* and a bloated federal budget that had an unsustainable revenue stream to fund government programs. Nixon viewed the Kennedy-Johnson era as a time of irresponsible experiments with economic policy. And with expenditure on the Vietnam War contributing to a ballooning federal deficit, he feared the erosion of the United States' economic superiority. Germany saw what was to happen to the value of the dollar and in 1970 decided to leave the Bretton Woods system. Around the same time many member countries lost their trust in US economic leadership and started to redeem their dollar reserves for gold. Soon thereafter many other European countries followed in Germany's footsteps in what was greatly regarded as the first sign of the fall of US economic hegemony and the beginning of the end of FDR's visionary ideology.

By the early 1970s the US had been in the decline phase of the Patriotic Prosperity cycle for a few years when temporary fixes that are designed from within the system could no longer nudge the system forward. The visionary Blue-Orange fourth to fifth-level system designed under FDR had served its purpose, but its continued use in *life conditions* that were vastly different than the ones under which it was created were doing more harm than good. A closed or arrested system of the Blue fourth level that assumed the presence of war as a super-ordinate goal in order to achieve economic prosperity and keep an alliance together was proving to be a toxic prescription that drove our allies away. The decline of this visionary and crucial era would continue through the decade as solutions fashioned from the values of the system only hastened its demise. Increasing the money supply to spur growth and fund wars and federal programs served to quicken the exit of our European allies out of Bretton Woods. The Federal Reserve, by targeting a specific interest rate to tame inflation without addressing its structural causes, hastened the end of the gold standard. In 1971, during the economic measures enacted in what became known as the "Nixon Shock," we announced to the world that we were no longer expected to honor a monetary system of which we were the primary architects and was a major pillar of a political and economic ideology that had rebuilt the world during the preceding four decades. This was the end of the gold standard.

The 1971 United States movement away from the gold standard, this false fourth-level global code of monetary regulation, brought along with it the ravaging effects of inflation. But, unlike past experiences, it was without the post-war economic order to dilute its effects. Although the dollar had been devalued and its redemption for gold had effectively come to an end, inflationary pressures continued to build, and a series of price controls by the Nixon Administration served only as temporary fixes.[75] The tools at the disposal of the most knowledgeable people in the system no longer provided the necessary fixes and the search for lasting solutions continued in vain. To add to the tumult of domestic challenges to price controls in all three administrations of the 1970s, the Nixon, Ford, and Carter Administrations had to contend with a whole newcomer to the inflation dance and that was OPEC. Flexing its economic muscles in 1973 and again in 1979 this cartel of the new (black) gold rendered the argument for price controls obsolete.

In value-systems studies as they relate to economics, the removal of the dollar from the gold standard was a natural step in the right direction toward a higher level of complexity in economic emergence. For centuries the arbitrary pegging of currencies to a precious metal ultimately meant that the nation with the highest levels of gold deposits by default had economic superiority over other countries regardless of what that country's measure of productive output was. Imagine the sudden discovery of gold in one of the poorest nations in the world that had very few other institutions that contribute to productive output. Under the gold standard, such a nation would have been considered an economic power. In memenomics, this is what is considered a false code of the fourth-level order system since it could falsely raise a nation economically without addressing the systemic developmental issues needed to build the institutions on which sustained economic prosperity rests.

The closest examples to this false code today are the OPEC countries that have done very little to diversify their economies away from oil and build the institutions that will sustain them once their wells go dry. In the analysis about the role of money in human emergence, it was seen that the United States has taken the lead role in leaving the false economic security of gold and had ventured into uncharted territories of a floating currency market that would require different metrics to justify its viability. This was the exiting of an antiquated fourth-level system in search for what might emerge as elements that would shape the foundation of a new fifth-level monetary system backed by the value of the productive output of the collective culture and its innovative genius and not by an arbitrary precious metal that is subject to daily and hourly manipulation by world commodity traders. The establishment of a stable dollar under these new realities had the potential of placing the United States at the helm of a new global monetary system that promoted the value of innovation and human capital above all else.

As often is the case with ᵛMEMEs emerging to the next level, dissonance from the dying forces within the current system attempted to block its emergence. As the economy became more misaligned with *life conditions*, we for the first time in modern history, started to question the bloated bureaucracy of our government. For close to five decades the building of fourth-level Blue institutions was an endeavor that very few questioned. The primary purpose of these institutions was to guard against abusive practices of the fifth-level system. With the increasing challenges of the 1970s this ᵛMEME that accommodated the fair and equitable spread of prosperity started to become a burden. Heavy regulation has crippled industry and made it uncompetitive. Unions who had wage rises and benefit guarantees in their contracts became the enemy in the fight against inflation. New environmental regulations made it tough for business to expand and remain competitive. With the fluctuations of a floating dollar that had become susceptible to free market forces, foreign investment was leaving the United States at a record pace.[76] Efforts to pinpoint the causes of the systemic decline of the economy grew more desperate by the day and the search for a new and vastly different economic paradigm was rapidly gaining acceptance.

FERTILE GROUNDS FOR IDEOLOGICAL SHIFTS

As the economy under the Second Memenomic Cycle entered the entrophy phase, there was little politicians or policy makers could do to ease the fall. These were fertile times when ideas compete to define the next system. This was also the time when different voices start to get louder. In the mid 1970s different peacetime memes started to emerge and began to drive culture in a new direction. With the creation of a society that had a strong center of gravity in Blue-Orange, fourth- and fifth-level systems, the new focus became the sustainment of prosperity. The sense of forward momentum to look beyond the accomplishments of civil rights of the 1960s and to address the social and economic impasses at a deep structural level started to take shape. The number of college graduates had continued to rise, and advancements in science and technology were blazing new trails and informing a new paradigm that was yet to be defined. In patterns that have repeated throughout history at times of social dissonance the 1970s were fertile grounds for new ideologies to be born. These were the final stages of entropy when pressure from the new system forces the old system to transform into informational units that empower a new cycle to search for a paradigm that sees new order beyond the chaos of the current system. According to Beck, the foundation for a value systems paradigm shift is a collective of memes that has such explanatory power it attracts the hearts and minds of people before going on to garner the political and ideological support of the establishment. Many social memes were born during the 1970s that reflected the changes in the culture among visionaries and called on its brightest minds to chart a new social and economic future.

Among the most prominent of these minds when it comes to memenomics, was Harvard University's sociologist Daniel Bell. In his seminal 1973 book *The Coming of Post-Industrial Society,* Bell articulated the primarily changes that were taking place *in Life Conditions* in the United States and in other industrialized countries in an elaborate and comprehensive way. He framed these changes in the context of what the future composition of the Western labor force would look like. Bell laid out the argument that in a post-industrial society the largest measure of productive output would come from the service industry, science, and technology.[77] The future construct of society's labor force would have less of the semi-skilled factory and blue-collar worker and more of the white-collar worker. Scientific discovery, knowledge, and information were the way of the future and the manufacturing of actual products was becoming the way of the past.

For the next decade critics and admires of Bell's thinking brought this intellectual debate to a level that questioned whether or not a society has to go through an industrial phase as a necessary stage for its cultural emergence. Much the way Adam Smith had foreseen in his day the effects of having the utopian construct for capitalism, Bell and other social critics of the 1970s laid out a utopian vision of what a service economy driven by science, knowledge, and information would look like.

In a span of a few short years, memes praising the coming of this new era were spreading and the hope for a new economic paradigm was emerging. These subtle shifts within the fifth-level system that considered a manufacturing economy a thing of the past and embraced a cleaner, smarter, more academically inclined information and knowledge- based economy, have created a very divisive discussion today. With the benefit of three decades of hindsight we can assess the lessons learned from a post-industrial economy. We can pick its best practices to design a second-tier economy that emphasizes the virtues of functionality and the important role that manufacturing must continue to play as one of the pillars of economic strength in any culture.

During the entropy phase of the *patriotic prosperity era* the Carter Administration put measures in place to deregulate much of the industrial sector in order to save it. Some of these measures made it into law after prolonged debates, but it was too late to overturn the emerging cultural memes that had become unstoppable. By the time Carter was serving his last days in office, the collapse of the system that had built America over the last four decades has reached its final phases and very little could done to save it. An out of control monetary system failed miserably to tame the beast of high inflation. Astronomical interest rates made it prohibitive for most businesses to expand. Slowly as the decade came to a close, the hulking, overregulated, and antiquated manufacturing sector, with its infrastructure and institutions that had defined the rise of the United States for a half-century, was regarded as at an end.

The *inquiry* and *introduction* phase of the emerging cycle was also being influenced by visionary and powerful memes that were emerging from the field of macroeconomics. The philosophy of monetarism was now informing this newly emerging paradigm in the historic context of the overall evolution of US culture. In October 1976 Economist Milton Freidman won the Nobel Prize for his achievements in the fields of consumption analysis, monetary history and theory, and for his demonstration of the complexity of stabilization policy.[78] In terms relevant to memenomics, Freidman's research was acknowledged for advocating a greater role of money in determining economic output. He is often quoted for saying "only money matters" which gave his ideology the name "monetarism."

The Chicago School of Economics with Freidman at its helm was known for the role it played in redefining money in our culture, but to put this in a historic memenomic context, the emergence of the monetarist ideology came as a natural outcropping of a new set of values that had fresh *explanatory powers* in contrast to ones from the previous system. "Explanatory power" is a term used in value systems to acknowledge the transition of culture through value systems and the new alignment of systems with *life conditions*. In the case of the monetarist ideology, Friedman's values and those of the Reagan era spoke to the emerging *life conditions* more than any other ideology at the time. In addition to the spread of the monetarist meme in influential circles, a different meme in monetary policy setting was being acknowledged. Due to the economic tumult experienced as a result of the US Dollar becoming a fiat currency, the powers granted the Federal Reserve up until 1977 were proving to be obsolete and ineffective in the fight against inflation. The ever-changing *life conditions* had rendered the limited powers of this institution out of touch and an overhaul of its responsibilities was long overdue.

As a part of the new and emerging economic paradigm that saw the fourth-level order system of government as a closed system that's unresponsive to the changing needs of the economy, the US Congress vastly expanded the powers of the Fed to accommodate the post-industrial economy. This again was a natural reaction to existential *life conditions* that required a complete shift from previous belief systems. Very few members of Congress understood the permanent departure from a fourth-level role these actions were going to create for the Fed. One could argue that once Congress placed the Fed in charge of insuring full employment, two major shifts in our society took place: The first was that Congress had acknowledged its incompetence in influencing monetary policy and had given a clear signal to the Fed to depart from fourth-level order responsibilities and embrace potentially unhealthy values of the fifth-level system for which the very same Congress was elected to guard against.

The second shift was within corporate America itself that no longer had to hire as many economists to do the difficult work of forecasting economic outlooks and identify the unique financing challenges that face their particular industries and segments of the economy. That fifth-level Strategic Enterprise responsibility was now in the hands of the chairman of the Federal Reserve. Except for an occasional testimony from the chairman, the government had absolved itself from any further responsibility towards monetary policy. This trend of eroding the powers of the fourth level order system and concentrating it in the hands of the few and the elite of the fifth level Strategic Enterprise system will become the hallmark that defined the next three decades of economic and political ideology. The values of the New Deal ideology were quickly reaching the end phase. In its memenomic cycle the older system had ceased to serve its original visionary mandate and had become a hulking hollow shell of its former existence. For the next three decades, the power of its institutions would slowly die off and much of their responsibilities would either disappear or get handed to a new system that had little regard to industrial-era values as it proceeded to define a new expression of capitalism.

The Third MEMEnomic Cycle

The "Only Money Matters" Meme

In this crisis, government is not the solution to our problem; government is the problem . . . It's not my intention to do away with government. It is rather to make it work—work with us, not over us; to stand by our side, not ride on our back. Government can and must provide opportunity, not smother it; foster productivity, not stifle it.

—PRESIDENT RONALD REAGAN
1981 Inaugural Speech

In November of 1980 America elected Ronald Reagan, one of the most prominent reformers, who as governor of California a few years earlier had brought the state back from the brink of financial disaster. America anxiously awaited signs of the country's new and promising direction under his leadership. This was the beginning of a love affair with new possibility. So much social change had taken place as we projected our hopes and aspirations on a new leader who would galvanize America's vision of the future. The virtues emerging from the debate about a post-industrial society were mingling with many of the memes that were spread as a result of the deregulation movement begun under the Carter Administration.

Any new policies designed to restore America back to prosperity after the ravaging effects of inflation and high interest rates would take many years to achieve their intended goal. After all, these were changes in ideologies and policies aimed to transform what America had been for close to half a century. Time and patience was required before they would be reflected in corresponding changes in *life conditions*. Just like the lag in time between the design, implementation, and the full realization of the transformative powers of the New Deal policies, the new platform would take several years to become an ideology that defined a new expression of capitalism. These social changes along with a newly empowered Central Bank would come together in a new platform that became known as Reaganomics.

According to William A. Niskanen, one of the architects of Ronald Reagan's economic policies, the main pillars of this ideology were reductions across the board in regulations, government spending, and income taxes, along with the effective control of the money supply,[79] Reagan went right to work in the pursuit of his ambitious reform agenda and proposed the Economic Recovery Tax Act of 1981. This new tax reform legislation represented the biggest tax reduction for both individuals and corporations in American history whereby the highest personal tax bracket was reduced from 70.1 percent to 28.4 percent[80] After being in office for less than a year, Reagan's first visible act to restore America was a resounding confirmation that the liberal policies that glued our values to the same fourth-level order ^{V}MEME had very little place in the newly emerging American memestack. In his first seven months in office, Reagan not only confirmed the end of the hegemony of the New Deal policies but had also consolidated the formation of the basis of his ideology that continued to spread its memes well into the future. Although other reforms would prove more difficult and take longer to implement, one thing was clear: the meme of laissez-faire capitalism was taking America by storm and would continue to be the driving force behind our value systems for many years to come.

Within the first year of Reagan's presidency the composition of the American memestack was reorganized from one empowered by patriotic communal values to one that championed individual success. A smarter, leaner, fourth-level order ^{V}MEME that sought to minimize the role of government replaced the old antiquated Blue order structure that towed the line of whatever our leaders decided the public would go along with. Gradually the old visionary motherboard of values that had defined America during a strong fourth-level order system gave way to one that empowered individuality and the pursuit of personal success. The year of 1981 tested the will of the old entrenched system as American labor and industrial relations proved not to be immune to the reach of this new ideology. On August 5, 1981, Reagan did what would have been unimaginable under the leadership of any of his predecessors since the end of WWII. In what became known as the iconic event that permanently weakened organized labor, Reagan fired over 11,000 members of the air traffic controllers union that were striking illegally and had ignored his orders to return to work.[81] The repercussions that this act had on permanently redefining America's fifth-level Orange code should not be underestimated.

Reagan approached this from a serious and systemic perspective. His administration used all the resources available to it to demonstrate—in no uncertain terms—its seriousness about its reform agenda. Lawsuits were filed in many courts against the union to force their members to return to work. Criminal charges were readied in nineteen separate courts against union leaders, the government seized the union's bank accounts, and petitions were filed to decertify the union permanently.[82] As this drama unfolded in front of the whole world to see, the manufacturing sector of America's fifth-level ᵛMEME got a good glance at how far it can flex its muscles with the American labor force in this new environment of reform and deregulation. This was an undeniable vision of the future of government leadership that backed its words with systemic actions. These actions were bent on making government leaner, and smarter by trusting in free market forces to be a far better regulator than bloated government bureaucracies.

This new era that sought the deregulation of industry across all sectors went from the *introduction* phase of this second cycle, which started under the Carter Administration, into the fast lane of the *growth* phase during the early Reagan years when it took on the mantle of his reform agenda. American manufacturers went right to work to extract new concessions from their labor unions in efforts to make their products more competitive with foreign imports and to improve their bottom lines. Soon the routine tasks of workers were taken over by efficient machines. Automation in factories increased and the unionized worker who had been such an important part of building America became increasingly marginalized. Laws that would have prevented companies from arbitrarily closing their doors and shipping their jobs overseas were reformed, or more aptly, were rendered obsolete. American manufacturers shamelessly picked up the ethos of the post-industrial philosophy and ran all the way with it to the bank while touting the virtues of white collar work over those of hard labor.

This newly empowered Enterprise ᵛMEME had found a partner in government that fully understood its right to make a profit over all other considerations. A business owner's decision to relocate a factory to China became merely an accounting matter without a struggle with the moral obligation to provide local jobs, or a consideration of the patriotic duty to participate in the collective prosperity of America as a whole. Those days were gone. The manufacturing industry's new motto became the enrichment of the white-collar worker over the blue-collar worker, as well as the stockholder over the stakeholder as high paying manufacturing jobs left the country in record numbers in pursuit of a better bottom line. During Reagan's first three years in office America permanently lost over 2.5 million manufacturing jobs.[83]

This was the beginning of the de-industrialization of America. The service industry, along with the other elements of a post-industrial economy, was still in its infancy stages. *Life conditions* could not change fast enough to re-educate and retrain a growing labor force. Reintegration of workers into an economy defined by science, knowledge, and a white-collar service industry did not include the factory worker who had a completely different set of skills. The high paying jobs in the new economy were designed for educated college graduates and had very little to do the old economy. As a result, most workers who weren't proficient in the skills of the post-industrial economy ended up with low paying service jobs. This phenomenon that was supposed to be a temporary problem in the transition of the old economy to the new economy had become a permanent stigma for the workers. It continues to be one of the primary reasons for the ongoing shift of wealth away from the working class and for much of the social unrest that is seen in the aftermath of the financial crisis of 2008.

TAMING THE BEAST

Most of the pieces of the puzzle for Reagan's reform agenda were in place by the third year of his first term. The only wild element that continued to rage out of control was inflation. Nixon and Carter's attempts at taming it through wage and price controls and other measures proved futile. Their simplistic calls on people to tighten spending did little to comfort an America that had become untrusting of the government's ability to do anything with the tools it had at its disposal. For an economy to effectively deal with out of control inflation, interest rates had to be considerably higher than the rate of inflation in order to slow spending. But to increase interest rates would have been political suicide and no president in the 1970s was willing to do it. The challenges the Fed faced throughout the 1970s were reflective of the enormous changes that were the results of a system in decay. According to Beck's theories of spiral dynamics, in the life cycles of memetic ideologies, a system that is in decline becomes susceptible to wild cards from outside the system itself. Plans to manage these unexpected events during the decline phase could create a reverse effect and serve to postpone the appearance of the new system while exposing the dysfunction of the old. The paradigm of the New Deal ideology was dying and the abandonment of Bretton Woods combined with the shocks to the economy from the oil embargo. Policy makers searched for answers within a dying system that simply did not possess sustainable solutions.

Inflation had made the job of Fed Chairman an undesirable one throughout most of the 1970s. Toward the end of the decade the virtues of the monetarist ideology were gaining more acceptance, but had not yet influenced policy making. In 1977, after Congress endowed the Fed with newly expanded responsibilities, subtle shifts started to take place that would eventually place it in charge of insuring full employment, but with the use of different tools. Government spending and taxation, a hallmark of the past fourth-level system, started to give way to a new expression of the same order ᵛMEME except that it was through policies that emphasized the effective control of the money supply.

Beginning in 1979 Paul Volker, the Fed Chairman who had played a leading role as Treasury Secretary in removing the dollar from the gold standard, took some steps that his predecessors had failed to take that would prove to be politically unpopular but were precisely what the economy needed. He started to contract the money supply while gradually raising the federal funds rate from an average of 11.2 percent in 1979 to a peak of 20 percent in June 1981. In the process this tamed the greatest threat to economic prosperity, as inflation dropped from a peak of 13.5 percent in 1981 to just 3.2 percent in 1983.[84]

This was a landmark development that had finally closed the book on a decade of transition in US modern economic history. The taming of inflation in the midst of the economic chaos of the past decade would have significant value-systems implication for the historic role of money in human emergence. This was the first glimpse of what the new metrics for the value of the US dollar would be as a fiat currency, or the first attempt at defining a fifth-level system of currency that is representative of true productive output. Volker became the lion tamer who had started a battle in the early 1970s to move money from its traditional false fourth-level expression of the gold standard to an embryonic but still emerging fifth-level expression that is a function of human capacity. With lightning speed, the taming of inflation by a strong monetarist Fed helped shove the principles of monetary policy into the forefront of a new economic ideology.

With all the pieces of the puzzle in place Reagan launched his "it's morning again in America" campaign that espoused the virtues of a stronger, leaner, and more economically agile America heading into the future. This easily got him re-elected. According to economist Joseph Stiglitz, Volker was a transitional figure at the Fed for the Reagan Administration because the policy makers didn't believe he was an adequate deregulator.[85] It was believed that the complete shift to Reagan's economic policies required more sophisticated metrics that had to come from an evolving and dynamic marketplace with an astute eye on economic efficiency and not from a place entrenched in past bureaucracy. In value-systems terms this meant that in order for the ideological shift to be complete the person in charge of money supply had to come from a fifth-level Orange system background and not from a parochial and often arrested fourth-level order system of the past. This role was to be identified more with a facilitator of and a partner in economic prosperity rather than with a regulator of economic policy. And no one fit this role better than the maestro himself, Alan Greenspan.

THE FINAL PIECES OF THE PUZZLE

Prior to becoming the Chairman of the Federal Reserve Alan Greenspan had been urged by one of his idols, Arthur F. Burns, to bring the pioneering economic metrics he developed in private practice to bear on economic policy. Burns had been an ineffective Fed Chairman himself during the 1970s, but he recognized the mathematical genius behind the modern forecasting models that his student had built through the years. In turn, Greenspan had also admired Burns' work on business cycles, but these were models that were reflective of an industrial economy at its zenith in the 1940s. Burns' work covered everything that affected the business cycle in an industrial economy from changing technology in the shoe-manufacturing sector to the effects of restrictions of money supply under the gold standard.[86] *Life conditions* had changed considerably by the time Burns advocated for Greenspan to be Ford's economic advisor. The times weren't right for his libertarian views to take root because the system needed a more radical reformist at the helm. After Paul Volker successfully brought inflation under control it was time for the Reagan Administration to drop in the last piece of the puzzle that would create the foundation for the ideological transformation of American capitalism.

When Alan Greenspan became the Chairman of the Federal Reserve Board In 1987, he presided over a full platform that viewed an economy from a liberal monetarist perspective that had taken full charge of the US economy. This was a man fully realized in the values of the fifth-level Orange system. The powers that shaped Greenspan's ideology along with a highly successful reformist agenda would be given free rein in directing the rest of Reagan economic policy and would be continually put to the test during Greenspan's three decades at the Fed.

This was America's full entry into the growth phase of the second memenomic cycle. With the newly found optimism that Reagan brought to America, the business model was primed for change. Insuring maximum productivity—the greatest task the Fed was charged with—became the Fed's primary obsession. The race was on to define a new financial model for capitalism, from Fed policies to capital markets. Measures that defined maximum productive output were changing from the industrial measure of manpower and machine output to a more subjective service-based valuation open to manipulation, as this segment of the new economy was still in its infancy stage.

Much in the new economy was still being defined in the 1980s and 1990s. Segments of the service industry, such as finance, real estate, transportation, and warehousing, were being codified, and the measures of their output was being standardized as primary contributors to the nation's GDP. This became the rise of the technical class that was made up of scientists, researchers, engineers, and economists. This evolved the professional and technical workers, who through education and training had the necessary skills to make the post-industrial society prosper.[87] This was the emergence of the healthiest expression of the fifth-level Orange system as it uncovered the secrets of life and everything quantifiable through scientific and mathematical inquiry. This held the promise to transform the US economy memetically if other exploitative sectors of culture didn't manipulate its transformative potential.

Information and knowledge had become the base from which all participants in this economy could effectively and with a great degree of certainty plan for the future. As prosperity spread under the values of the new economy, the old beliefs about the role that an invisible hand played in it were becoming obsolete. With information and knowledge as the new hallmark of productive output, everything about this economy was subject to quantification. Knowledge contributed to the measurability of production. The more measurable a product or service became the more predictable the future of the economy became. Knowledge was power, and once that meme started spreading it became a quantifiable commodity. By the 1990s knowledge and its use through computer networks and other technological advances had imbedded its meme into every business model in every sector of our economy. The very definition of labor became muted as hard work was now being reflected in higher levels of knowledge.

This was the corporate revolution brought about by the age of information. The more knowledge the individual acquired, the more valuable he or she became to a potential employer. The more knowledgeable employees of a company were, the higher the valuation of a company was. In the views of political leaders and regulators, there was nothing to regulate and everything to claim credit for as prosperity continued to spread. Policies at the Fed touted the virtues of this new prosperity as the chairman himself so rationally and convincingly articulated in his appearances in front of Congress to reinforce the steady direction of the new economy.

Financial analysts on Wall Street took notice of these changes as they threw out their old valuation models and adopted new ones that saw the unlimited potential of a knowledge-driven economy. This became the precursor that revolutionized the financial industry because it made capital for new knowledge-based ideas easily available. As liberal lending policies became a part of the new economic landscape, the new valuation models rarely received any scrutiny, since very few institutions and regulators had the competencies to know what to look for. This passive negligence was helped by the substantial rise in wealth in the coming decade that cemented Wall Street's role as a prominent player in the future of the post-industrial economy. This further reinforced the myth that the new economy was capable of self-regulation. This era also became known as the "Great Moderation" as volatility was tamed through effective use of monetary policy and a reformist agenda that reduced taxation and the role of government.[88] As we continued into a prolonged *growth* phase of the second memenomic cycle, *life conditions* continued to be tightly aligned with the system. The rise of the professional and technical class had become a reality, and a whole financial system was in place to bankroll it. These were happy times at a party that lasted two decades, and no one wanted to suffer the ridicule of taking away the punch bowl too soon. The systematic reordering of culture has been achieved and its economic engine hummed along quietly for years.

FINANCE VS. PRODUCTION

With advancements in scientific thinking and mathematical modeling in the private sector, the financial industry started venturing into new and exciting areas of financial innovation. The 1990s witnessed the birth of the concept of securitization, which called for the systemic monetization of everything that had value or was perceived to have value, or with proper guidance can have future value. According to one of its strongest advocates, professor John C. Edmunds of MIT, "in a post-industrial world securitization has become the most powerful engine of wealth creation wherein economic policy that aims to achieve growth through securitization does not attempt to increase the production of goods and services, rather it finds ways to increase the value of its stocks and bonds."[89]

This was an influential manifesto since Edmunds was also an advisor to many governments in emerging economies that embraced his views without much scrutiny. From a value-systems perspective this huge leap forward had tremendous ramifications. Suddenly the emerging world was being told that the values of the Industrial Age that the West went through and the journey that helped build the foundation of the fourth- and fifth-level Blue-Orange systems and which defined much of the character of the West and the middle class, were no longer necessary steps in cultural emergence. *Life conditions* in places rich in oil like the Middle East had remained primarily in the second and third Tribal-Egocentric ᵛMEMEs and had not experienced prolonged presence in a strong center of gravity in fourth or fifth levels. Suddenly these cultures were being told that these important stages could be skipped altogether in favor of making the size of the checks from oil revenues bigger without increasing levels of production or without the need to diversify their economies from that single and finite source of revenue.

In turn, these checks were reinvested in newly inflated stocks and bonds from a belief in the securitization process. This fallacy had only short-term benefit to whoever adopted it and was of considerable benefit to the credit enhancer who was facilitating the channels to fund it. This shift in economic focus from innovative ways to pursue production to the pursuit of financial innovation without production, laid the grounds for a potential global asset and commodities bubble if the practices were to be adopted by these economies. This securitization meme had the potential to leave a profound mark on advanced economies as well. In general, this new innovation redefined companies strictly as financial instruments without their having to contribute a single additional product to overall output. The rising belief that capital assets used in production can be securitized to many times their actual value, and the notion of creating something out of nothing, gave Wall Street the impetus to securitize everything it could possibly get its hands on without having to patiently wait for a venture to prove its viability in a competitive marketplace.

As securitization moved into small and medium-size enterprises, it had a profound effect on how traditional business decisions were made. Under the traditional model, businesses regarded themselves as stakeholders in their communities and acted as good, responsible corporate citizens answering as much as possible to the collective needs of the community while keeping an eye on their bottom line. Under the new model, these companies became indebted to the wishes of the securitizer, be it Wall Street or the smaller private equity firm. This was the classical example of how a finance-driven economy began to shift wealth from Main Street to Wall Street. The distributed model that provided cultural prosperity for the working and middle-class with proven generational presence was now being exploited for short-term gains orchestrated by elite financial wizards who cared more about short-term profits to provide more wealth to themselves, their investors, and stockholders.

For Wall Street the use of securitization was a heaven-sent proposition. It allowed fund managers and analysts to perform value enhancements that increased valuations based on regression, and presented projection models that were the sole creation of the financial industry. This was one of the biggest visible shifts in the new economy away from diverse, measurable, and objective valuation methods specific to each sector of the economy to ones that were speculative, notional, and in the hands of the powerful financial industry. This shift announced the system's entry into the *maturity* phase and signaled the beginning of the decoupling process from *life conditions*.

In memenomic terms, the newfound prosperity confirmed that a considerably muted fourth-level order system was essential in the continued success of the economy. Moreover, the complete independence of the Fed from any government influence was essential. As everyone was prospering, no one paid attention to the rising power of the Fed as the accommodator of prosperity and the potential for collusion of the largest central bank in the world with the emerging field of financial innovation. While these changes in the financial industry were taking place, there was no corresponding rise in new fourth-level system laws to intelligently articulate the new role of finance in the new economy. The prevailing thinking in government at the time was to maintain the status quo on two fronts. The first was not to rock the boat under a successful reformist ideology that believed in liberating the private sector from obsolete industrial-age laws. The second was the emerging belief that government and its antiquated institutions were incapable of understanding the dynamics of the new economy and that by its very nature this new expression of the fifth-level Orange system was self-regulating.

Both of these premises would prove to be dangerously false in later years. The long-term effect of a diminished regulatory ᵛMEME cannot be underestimated, because collusion with the unhealthy versions of the fifth-level Orange system would be inevitable. *Aesthetic change* undertaken by the Orange system during the *growth* phase of a cycle that tweaks the system forward works well. But as a system moves to the *maturity* and *decline* phases, the Blue system within the cycle must be aware of the nature of these tweaks as they effect the health of the entire system. During the *only money matters* cycle a highly diminished Blue system has little understanding of what these a*esthetic changes* are. As it reposes into complacency, it becomes increasingly difficult for it to regulate when it comes time for it to do so.

Under an information-driven post-industrial economy not everyone sought to rise into the technical, college-educated class. *Life conditions* still showed that over two-thirds of America's labor-force held lower levels of education and not all could become scientists, bankers and economists. The question became which fourth-level Blue structure of the post-industrial economy, whether a labor union or government institution, would insure fair labor practices and full employment for this majority of society. Manufacturing had continued its exodus into the emerging economies and the Fed's answer to this was to provide more money to the new economy. Globalization and outsourcing started to drain even the small number of jobs in the service sector created for the non-technical working class and the Fed's answer was to provide the economy with even more money. The Fed, which was in charge of insuring full employment was acting as if the US labor force had reached that Utopian dream of the post-industrial society. Of course, this couldn't be further from the truth. This disconnect between the elitists, who pursued success only through proprietary fifth-level financial innovation, and the rest of society grew by the day. The diversion of the entire post-industrial economy into this narrow but lucrative field of financial innovation would alter the very nature of capitalism and nudge the system forward through false *esthetic changes* that would temporarily prolong the maturity phase of the memenomic cycle.

SETTING THE CONDITIONS
FOR THE PERFECT ᵛMEME STORM

The 1990's decade was a time when the commodities and trading industries were being redefined in response to emerging trends in the new economy. By mid-decade the trading floor of every stock exchange was transformed from what it used to be just ten years earlier. This wasn't your father's Wall Street anymore. This was an industry, like other parts of the new economy that had parted ways with old industrial-age metrics and had embraced the new values of monetarism and the new economy. During the 1980s the trading profession had experienced a shift away from the old routine of selling stocks and bonds to the more complex and profitable financing of leveraged buyouts and facilitating mergers and acquisitions. Finance was playing a far more prominent role in the lives of every American. The very definition of prosperity was changing in accordance with the dictates of Wall Street.

The old philosophy of purchasing blue chip stocks on the premise that buying and holding them as long-term investments would spread prosperity to the middle class was being replaced by more speculative short-term practices that attracted predatory behavior by people with little interest in the qualitative long-term value of the stock. Most Americans understood what a profitable quarter for GM meant to the value of the stock, but in the 1990s investors had no patience to think of things like P/E ratios or actual generation of revenue. The catalyst to this change in the marketplace was the creation of the Internet. Wild speculation about its potential in transforming the future combined with easy access to capital allowed financial analysts to value Internet companies at multiple times the normal valuations without the proof that they could generate a single dollar in revenue. Objective evaluation of the fundamentals gave way to hype and speculation. Venture capital money allowed these companies to develop a business model to carry them long enough to garner an initial public offering while the hype sold the stock for many times its initial value. This was a preview of what became known as a "bubble economy" under the monetarist ideology. The more money the economy had, the bigger the bubble was, and the more the speculative element took hold of the culture. Lending rules and debt margins were relaxed so that more of the rising liquidity could be put to use. Investors who in the past were prevented entry into certain investments due old rules such as minimum equity requirements, net worth and credit worthiness found their ways to unprecedented opportunities.

In short, the diminishment of the fourth-level order system that started with the dawn of the Reagan ideology had worked its way through government institutions, the private sector, and had now started spreading its values at a systemic level to the entire culture through financial institutions. By the late 1990s the threat of money corrupting the very values of capitalism was like an ominous dark cloud hanging over the future of the US economy.

The list of events detailed below represent the systemic spread of the *only money matters* meme that accelerated the movement of the cycle from the maturity phase into the decline phase. Capitalism during this phase was presented with its greatest challenge since the days of Adam Smith. During the Clinton-Bush era the financial sector of the new economy was charting a new direction for capitalism. As the obsession with Reagan's reformist agenda continued, the Clinton Administration ventured into an area of deregulation that, from a value-systems perspective, would prove to be disastrous. Much analysis has been made about the causes of the financial crisis, but the following chronology of events section is specific to the value-systems dynamics as they demonstrate with a degree of clarity how crucial it is for a fourth-level order system to anticipate the exploitative potential of the strategic fifth system.

1. The Disappearance of the Order ᵛMEME from Banking

In 1999 the US Congress passed, and President Clinton signed into law, the Financial Services Modernization Act. This act repealed much of the Great Depression era law known as the Glass-Steagall Act of 1933 that separated the activities of investment banks and insurance companies from those of commercial banks. Suddenly there were no barriers preventing banks that were insured by the taxpayer from participating in the risky investment activities of Wall Street. The new Wall Street had friends in high places that not only could be called on for a favor or two, but ones that were part of the long-term decision making and policy shaping process. The Financial Services Modernization Act was also known as the Citigroup Relief Act.[90] United States Treasury Secretary Robert Rubin, who had a storied career with one of the most venerable firms on Wall Street, Goldman Sachs, was one of the main architects behind the legislation.

This was the appearance of a new and dangerous form of regulator for the fourth-level system. To understand the complexity of the new economy, a regulator had to be thoroughly knowledgeable of its intricate microeconomic functionality. However, under *life conditions* that sought the elimination of laws as a positive step for the economy, the potential for collusion and corruption was muted. The deregulation of traditional banks opened the floodgates to what became the hallmark of the new fifth-level Orange system of that era—the acquisition of smaller banks and the integration of non-lending activities into one big umbrella of financial services that promised the consumer a more diversified and less expensive product line. The activities that were hidden from the consumer-friendly face of this act were the risks that commercial banks started to be involved in without this being noticed. Traditional financial channels for making investment capital available were no longer satisfactory since they couldn't compete with what Wall Street had to offer. After the change in the law, commercial banks started venturing into the untested waters of new financial instruments that were being created by Wall Street. The mad science of algorithms and financial derivatives was taking the investment banking industry by storm. The more complex a financial instrument was, the more appeal it had to investors, and the more the appetite grew to monetize any liquidity that became available anywhere in the world. The increased degree of sophistication in the fifth-level ᵛMEME became less and less detectable by an increasingly diminished fourth-level ᵛMEME.

2. The Rise of Notional Money and Speculative Investments

Nowhere had the rise of the technical class of the post-industrial economy been more noticeable than on Wall Street. Geniuses with highly advanced technical skills and PhDs who should have been working in the fields of space exploration, epidemiology, and other obscure areas that are critical for the of future of humanity, were lured by much higher pay to companies like Lehman Brothers, Goldman Sachs, and JP Morgan. Investment banking was attracting the best talent in the world in order to create a bigger and more profitable line of investments. In a nutshell, what these scientists on Wall Street were doing was creating mathematical algorithms that attempted to predict the future performance of certain economic activity or the future price of certain commodities and sell these findings to investors in the form of contracts. The possibilities for experimental combinations for these contracts were unlimited.

There were no actual products or services being added to benefit overall society; these products only manipulated the prices of world's existing resources and output under varying scenarios. This is how the financial services industry came to define growth, not by adding to actual productive output, but by manipulating the world's existing resources through clever betting games. This new and highly sophisticated form of betting on the future borrowed quite a bit of its practices from the long-established actuarial models of the insurance industry, which gave it the cover of long-term stability. It was called derivative insurance, which had been around for decades. Actuarial mathematicians in the dark basements of insurance companies would produce risk assessments models that determined the rates their companies would charge for a variety of products from crop insurance to a life policy premium for an 80-year-old smoker. This became known as the derivatives market and had the cover of safety to within 95 percent of historic accuracy.

The industry was largely unregulated and had served the role of muting the effects of risk in the past, but its increased use as a standard investment product posed the dangers of systemic risk. As there was little scrutiny of these types of contracts, they became Wall Street's favorite mode of investment. The derivatives market was a whole new area of financial innovation and the fear of the potential damage it can cause to the economy grew by the day as no one in government was willing to challenge the gray area it operated in.

The Securities and Exchange Commission is charged with regulating the investment banking industry, but there was very little reference in law that identified the nature of derivatives as an item that fell under the jurisdiction of the SEC.[91] Investment banking historically receives little scrutiny from the fourth-level system, because there's an underlying belief that protracted inquiries can have unfavorable effects on markets. These were paper contracts and the firms who underwrote them rarely owned any of the underlying security. Derivative contracts of every kind were being created and sold, from betting on the future of oil prices to the performance of sub-prime mortgages. If there was an appetite for it, Wall Street made it into a derivative and sold it.

By June 2008 the value of contracts in the over-the-counter derivatives market was estimated to be around $684 trillion.[92] In comparison, the total value of goods and services exchanged in the United States in that same year was under $15 trillion. Most of these contracts were what's called counter-party contracts and had little bearing on systemic risk. The one type of derivative contract that did was the Credit Default Swap (CDS). This was an insurance policy taken out by both parties to the derivative contract. In case the losing party becomes insolvent, the holder of the CDS insurance policy was made whole by the insurance provider. The Bank for International Settlements estimated the value of these CDSs to be around $63 trillion in June of 2008.

Not even a year had passed since the Financial Modernization Act went into law, when new concerns started to appear about insurance firms becoming major providers of coverage in an unregulated industry. With just a small notional value assigned to the assets as collateral for the insurance provider, multiple losses could spell disaster for an insurance company that also provided other conventional coverage like home and auto. Many consumer protection groups lobbied Congress to place "credit default swaps" under state gaming regulations, but the calls went unheeded. The inability of this segment of the fourth-level system to regulate financial innovation grew exponentially as Wall Street entered uncharted waters in its pursuit of profits that contributed very little to productive output. The expression of the fifth-level system at this stage was gambling, pure and simple.

It hid behind the sophisticated façade of math and science, but at its core it was no different than sitting at a Las Vegas Casino and rolling the dice. The rise of the technical class under this expression of the new economy was beginning to take on an unhealthy direction that had the potential to downshift the entire culture into opportunistic and exploitative practices of the third-level RED system. This change in focus away from productive pursuits in the presence of a diminished fourth-level system was also a prescription for the rise of unhealthy practices of the fifth-level system, since it had the potential to take hold of the world's natural resources and productive output and monetize them according to this new gambling platform that became the foundation for the financial crisis.

3. The Largest Global Pool of Money in Human History

In the early 2000s the world was becoming an increasingly smaller place. The rise of globalization had brought unprecedented levels of wealth to emerging economies like China and India and to many in the oil-producing region of the Middle East. The West had seen a steady climb to new levels of prosperity after the fall of communism in Eastern Europe. The promise of the new economy's knowledge sector, coupled with low cost of capital, brought new innovations to markets in record time. Everyone was sharing in this newfound prosperity as the tide of capitalism was lifting all boats. The wealth in emerging economies was growing at a much faster rate that what their respective systems could absorb. Although investment in actual infrastructure projects at home in these countries was lucrative and essential in developing a viable presence on the global stage, the development of capital markets needed considerably more time and political stability to become as viable as those in Western economies.

Among all Western models the United States and the United Kingdom had the most developed investment infrastructure that had become the envy of the world. The proven track record of sophistication, discipline, and consistent returns over many decades had made Wall Street and The City of London the preferred choice for managing global wealth. One of the most crucial events leading up to financial crisis would test the moral framework of these two centers of global power and become the ultimate test that would determine their future and that of the newest innovation in financial engineering. Between 2000 and 2006 a sudden rise in global liquidity in search for a safe haven tested the limits of finance as a viable discipline. According to the head of capital markets research at the IMF, the amount of cash that was looking for a safe investment home had risen to approximately $70 trillion, which was twice the normal buildup in the global pool of money.[93] At the current levels of productive output, it would have taken more than a decade to employ all this added liquidity because traditional investment vehicles simply couldn't absorb it. United States treasuries had been a traditional favorite investment in the past, but after the attacks of 9/11 the Fed has artificially brought down interest rates to avert an imminent recession, forcing global money managers to look for better returns elsewhere.

HOW THE OLDEST FOURTH-LEVEL SYSTEM WAS CORRUPTED

Growth of Global Fixed-Income Assests (Cash) Looking for a Home (in Trillion USD)

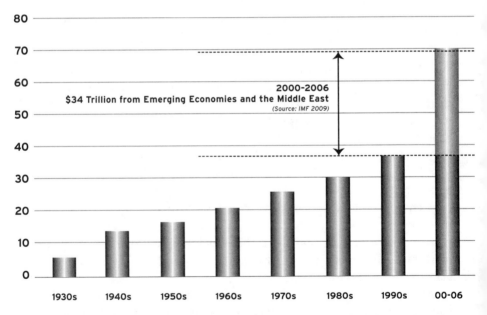

Legitimate investment vehicles can only absorb $1.8 trillion/year of added infusion of liquidity. Wall Street created shady investment vehicles designed to absorb the excess and enrich themselves.

From a values-systems perspective, this was a crucial stage that is often overlooked by many analysts offering explanations for the causes of the financial crisis. Financial innovation was at a cross roads in its evolution. On the capital deployment side, with $34 trillion at hand, the infrastructure to transform capitalism to its next expression was fully in place. The biggest question was whether it would be deployed into productive areas of innovation in the constantly evolving knowledge sector of the new economy to fund much needed research and development projects that would chart a new course in sustainable capitalism, or if it would it be deployed into the exploitative channels of which we had already had a glimpse. The former represented the highest expression of a healthy fifth-level system, while the latter represented the dominance of the exploitative and toxic form of the same ᵛMEME.

With that level of funding, capitalism stood at a very crucial stage in its history. Under the virtues of the post-industrial economy, the securitization meme had created much wealth out of clever ways of reframing the perception of value. The notion of creating something out of nothing had already been tapped to its maximum possible benefit. The existing values of stocks and bonds couldn't possibly be stretched any further than they already were. With just a fraction of that $34 trillion available earlier in the decade, capital markets used it to finance Internet startups that resulted in the tech bubble and a crash that gave the world a glimpse of who benefits financially from these escapades.

Meanwhile, by 2003 the dangers of the derivatives sector of financial innovation had claimed the largest bankruptcy in US history. Enron, the energy company, had been the pioneer in using energy contracts in counter-party biddings to manipulate energy prices. This was the canary in the coalmine for this highly sophisticated game of betting and resource manipulation. If Enron succeeded in manipulating energy derivatives, the rest of Wall Street was ready to apply the method to everything else in the global economy. With Enron's devastating failure, Congress passed the Sarbanes-Oxley Act that held officers of publically held corporations personally accountable for the disclosures in their companies' financial statements. For the first time in recent memory, this was the appearance of new fourth-level order system that attempted to make its presence known, and only time would tell if this was the return of a visionary regulatory structure that understood the inner workings of the new economy. But, alas it had been too long since a diminished regulator ᵛMEME had confronted the unhealthy expression of a far more sophisticated fifth-level system because Wall Street was already too invested in this infrastructure of the derivatives market. Shortly after the passage of Sarbanes-Oxley, Wall Street firms like Lehman Brothers moved the engines that ran their derivative operations to London where such activity was not regulated.

IN THE EYE OF THE ᵛMEMETIC STORM

The decision about which road to take that would decide the future of capitalism had just taken a grave turn for the worse. This wasn't the deregulation of an industry that affected a minor part of the culture. The money supply had been to human emergence what oxygen had been to every life form. It has shaped our lives for over 8,000 years, and the stage had just been set for it go through profound transformation. The very historic role of money as a function of productive output was just about to be tested by a brave and risky experiment in capitalism. The old metrics that required some degree of fourth- level Blue discipline were suddenly put out to pasture. Everyone along the memetic stack, from second-level tribal values to sixth-level egalitarian values was enticed into taking part in this new global wealth as the virtues of hard work gave way to speculative and short-term investment behavior. The floodgates of money had just been opened to the entire global memestack, as the world indulged in one of the biggest orgies of easy consumer spending it had ever known.

One of the last remaining industries that was immune to the securitization and derivatives practices of Wall Street was the real estate industry. The residential sector had played a major role in establishing the wealth of the American middle class while the commercial sector has been defining the character of urban growth and the shape of our cities' skylines for decades. With $34 trillion in unregulated money, Wall Street went right to work to create securities and derivatives that would knock down the walls of this last stronghold of traditional wealth. Endless products from sub-prime to Alt-A, and everything in between with investment-friendly sounding names, funded the purchases of homes. Then they were sprinkled with the magic dust of derivative algorithms and put into huge pools of securities and given fancy names like RMBS and CMBS. Armies of Wall Street analysts were giving their sermons to all those who would listen on how the new American dream was now open to everyone. All a potential homeowner needed was a social security number and a pulse and the dream was theirs. The race was on to pump this excess liquidity into a housing market worth trillions of dollars and to allow homeowners to use their equity as the biggest source of wealth to fuel an economy that was becoming increasingly dependent on debt financing.

THE BLOODY DANCE OF THE ᵛMEMES *A ᵛMemetic Summary of the Predatory Values That Caused the Housing Bubble*	
Players on the Demand Side	**Players on the Money Supply Side**
• **RED/UNHEALTHY ORANGE ᵛMEME** agents, brokers, appraisers, fraudulent document preparers • **RED ᵛMEME** straw buyers, speculators, buyers using stolen identity • **RED/PURPLE ᵛMEME** victims left holding the bag when it all came crashing down	• **RED/UNHEALTHY ORANGE ᵛMEME** mortgage brokers and originators • **RED/UNHEALTHY ORANGE ᵛMEME** Wall Street securitizers (subprime, ALT-A, CDO, MBS, CMBS, etc.) • **RED/PURPLE ᵛMEME** and unsuspecting **BLUE/ORANGE ᵛMEME** victims/ securities buyers: institutional investors, sovereign wealth funds, pension funds, mutual funds, teachers and government employees, labor unions ... (lots of cash)

With rising values, homes became super ATMs that spit out $10,000's if not $100,000's in equity that greased the wheels of an economy that had become 70 percent dependent on consumer spending. This became a new American meme that affected every value system as we all tried to keep up with the Joneses and do our share to keep the economy moving. By 2004 this fallacy of wealth had taken full hold of our culture as Wall Street lured everyone with access to debt into thinking he or she were investment geniuses. This was also the end of the *maturity* phase of the third memenomic cycle and the entry into the *decline* phase.

From a value-systems perspective there were two distinctive ᵛMEMEs in operation during the buildup to the financial crisis. In absence of a visionary fourth-level regulatory structure, the fifth-level Strategic Enterprise ᵛMEME downshifts to unhealthy exploitative practices, and the third-level feudal system rises to break free from the forces that have kept it down. Historically, there has always been a relationship between these two memetic expressions, as they both seem to rise in absence of law and order. The unhealthy expression of the fifth-level system is far more dangerous than that of the third level as it has the patience to be more strategic and systematic about its abuses.

To draw a comparison from contemporary life, this is the difference between an individual like Bernie Madoff and the character of Tony on the TV series *The Sopranos*. While Tony's thugs hit up neighborhood businesses

ANATOMY OF THE THIRD MEMENOMIC CYCLE
1999-2002

In the Eye of the ʸMemetic Storm
Entering the Entropy Phase of the Current System

1
THE RISE OF THE
WESTERN UNHEALTHY ORANGE

The World becomes flat and Emerging Economies flood the U.S. with liquidity looking for safe Investments other than U.S. Treasuries— giving rise to Wall Street Securitization.

2
THE DISAPPEARANCE OF BLUE
FROM BANKING REGULATION

A: In November 1999 Congress repeals the Depression-era Glass Stiegel Act that separated investment banks from commercial banks who then entered into SECURITIZATION.

B: In 2000 Congress fails to regulate financial derivatives and exempts Credit Default Swaps from state gaming regulations. Risky securities were now insurable and the appearance of risk was muted.

3
THE POST-ENRON REVENGE
OF THE UNHEALTHY ORANGE

Sarbanes-Oxley Act leads to offshore/off books activities by major banks and to AIG London and Lehman Brothers London which underwrote most risk without detection.

4
POST 9/11 ECONOMIC POLICIES OF
THE BUSH ADMINISTRATION (RED/ORANGE)

A: Need inexpensive ways to finance wars in Afghanistan and Iraq.

B: Call to arms: "BUY, BUY, BUY or the terrorists win."

C: Fed drops prime rate to 40-year lows.

for a few hundred dollars of protection money, Madoff takes twenty years to defraud investors out of tens of billions of dollars. The behavior of the third-level system is easily detectable by law, while that of the unhealthy fifth-level can go unnoticed for years. The unhealthy fifth-level system did its work at macro, large scale and institutional levels, while the third-level Red system did its dirty work at the street retail level. Financial advisors procured capital in the billions from all across the globe. There was money from sovereign wealth funds, labor unions of all types, pension funds, advisors to emerging economies, and any global investor looking for the stability and safety of US capital markets.

On the retail end in housing, the third-level system mobilized itself, and anybody else who wanted to become wealthy, overnight. Identities were sold for a few thousand dollars. Back room document preparers produced anything a borrower needed to get a loan—fraudulent tax returns, false bank statements, W-2 statements with phony credit reports, and the list goes on. The more they got away with, the braver and more systematic their practices became. Properties were selling within hours of being listed as bidding battles drove price beyond the list price. New homes were being sold even before ground was broken and were sold again several times for hefty profits on the contract without any of the interim buyers taking possession when construction was complete. The more loans were given, the more capital poured into Wall Street as investors became attracted to the high returns.

These were the predatory value-systems dynamics of a bubble. Similar pattern of investment behavior repeated in equity and commodity markets as ambitious traders were lured into the overnight wealth mantra of the Red system. Because of the levels of liquidity available along with accommodative Fed policies, speculative behavior didn't crash when it was supposed to. Political leaders mistook this as a confirmation that the new economy was capable of self-regulation. This thin cover of safety for these toxic securities spread to institutions that were formally immune to their allure. Fannie Mae and Freddie Mac, the largest buyers of traditional mortgages who had stayed out of the securitization game, started buying mortgage-backed securities in the billions as systemic toxicity reached ever-higher levels. The only voice of a regulator ^{V}MEME that the world ever heard from during these days was that of Alan Greenspan, the maestro himself, who applauded the success of the new monetarist ideology at every chance he had while presiding over its full implementation over the preceding three decades. The deregulation of the financial industry was supposed to be his crowning achievement as he prepared to exit a storied career no other central banker has experienced in history.

The success of the securitization meme has shifted power from a traditional distributed system of funding that had been decades in the making to one that had concentrated the power in the hands of the few on Wall Street. In less than a decade a highly sophisticated expression of the financial innovation sector of the fifth-level system had unraveled what took the old system decades to build. Suddenly, at a cultural level, money wasn't representative of work anymore or of long-term strategic planning. The addictive nature of a get-rich-quick system made it difficult to reflect on the virtues of the past that build our fourth-level institutions step by step and brick by brick. Predatory lending and speculative investing had created a culture of predators that had gotten addicted to immediate gratification. When it came to new ways of wealth building, there was no longer a belief in traditional American values that were built under the *patriotic prosperity era.* Finding meaning in work and in other forms of higher calling gave way to over-consumption, indulgence, and gluttony. Personal influence and the power of the ego supplanted the collective emergence of a whole society. Contractors showed up to job sites driving $70,000 Hummers with a flatbed Hummer behind delivering supplies. It was inspired by the glitz from the spontaneous impulse of wanting to be seen in such high profile vehicles without any regard to where the next auto loan payment was going to come from.

Wall Street had already taken millions of these loans, packaged them into what's called a "Collateralized Debt Obligation" security and sold them to some unsuspecting wealth fund manager in Dubai or Soule, South Korea making millions in fees in the process. The professional class wasn't immune to these cultural shifts either. Doctors were spending less time with their patients and more time checking on their growing portfolios, talking to their brokers, and playing the market. Scientists were creating more algorithms on Wall Street because of the high pay instead of finding cures for diseases on Main Street or exploring space and scientific inquiry. Retired teachers were lured into refinancing their homes, with initial payments lower than they were under their old loans after taking out $100,000 in equity. No one explained to them that their interest rate would adjust in eighteen months to triple the monthly payments.

College students became reckless in their borrowing as Wall Street gave them 100s of millions in student loan and created more CDOs and sold them to more unsuspecting investors. Institutions weren't immune to the flood of greed as this meme cemented itself as the new normal. Financial services as a percentage of corporate profits rose to all time highs. In-house financing became as important a business tool as that business's area of specialty. Again, Wall Street was there to securitize, package, sell, and provide more liquidity to a world that couldn't stop its addition to debt financing.

THE HISTORICALLY INVERSE RELATIONSHIP
BETWEEN THE BLUE-FOURTH LEVEL REGULATOR ᵛMEME
AND THE FIFTH-LEVEL ENTERPRISING ᵛMEME

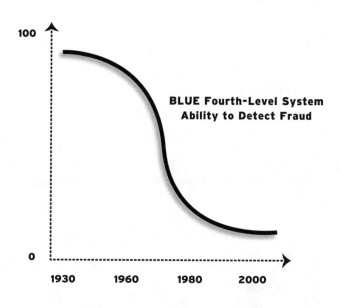

BLUE Fourth-Level System
Ability to Detect Fraud

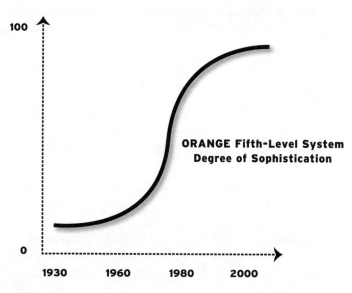

ORANGE Fifth-Level System
Degree of Sophistication

After much of the global liquidity was securitized, refinancing into new loans became harder to do and borrowers started to default. The game of smoke and mirrors was over as the thin cover of safety on these assets began to fade and expose their toxic nature. By the time Lehman Brothers failed, banks were so leveraged that third party checks wouldn't have cleared. In five short years the abuses the world endured as a result of the predatory lending behavior of the third- and fifth-level systems had brought the global economy to the brink of disaster.

BAILOUT: THE FINAL PHASE OF THE CURRENT SYSTEM

The financial bailout of 2008 was intended to avert a catastrophic collapse of the US economy and global financial markets, or so the story went to convince members of an oblivious fourth-level system that had no viable ways of verifying these claims. Government service had become the natural springboard into a lucrative career that lobbied for the deregulation of the financial industry, and no one saw the potential collusion between the interest of the industry and the consumer. The SEC was repeatedly determined to look the other way when evidence of fraud committed by investors like Bernie Madoff was handed to them on a silver platter.

Hank Paulson, a critical figure in the fifth-level system that understood the practices of the financial industry, was now Treasury Secretary. His presence there was not to warn of the impending disaster, but to cushion the fall through a government rescue should that day come. In the history of fourth-level ᵛMEMEs, there is one day that lives in infamy as a testament to how ineffectual the order system had become in stopping the abuses of Wall Street. That day, October 3, 2008, was when the American people through their Congress gave Wall Street a blank check with which it returned to the gambling table and started the final phase of the collapse of the current system, the *entropy* phase. In value-systems studies, a diagnosis of a substantially diminished fourth-level ᵛMEME that is incapable of regulating can easily be differentiated, and specific prescriptions could be recommended for the rescue of the entire system before it reaches the point of no return.

But, this was a system that has bought into the belief that what is good for Wall Street is good for America. For over three decades it had filled top key positions, such as Secretaries of the Treasury, the Fed Chairman, and the Head of Economic Advisors with individuals who were more concerned with the growth of financial markets and accommodating fifth-level system power brokers than they were with the changing needs in *life conditions* and operating as regulators to insure against predatory behavior. The invisible hand of the market was rendering many industries obsolete and shifting the wealth from Main Street to Wall Street. A fourth-level system was not only clueless to what was happening, it was in direct collusion with it.

By the time Hank Paulson walked up to the steps of the Capitol, our fourth-level regulator ᵛMEME had no independent sources of information that was available to it that hadn't been shaped by Wall Street. This was the addict who had run out of money and was coming home begging for more cash to support his habit and placed a gun to the head of Congress. By voting for the bailout, the fourth-level system became a party to the heist of the American taxpayer. Regardless of how the repayment of the bailout money turns out in the end, the fourth-level system has lost credibility with the very people it is supposed to represent. The US economy and the American worker continue to suffer greatly as their homes are foreclosed on in record numbers. Banks and Wall Street, in confirmation of an ineffective regulator ᵛMEME, continue their addiction to non-productive and highly risky betting games and turn away from lending to the consumer and small businesses who are the lifeline of the economy.

Voter anger remains at an all time high as the pathologies of the old system become exposed to the taxpayer who is far more interested in learning about the collusion of Wall Street and our government than they were before the bailout. This is a system that was placed on life support through the bailout, but has now become a system of the walking dead with its institutions toxic, bankrupted, obsolete, and now incapable of reforming itself. Exploitation of resources and the shift in wealth continues as the stock market recovers to pre-crisis levels, while poverty reaches the worst levels in three decades. A government that had given the regulation of the economy to the fifth-level system under the belief in self-regulation is finding itself incapable of passing meaningful laws. This is all a painful confirmation that our culture had become polarized, and the only way out is the added popular pressure that will push the system into final stages of entropy where its values transform into informational codes that inform the new system. Much like this phase in the previous system, the emergence of the new system has already begun, but its values won't come in sync with *life conditions* until all the toxicity from the current system disappears.

THE SECOND AND THIRD MEMENOMIC CYCLES:
HOW ECONOMIC VALUE SYSTEMS RISE AND FALL

FDR'S NEW DEAL
THE PATRIOTIC PROSPERITY ERA

"The test of our progress is not whether we add more to the abundance of those who have much; it is whether we provide enough for those who have too little."

	1930s-1950s	1960s-1970s
BLUE	**VISIONARY**	**BURDENSOME**
	Built Modern New Deal Institutions • Social Security • FDIC, HUD, SEC, FTC, FHA, Fannie Mae, Freddie Mac • Fair Labor Act	**Heavy Cost of Visionary Mandates** • War and European Reconstruction • Social Welfare • Sustained BLUE Presence
ORANGE	**HEALTHY AND INNOVATIVE**	**BURDENED AND NON-COMPETITIVE**
	Encouraged to do Good by Visionary Blue/Orange • Established U.S. as non-disputed industrial superpower • Created the most economically powerful middle class in world	**Inflation, Gas, and Trade** • Inflation diminished profits • Expensive capital for expansion • Imports gained competitive edge

THE SECOND AND THIRD MEMENOMIC CYCLES: HOW ECONOMIC VALUE SYSTEMS RISE AND FALL

REAGANOMICS
THE "ONLY MONEY MATTERS" ERA

"Government is not the solution to our problem; government is the problem; it can and must provide opportunity not smother it. Foster productivity do not stifle it."

	1980s-1990s	2000s-2010s
BLUE	**DIMINISHED INFLUENCE**	**SYSTEMICALLY INEFFECTIVE**
	Government is the Problem • Deregulation of entire economy: banking communication, transportation, energy . . .	**No Bark, No Bite** • Clueless to banking • Clueless to capital markets • Clueless to derivatives • Clueless to high-tech
ORANGE	**MOSTLY OPPORTUNISTIC**	**SYSTEMICALLY DAMAGING**
	Dawn of Financial Innovation • Stock markets • Commodities markets • Built infrastructure for securitization/derivatives • Global finance • Outsourced for profit	**Destroyed New Deal Institutions** • Bankrupted Freddie and Fannie • Offshored labor-intensive jobs • Shifted wealth back to the wealthy • Gutted SEC and Federal Reserve

SEVEN

In Search of a New Paradigm

In the wake of the devastation caused by financial crisis, the cultural debate has transformed from discussion of the traditional role that money played in human emergence to a sobering and often contemptuous discussion about the abusive powers the financial industry wields over the lives of so many around the world. This wasn't about the upward enfoldment of human values under the capitalist system anymore. This became a study in how values become corrupted in the absence of law and order in any given area of culture. The current expression of capitalism became a system so disconnected from the original virtues of the ideology that it was no longer recognizable. The conception of money that started 8,000 years ago in the form of gifting and a simple act of exchange had developed into a complex global monetary system that built nations. All these developments, as complex as they are, were built on the premise that money or the future promise of money will always act as a function of productive output.

Rural and agricultural values gave way to industrial values, and money as a function of innovation acted as catalyst to facilitate the change. Industrial values in turn gave way to post-industrial values, and again as a function of change in innovation and productivity, capital acted as a catalyst. Rigid and antiquated metrics of industrial economies gave way to new and more complex metrics of knowledge-based economies. Somewhere in attempting to redefine innovation in the new economic landscape, the post-industrial era ushered in the intellectual elites who viewed the rise of the technical class with more liberal and subjective measurement. Liberal social thought merged with the values of the monetarist ideology that spread the meme of "only money matters" to create an economic platform that was vulnerable to many outside factors. Capital parted ways with being a function of productive output and became innovation itself.

The language that interpreted employment under the monetarist ideology was reframed in such a way that news about 10,000 workers losing their factory jobs due to automation sounded as if 50,000 jobs were being created. A machine that produced one hundred widgets an hour with one person

153

running it was considered by the Fed to be ten times as productive as five workers producing ten widgets and hour. Productivity parted ways from its historic correlation to levels of employment under new Fed policies, as did much of the metrics of the old economy and Wall Street, and the financial markets loved it. There wasn't much heavy lifting or need for hard hats in the new economy. Instead of dealing with out-of-work factory and auto industry workers, and creating retraining programs to bring them back into the fold of productive output, the Fed simply adjusted that measure to show increase in productivity through improvements in technology and efficiency. The worker was becoming less and less relevant to productive output and this became the meme that symbolized the post-industrial economy. And, again, as a sign of cost efficiency, financial markets couldn't be happier.

The absence of regulation in the financial industry was the proof of how an opportunist predatory culture with too much money was able to hijack all the other virtues of the post-industrial economy. As our values were being reshaped over a two-and-a-half decade time span, the liberation of the financial sector poisoned the entire knowledge-based ideology by having far more liquidity available to it than the global economy could legitimately absorb. This excess liquidity created a new global economic meme called the "bubble economies" as speculators inflated prices, took profits, and moved on to the next bubble. The entire global memestack of values has shifted from being characterized by the distributed safety under the pre-monetarist era to one that concentrated power in the hands of the financial sector. This shift has caused stock markets around the world to decouple from being representatives of productive output and become servants to the exploits of the third- and fifth-level systems. This is also the memenomic description of how the shift in global wealth continues to take place. A highly sophisticated, but unhealthy expression of the fifth-level system continues to sell notional assets as it manipulates the price of anything that can be manipulated without anyone forcing it to justify prices based on real demand.

More than four years after the financial crisis the financial services industry still identifies with betting on failure as a legitimate investment vehicle. Stock markets have recovered their losses from 2008, as this pathology has become the norm that continues to define global economic activity. After a global financial collapse was averted, financial innovation remains the tail that wags the dog as one sovereign debt crisis after another continues to erupt. The global economy continues to be defined as a culture of speculation and debt, and the search for a new economic paradigm continues to be elusive. The raw ideals for that new paradigm are represented in the *inquiry* and *identification* phases on the new cycle that is emerging. It is informed by the virtues of the knowledge economy and the disruptive forces technology is bringing to entrenched Orange practices. But would these embryonic values define a sustainable future economy?

Since the invention of modern economic thought, the way to insure against severe corrections in output and the negative effects of prolonged recessions was to have a policy of economic diversity. Never put all your economic eggs in one basket. Never risk the possibility that one sector of the economy can hijack the future. Yet under the monetarist ideology, this is precisely what happened. As long as the finance sector acted as a function of productive output, economic cycles represented an organic form of efficient market behavior. If a certain company's products or services were becoming obsolete, a natural function of corporate finance would drive the company's stock value down, forcing it to invest in new innovation or face reorganization and bankruptcy. Under the monetarist ideology, the increasing role of liquidity substituted for the need to seek diversity.

Over a three-decade period, the *only money matters* meme altered the drive to diversify in two risky steps. The first was the onset of the securitization meme that allowed corporation to be much more leveraged. As long as there was capital available to fuel the fallacy, stocks continued to sell at considerably higher valuations that the pre-securitization era. The second blow to economic diversity came when the giant pool of global cash flooded already speculative and highly-leveraged financial markets and overextended consumers. The metrics that had not been tested under an already loose money supply were suddenly thrown out altogether and money, as the oldest form of fourth-level system of accountability, was no more. This represented the perversion of the capitalist ideology, pure and simple. Capitalism's greatest vulnerability that Vladimir Lenin warned us about in the past was at hand.

By 2008, less than two decades after the fall of communism, capitalism was knocking on death's door. The perversion of the currency was taking center stage in the most grotesque forms that had nothing to do with innovation. Under financial engineering, capitalism looked nothing like what Adam Smith or Ayan Rand prescribed for in a virtuous society. Their philosophies exalted the merits of moral sentiment and the power of human ingenuity and self-reliance. As Rand's philosophy of separating government and business became the rule under Greenspan's new Fed, government became powerless and incapable of detecting systemic risk. Nothing stopped the fifth-level system from getting into unhealthy business practices under the guise of innovation. Financial engineering as it went undetected had lulled the culture into a numbing comfort and an air of complacency.

By flooding the entire memestack with money, job and wealth creation were fictitious and unnatural. A party planner making over $500,000 a year in 2006 was not representative of organic job growth. A home tripling in value between 2004 and 2006 was not representative of normal appreciation in the housing market. The newfound equity in that home was not representative of hard productive work. A chef taking diners in a hydraulic lift 1,600 feet in the air and charging $1,500 per customer should not be regarded as a new platform for economic growth in the service industry. Yet these were the kinds of jobs being created under a perverted money supply. Tapping into the newly found equity in homes enabled homeowners across the globe to take part in these indulgences, and when they could no longer kick the can down the road by refinancing their homes, they found themselves trapped in unbearable levels of debt. The taps to easy money were turned off and the only way to eliminate the debt was to avoid payment, file for bankruptcy, or endure the long-term pain of paying over many years.

Money by its very nature is the lifeline of every sector of the economy. Much like the bloodstream in the human body that provides essential nutrients to its different organs, money provides essential liquidity to the various industries that make up the economy. When nutritional intake exceeds the levels needed for good health the human body tolerates the excess for a while until a variety of symptoms make it impossible to ignore. An economy with too much money available to it is like an obese human being. When eating habits decouple from nutritional needs, different organs start deteriorating as the body develops metabolic syndrome. Gone unchecked, this could lead to stroke, heart disease, and diabetes. What happened between 2000 and 2006 with the economy was as if doctors reversed their views on the virtues of good health, started giving out prescriptions for fattening foods, and after seeing their patients reaching levels of morbid obesity in 2008, left them on their own to deal with the dangerous consequences.

Much like a human body out of balance dealing with metabolic syndrome, our entire economy had become a system out of balance. It had spread its toxic excess at epidemic rates and needed a good doctor to stop it before reaching a critical tipping point from which there can be no return. Because of the absence of the fourth-level system the window of time to heed the warning signs had passed without detection of them and the system reached its final state of decay and collapse. In the absence of a guardian of good health, in the absence of an effective fourth-level system regulator, collapse would have been the natural course for the entire system as toxicity had poisoned the very virtues it stood on. By the time Lehman Brothers collapsed, the fourth-level system was not only incapable of knowing what was happening, it was vulnerable to the abusive practices of a system that has run out cash to support its betting habits, much like people on the inside who paint a horrifying picture if cash is not infused into the gambling table. The needed collapse was averted and a toxic and addicted system lived to see another day.

Albert Einstein is often quoted as having said that we cannot solve our problems with the same thinking we used when we created them. Yet the same metrics, the same assumptions, and the same people who created the problem, are still the ones telling the world they have the solutions. Today we are experiencing a complex system in final stages of entropy. We continue to deal with the aftermath of a decade of abnormal indulgences and abusive financial practices with outdated and ineffective tools that are an extension of the thinking from the system that created the problem. Regulations to limit financial risk and provide consumer protection under the Dodd-Frank reform act was diluted a great deal from its initial intent: it does not offer full assurance against systemic risk. Since its initial passing, lobbyists and special interest have opposed the appointment of most nominated regulators to head the new agency, and Wall Street sent back its lobbyists to further pacify the small amount of the initial proposed legislation that made it into law. If the house of cards that Wall Street built were allowed to collapse in 2008, an entirely new and organic system would have risen from the ashes with a new and visionary fourth-level ^{V}MEME to guide it along that path.

But, alas, the bailout had lulled us into thinking that what we needed was some minor tweaking of the existing practices within the system and all would be well. What we really needed was profound structural change to set us on a new path for sustainable pursuits from a diversified knowledge-based economy. What we got was more of the old exploitative financial innovation in decay. The financial crisis was the confirmation that the ship had split in half after hitting the iceberg, but without a dutiful captain at the helm, an out of touch management of the cruise liner started to immediately cover up the truth and promptly proceeded to rearrange the deck chairs on the sinking ship in an attempt to convince everyone that everything was fine. Since the onset of the financial crisis there have been many confirmations that the ship of financial innovation is indeed lifeless and continues to sink at a slow pace.

Long after Alan Greenspan testified to the US Congress about the short-comings of the ideology of the era, predatory value systems are still running the global economy. The societal rifts these changes brought are palpable on every street corner in America and Europe. Since the bailout the toxicity of the system had been in full view of an angry public that has taken to the streets through the Occupy Movements all over the globe. Investors in credit default swaps are doing everything in their power to make sure the Greek, Italian, and Spanish banks and governments default on their debt payments so they can win bets worth billions. Wall Street wanted the auto industry to fall for these same exact reasons. Meanwhile, meaningful alternatives to deal with the fallout from the massive amounts of debt that is classified as toxic assets remain elusive. Many have been reincarnated in the form of assets that central banks around the world own.

In addition to the bailout money, the Fed has acquired questionable or non-performing assets worth trillions of dollars where very few can voice their concern about their real market value. The Fed also bought many other assets that were not a part of the TARP program created by the bailout. They were purchased directly from Wall Street without allowing the market to determine their value and thus risking the chance of collapse again. As entropy continues towards the end point of this particular expression of capitalism, the Fed has become a black hole into which the most toxic of assets are thrown and are never to be heard from again. During this phase of collapse it seems that the Fed, the most powerful financial institution in the world, had run out of tools at its disposal. To help stimulate the economy, it has lowered interest rates to levels where they can no longer be lowered and has boxed itself into a non-functioning monetary policy. The economy needs the housing market to stabilize as a sure sign of recovery, which removes from the Fed's toolbox the options of the raising of interest rates and tightening the money supply. Meanwhile in Europe, the system is dying in a slightly different manner. With every country that gets near default on its sovereign debt, the owners of the sovereign debt bonds impose more interventions on its internal affairs. The more control they get through concessions, the bigger that rescue package becomes, and the perpetual cycle of debt keeps kicking the can down the road towards a predictable end point.

THE FOURTH MEMENOMIC CYCLE:
THE DEMOCRATIZATION OF INFORMATION MEME

Technology has always been a memetic agent of change. The question that value systems experts always ask is which ^{V}MEME and which expression of that ^{V}MEME will end up using the technological advances and for what purpose. Before the personal computer and the onset of the knowledge age anthropologists always argued about whether technology moves culture or culture moves technology. The overwhelming conclusion, it seems, was that cultures move slowly in adapting to new technologies as other ^{V}MEMEs act to soften the pace of change in accordance with *life conditions*. There is no denying that the knowledge economy is having a profound effect on this ongoing debate. While the focus so far has been about a macromemetic analysis of the US economy, the ᵛMemetic dance of the third-, fourth-, and fifth-level systems has greatly determined the US's economic expression. We have seen how advancements in technology through computerized algorithms and derivative models were used by Wall Street to create trillions of dollars in toxic assets—an unhealthy expression of the fifth-level system that used technology as a catalyst that eventually lead to the financial crisis.

What was overshadowed in the debate, was the use of these same technological advancements by a healthy expression of the Green sixth-level system. This system was heavily populated with many more individuals, groups, and start-up corporations with similar qualifications in mathematics, theoretical physics, and actuarial sciences that were focusing on the use of these advances in expanding the reach of the World Wide Web and a limitless number of other uses. The healthy expression of the sixth-level ᵛMEME that includes all the complexities of the levels below it has made its debut in the shadow of a dying expression of the fifth system. We are today in the *introduction* phase of the fourth memenomic cycle and we're moving through it at the speed of light compared to previous cycles.

Suddenly, the historic debate on the role that technology plays in culture was significantly altered. While financial innovation under the *only money matters* meme concentrated power in the hands of the few, technological advances in the knowledge sector were moving other parts of the economy in the opposite direction. The digital age has brought about the democratization of knowledge. In the process, most economic activity and social interactions around the world underwent profound change. Today, anyone with a laptop or a smartphone has access to information that can be used to accommodate global trade, facilitate research for a PhD thesis, or simply chat with friends. The rapid rise of technology is causing long-established fifth-level system practices to become obsolete. It is redefining corporations at their core while at the same time allowing social networks to play pivotal roles in affecting social change. This is the good side of theoretical mathematics, algorithms, and derivative modeling. Open source and collaborative technologies drive much of the innovation in the knowledge economy today compared to proprietary and secretive practices of most past economies predominated by fifth-level system values.

Significantly more aspects of the knowledge economy are characterized by values of the Green sixth-level system. Open-source models of innovation are available to everyone for free and are becoming a standard way of operation. Creativity in designing and producing products is leveraged in an egalitarian, group-centered way to serve the overall good of the culture. The very nature of intellectual property is changing under the sixth-level driven knowledge economy. Compared to values predominated by Orange ways of thinking that would have placed patent rights and licensing revenues ahead of all else, collaborators in the knowledge economy are giving away their intellectual property. The knowledge economy has not only democratized the access to information. It has torn down the walls of systems and processes of institutions and ways of thinking that have resisted change for decades. Through the spread of knowledge the digital revolution is introducing creative destruction to every segment of the economy just as economist Joseph Schumpeter initially envisioned it in 1942. The entrepreneur who has the technical knowhow and the skills to undertake the change is finally the one who's doing the change and not the businessman or the Wall Street analyst whose primary interest is maximizing profit.

As elements of the sixth-level system rise to redirect the motivation of economic systems away from the bottom line and to the deeper understanding of the human bond would the need for equal distribution of resources overshadow the capitalist system's need to make a profit in order to survive? Would the capitalist model be able to survive on values that are less concerned with the bottom line? This will be the ultimate test that will determine if the capitalist system can reinvent itself as the changing *life conditions* are making its past institutions obsolete. One of the starkest examples of change that has been brought by the knowledge economy is the media industry. Online access to news as it happens and accessibility to it 24/7 has put hundreds of newspapers and magazines around the world out of business. Random abuses of power that would have been hidden by entrenched systems of the past are exposed for the whole world to see by someone with a cell phone. The entrenched systems themselves, not just the media, are under threat by the deluge of consumer products that are decentralizing the old command and control structure and turning it to a decentralized assembly of communities.

Increasingly, people are giving away their creations and expressing their monetary and non-monetary support for things, events, and the values they appreciate.

Whether thousands of miles away or at the local coffee shop, real or virtual, human communities are becoming the ideal form for catalytic change. New patterns of power distribution and shifts in past hieratical relationships are emerging. We are on the cusp of a healthier cultural shift that is empowered by a deeper appreciation for human values. Could the change the digital age brought to media today transform technology that affects the physical production of goods tomorrow? Could desktop manufacturing become a reality in the near future, and what would everything else in between look like under a system with no walls and artificial barriers?

For all the wonderful things that a Green 'MEME has brought to culture, its prolonged expression through the digital age has only been possible because of the infrastructure of capital markets that was built by the Orange system before it. The globalization of trade the implementation of efficient distribution systems and the adoption of Orange values worldwide has paved the way for the Green 'MEME to further level the playing field on our endless quest towards upward emergence. We have seen how financial innovation and the over-supply of global capital corrupted the very virtues of the fifth-level system. These same dynamics helped spread the values of the Green 'MEME by turning a blind eye to valuation metrics of companies that existed in the virtual world without having generated much revenue to justify their astronomical worth. Wall Street would value a social networking company at hundreds of times the worth of a long established blue-chip brick and mortar company based on the promise of its future rather than on its proven track of profit generation.

It's Wall Street's permanent suspension of applying strict valuation metrics to the knowledge industry that have enabled many of its Green stakeholders to spread the virtues of the Green 'MEME to the global level we see today. The sixth-level 'MEME remains a communal value system where energy is spent on building relationships and exploring the inner self. Equality for all humanity is its primary driving force. Fair and equal distribution of resources comes from a far higher place than the strategic nature or philanthropy of the fifth-level system. On the unhealthy side, Green often loses the awareness of the hierarchy of values that got it to where it is and kicks the ladder that got it there out from under it. This value system believes that its own stage of development is the highest form of expression for human existence and as a result rejects the complexity below it.

What will happen to the spread of Green values if capital markets dry up and the net worth of its creators plummet? Would productive output have to be redefined to include the old Orange metrics to prevent the system from collapse, or would Green render the old economic metrics obsolete? Still, with the feeling of community that has been created under this value system, we are coming together to ask far deeper questions about the nature of humanity, about the exploitation of capitalism and the plight of the disadvantaged. We are building relationships and exploring our inner selves. We sit in circles and give everyone an equal opportunity to deepen our understanding as far as what to do.

The catalyst that knocked down the walls to this value system is the Internet and the primary goal of the Internet is to democratize humanity's access to information. Have the Internet and advancements in technology run their course in equalizing the global playing field? Is the reservoir of endless information a better teacher than a teacher in a classroom providing direct and specific instruction? Has the democratization of knowledge allowed proprietary technologies to fall into the wrong hands? Has military and industrial espionage become much easier as a result of our emergence into the information-laden Green ᵛMEME? Does the same information in the hands of a Google engineer mean the same to a Wall Street trader, a zealot prosecutor, and a dictator in an oil-rich country? The knocking down of the walls of the old system has flooded *life conditions* with all kinds of pathologies that require a new perspective.

In its drive to make everyone equal under a capitalist system, Green values are often in direct conflict of Orange values. The sixth-level Green system creates victims out of the second and third-level systems and blames the fourth- and fifth-level systems for their inability to have a seat at the table. Beck often calls the unhealthy expression of Green *the mean green meme* for its inability to see hierarchy. It is only when our cultural capacities exit the egalitarian ᵛMEME and reach the point where we see with clarity that a stratified approach is needed to resolve our economic issues, that we abandon economic policies that are set by the value systems of economic subsistence that have ruled humanity since tribes started gifting each other in the very first forms of exchange.

Capitalism is at a crossroad of unprecedented proportions. Its past historic emergence has been defined by shedding one ideology for another with higher complexity and level of sophistication. At every stop along the way its ideological shifts have left culture in a more prosperous place than where it was before. But with the speed at which change is taking place at the level of competing values and ideologies, is it possible for the system to emerge to higher levels of expression? Ideological shifts generally don't happen quickly as we have seen in the memenomic reexamination of the forces at play during the Great Depression. It was more than two decades of events, an existential World War and powerful and visionary leadership, that began the transformation of America. By the 1950s American value systems looked nothing like they did in the 1930s.

Similarly, the 1970s transitioned from a system burdened by the mandates of its visions to one that championed the virtues of free enterprise. By the 1990s American value systems looked nothing like they did in the in 1960s. Today, while the US economy goes through a contraction to correct the excesses of the last decade, unemployment remains high, consumer debt is close to record levels, savings accounts are tattered, and economic

HISTORIC MEMESTACK OF ECONOMIC VALUE SYSTEMS

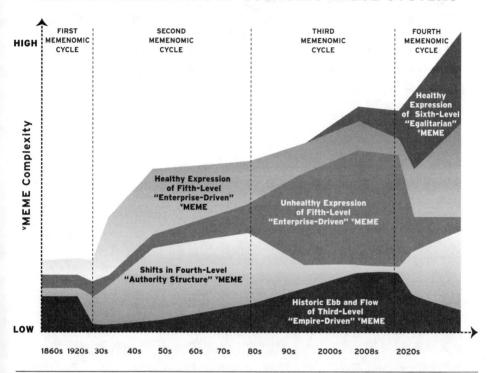

growth remains at anemic levels. Meanwhile financial innovation is back, commodity prices are reaching pre-crisis highs again, IPOs for technology companies are on the rise, and stock markets are confirming the decoupling of the financial system from reality. The ideology that made money matter most has been exhausted down to its last virtue, its principals bankrupted and its leaders spent.

The knowledge economy has leveled the playing field and allowed humanity access to information and technology to be equal participants in economic prosperity. As more and more technological advancements become the driving force behind the new expression of capitalism, old skills are being rendered obsolete at alarming rates. Institutions of the past are becoming hollowed silos as the faith in the capitalist system is gradually waning. Meanwhile, social discontent with the current system in Western economies is forcing leaders to think differently as the search for a new economic paradigm slowly gathers steam. Systems and ideologies almost never die with a bang; that could spell a swift end to a career in politics for many. Ideologies whimper off to a shallow grave in prolonged agony of people, institutions, and cultures. During this agonizing stage, a new ideology is being born that is reshaping the worker's belief systems and making them more resilient. If history is any indication of our bumpy economic journey, American value systems in 2030 will look nothing like they did in 2013.

PART THREE

The Platform for Functional Capitalism

EIGHT

Value Systems and Functional Flow

Herein lies the Global knot: The seemingly irreconcilable conflict between and among the haves, the have nots, the have a little but want more, and the have a lot but are never content. There must be a better way.[94]

—DON E. BECK, PhD

THE EXHAUSTED ECONOMIC VALUES
OF THE FIRST TIER

While reframing the modern day history of the US economy through the prism of value systems, we have seen the crucial role that money historically played in being a primary catalyst to propel humanity to higher levels of existence, while at the same time providing the functional role of a fourth-level order system that gave work meaning and allowed humanity to take a great leap forward from the impulsive third-level system to an ordered world created by temperance. The exchange of value that money represented throughout the centuries has plugged humanity on the motherboard of productivity through our arduous journey towards prosperity and comfort. We have also seen how superordinate goals that are set by visionary leaders have the potential of transforming culture while providing prolonged economic sustainability.

Through the Patriotic Meme of the New Deal ideology we witnessed the complete transformation of the country and the world after the Great Depression and WWII. As visionary as the era was, we saw how its lofty goals eventually lost touch with life conditions, as the shifts in cultural values brought an end to the ideology. While new values took hold, over a decade-long period we witnessed social and economic upheaval that shaped a new paradigm. The end of the Patriotic Meme ushered in the uncertainty of 1970s that closed the doors on the industrial society and ushered in post-industrial or post-modern values. Visionary mandates moved from the hands of the fourth-level system to the hands of the fifth-level system. The regulatory ᵛMEME was rendered mostly obsolete by the new ideology as the promise of the new knowledge-based economy was hijacked by advancements in financial innovation. The setting of superordinate goals was given to the free markets that redefined the ideology under the *only money matters* meme that eventually led to the financial crisis.

If there are lessons to be gleaned from this analysis, it is this: whether economic policies are liberal or conservative, whether they call on government to increase spending during recessionary times, or stand by and let free market take its course, whether Keynesian, monetarist or anything in between, without having mechanisms built into the system that take into consideration the constant changes in *life conditions*, all economic policies are doomed to fail.

We have seen how burdensome and out of touch the heavy-handed ideology of the New Deal was towards the end, and in reaction to it we've seen the pendulum swing the other way: from heavy regulation to no regulation. The end phases of both ideologies had similar consequences and that was the prolonged suffering of the worker. While the worker who suffered in the 1970s was predominantly identified by blue-collar work, the definition by 2008 expanded to include the teacher, the architect, and the real estate broker—the very people that the post-industrial manifesto proclaimed to make up the future of advanced societies.

Meanwhile politicians have had a great degree of success in blaming failures on their adversaries and claiming credit for successes that happened on their watch. The Obama Administration gets blamed for the bailout of Wall Street and the auto industry while it was the Bush Administration that authorized it as the *only money matters* meme reached final stages of decay on Obama's watch. George W. Bush's Administration gets blamed for leading us to the near collapse of the banking system while it was the Clinton Administration that deregulated banking effectively killing the fourth-level order ^{V}MEME and looked the other way as derivatives and credit default swaps allowed Wall Street to hijack the future of our economy. The Carter Administration gets the blame for high inflation and ineffective leadership while it was the death of a system that had been four decades in the making that reached the final stages of collapse on his watch. The Reagan Administration gets all the credit for reviving America and ending communism while it was the budding rebirth of a new system from the ashes of the old that should get most of the credit for the former, and it was the decay of a bankrupted and hollowed ideology that brought a swift end to the latter.

In the study of memenomics, policies and political ideologies are viewed as parts of a complex system that takes years to form, lasts for decades, and collapses over many years as a new ideology starts to take shape in order to reflect cultural changes. Conservative and liberal views are varying expressions of the fourth and sixth-level systems respectively and need to be plugged into the motherboard of a superordinate goal that makes the entire spectrum of values reflect healthy expressions. In order for economic policy to be designed effectively, one must acknowledge the multitude of other ᵛMEMEs and their motivations and begin to design accordingly. One must also acknowledge what combination of value systems make up his or her own memestack of values, or belief system and have the courage and the foresight to set it aside in order to begin a design approach from the second tier of value systems—the tier of "Being."

What if economic policies evolve in such subtle ways that their functioning becomes automatic without being hijacked by one ideology or the other? What if every president regardless of party or ideological affiliation can claim credit for continuous economic prosperity? Since Adam Smith pronounced the virtues of Moral Sentiment, the subsistent economic value systems of the first tier have hijacked the true meaning of capitalism and exploited it to fit their narrow political and economic needs. What if the new expression of capitalism places innovation, and research and development ahead of resource and financial manipulation? What if the US manufacturing sector is empowered by a new paradigm shift that revives its past glory in light of technological advancements and makes all its stakeholders aligned to the same goal? What if the virtues of the knowledge-based economy come to full fruition? What if financial innovation regains its functional role in making all this possible?

What if economic policy adapts seamlessly to changes in *life conditions*? What if economic policy is designed from the second tier of human existence? This is the *inquiry* and *identification* phase of the fifth memenomic cycle that must answer to systemic and functional challenges represented by the lower four cycles. These are the issues that will be further defined as we reframe modern day economic history through the prism of value systems and learn through the benefit of hindsight to restructure competing ᵛMemetic ideologies into a cohesive platform and identify the elements of a sustainable and functional economic ideology that will take us into the future.

HUMAN NATURE PREPARES FOR A MOMENTOUS LEAP

In 1974 my colleague and mentor Dr. Don Edward Beck was a tenured professor at the University of North Texas in Denton when he read an article in *The Futurist* magazine that changed his life and the lives of thousands around him. Professor Clare W. Graves had just published a summary of his life-long work on the theory of human existence, which declared that human nature is preparing for a momentous leap. Below is part of Grave's own description of the stage at which existential reality becomes an awakening that drives humanity to abandon its subsistent past and embark on a great leap forward:

> When man is finally able to see himself and the world around him with clear cognition, he finds a picture far more pleasant. Visible in unmistakable clarity and devastating detail is man's failure to be what he might be and his misuse of his world. This revelation causes him to leap out in search of a way of life and system of values which will enable him to be more than a parasite leeching upon the world and all its being. He seeks a foundation of self-respect, which will have a firm base in existential reality. He creates this firm basis through his G-T value system,[95] a value system rooted in knowledge and cosmic reality and not in the delusion caused by animal-like needs. At this level the new thema for existence is: "Express self so that all others, all beings can continue to exist." His values now are of a different order from those at previous levels: They arise not from selfish interest but from the recognition of the magnificence of existence and the desire that it shall continue to be. [96]

After meeting Graves and seeing the decades of academic research and the breadth of his theory, Beck left the security of his tenured post, cashed in his retirement, and embarked on a journey to inform the world of the nature of human existence and the much brighter future that awaited it. It is clear now that both men were way ahead of their times. Imbedded interests in the First Tier political and economic establishment had delayed the onset of Second Tier change. At the time Graves wrote his groundbreaking article, culture was transitioning through the post-industrial ideology that projected an end to the ecological degradation caused by our disregard to the environment during the Industrial Age. The brightest element of the new economy was its knowledge sector that Graves viewed as one of the most essential tools that will reshape our behavior and define our cosmic reality. The knowledge economy was at its infancy stage where a normal, healthy trajectory of cultural values would have made Grave's prediction a reality today.

But, as we've seen from the memetic analysis of the third memenomic cycle, the promise of the new economy was hijacked by the monetarist ideology that was born out of cutting edge thinking of the fifth-level system at the time and became pathological towards the end. The shift to systems-thinking would have to wait. More than three decades later the fallacy that sidetracked the post-industrial economy may not have collapsed our ecological systems, but has created equally dangerous fragments in the fabric of Western civilization. The *only money matters* meme has financially and morally bankrupted much of contemporary Western values. This is reflected in the appearance

MEMENOMIC CYCLES (MCS) AND THE MOMENTOUS LEAP

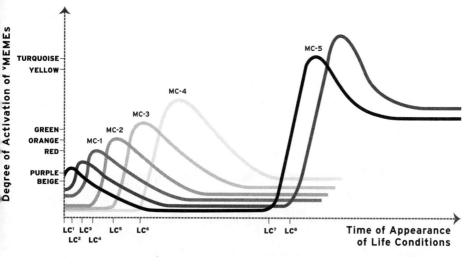

Based on the Graves/Beck framework, the appearance of seventh-level values (YELLOW) represents a quantum leap for humanity that is like nothing we have experienced. This explains the prolonged presence of our current economic contraction (represented by the gaps between MC-4 and MC-5) as the new system continues to be defined. MC-5 will take decades to be fully articulated. It is represented by the functional and systemic values of the MEMEnomic *Platform for Functional Capitalism.*

of a new global meme on the streets of every Western city in acknowledgment that the current system is in need of profound change. Today, every vMEME from second-level Tribal to sixth-level Egalitarian is at its highest intensity, asserting that its way is the only way forward. Through our use of social media, we see these various levels of systems all throughout the West shouting at us in vibrant and dynamic layers in many waves and cultural codes, their different beliefs and behaviors. How can economic policies of the future accommodate so much diversity? How can leaders under a capitalist ideology be made to include all the viewpoints in their economic policies and still allow for prosperity to remain the guiding light?

Since both Graves and Beck claimed that problems with existential *life conditions* can no longer be solved by the current system, solutions from a higher value system are not embraced or even understood and therefore dismissed. One could add to that observation that if a system is too invested in its current values it fears the uncertainty of quantum change. It chooses instead to nudge the current hollow and often obsolete system forward through *esthetic changes* expecting different results. This is where much of the old system is today, and the time to usher in a new systemic economic model is now. Our problems today can no longer be solved from a first-tier subsistence toolbox that has been exhausted and corrupted. That system is in decay and the final stages of entropy are at hand. Will humanity decide to take the momentous leap forward and begin to design from a systemic perspective that is informed by the lessons learned from the subsistence value systems and past human behavior or would we continue to squander our human potential by providing band-aid solutions and hope for the best? If we choose the former we will evolve to the "being" level of existence on our upward journey of human emergence. If we choose the latter, we will condemn ourselves to becoming a footnote in the universe's cosmic reality.

THE SYSTEMIC ^{V}MEME REVISITED

When we were first introduced to the seventh-level system in Chapter 2, most of the information about it was innocuous and presented with a general view of how its principles could be applied in theory. Now that the history of our modern day economy has been reframed through the prism of value systems, and we have experienced the varying expressions of the lower six levels of the first tier system in our economy, *life conditions* are triggering the codes of the seventh-level system to appear. All the levels of the lower sub-systems are incapable of designing solutions that work for the whole as each level sees itself as the sole provider of solutions and all the ones below it as pathological, ineffective, exploitative, or inferior.

The seventh-level Yellow surfaces as a natural solution once the competing lower ^{V}MEMEs have exhausted themselves and by default have agreed to disagree. Each ^{V}MEME's focus moves from a my-way-or-the-highway attitude to the quiet acknowledgement of we all have to share the same space. Like a good physician with proper diagnostic tools and the right medicine, Yellow comes to heal and restore order to a world endangered by the past practices of the lower six systems. It inoculates the diseased parts of each level against future unhealthy practices and stitches together a world that has been long divided. It is primarily concerned with the survival of the human species and therefore places that above all else in designing functional solutions that emerge naturally for the entire system.

A Second Tier approach to economic policy takes the healthiest expressions of all the First Tier systems and places them into a functional flow that serves the long-term sustainability of the culture. This is an approach that understands the motivations of all the lower ^{V}MEMEs and sees far beyond their limited subsistent impulses. As Beck often says, if Red is running amuck, Yellow must

THE SYSTEMIC DESIGN OF THE FIFTH MEMENOMIC CYCLE

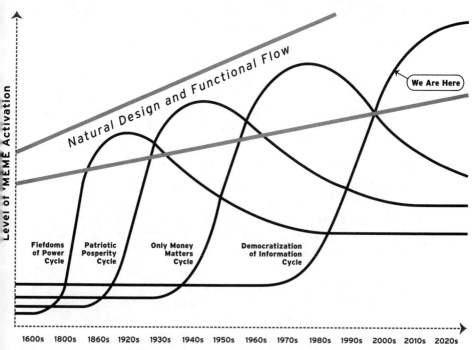

channel its raw energy. If Blue becomes too punitive Yellow must reform it. In the case of financial regulation today, if Blue is too diminished, Yellow must rebuild it. If Orange practices become toxic, Yellow must make them healthy again. It performs all these functions, but it does not favor exclusive solutions from one lower ᵛMEME over the other. That is what created the problem in the first place. Yellow is informed by the dynamics of all the first tier-level systems and treats them all as subsystems to its own superordinate goal. When designing functional solutions from Yellow, all the lower levels contribute in a "natural design" that in and by themselves begin to shift individual behavior and cultural values. Once a superordinate goal becomes more visible to the culture, Yellow leadership starts to rise out of long dysfunctional *life conditions* acknowledging the need for more complex and natural solutions.

In the 2008 race for the White House President Obama held the promise of being a Yellow seventh-level leader. Patterns of second-tier language in his speeches mesmerized voters and gave them the hope for a seventh-level revolution that was going to plug all Americans on a new motherboard. But, alas, his election was not a full reflection of where the current system was in relationship to *life conditions*. His first term fell into a polarizing dynamic, the likes of which the country hasn't seen in decades. What we continued to experience in 2012 with a new election cycle were the final stages of collapse of the current system out of which very few sustainable ideas have emerged. Romney, the Republican candidate, had a belief system that was fully realized in fifth-level values and attempted to realign the emerging *life conditions* with a memenomic cycle that was in its decay stage. Although many of his ideas for the economy were valid, they simply could no longer play the dominant role in the composition of the newly evolving system.

In the study of value systems the shift from First Tier to Second Tier is thought of as the most painful. This is not a shift from an order-dominated fourth-level culture to an Enterprise-driven fifth level. This is a shift that recognizes the varying difference, motivations, aspirations, exploitations, and dysfunctions of all the lower six levels of subsistence and aligns the fullness and the uniqueness of the entire mosaic of values and designs accordingly. Many of President's Obama's Yellow ideas about financial reforms were sidelined by the imbedded interest of the financial industry once he became Commander-in-Chief. The diverse Yellow thinking of the entire Chicago Group lead by Paul Volker in the fall of 2008 was replaced by Larry Summers who had become the poster child for the old and toxic system and a catalyst in the erosion of the order ᵛMEME of the financial industry. Seventh-level leadership ideas got shot down one after the other, not because they weren't great, but because the Obama ideology might have been about a decade ahead of where *life conditions* in America were.

SUPERORDINATE GOAL OF A FIFTH MEMENOMIC CYCLE

Since Yellow ideas fail to manifest while *life conditions* are exiting first tier, they become an incubator that houses and projects the early expression of the shift that is taking place. The dysfunction becomes a call to reform and transform structures. The weak signs that are emanating from the levels below feed the Yellow platform that begins to design structures that speak the language of each specific level and perform functions that align its values and the values of all the other levels on the motherboard of Yellow's superordinate goal. JFK's call to pursue an Orange superordinate goal of placing a man on the moon was the catalyst that aligned all the ᵛMEMEs prevalent at the time from second to fifth level on the same motherboard. Although that alignment was an *esthetic change* that kept the system in sync with life conditions in the middle of the second cycle, the outcome was the superior advancements in science and technology that the US still benefits from to this day. A Yellow superordinate goal must have in it the elements of systemic transformation and not one that just leads to another Orange expression. If it speaks to all the first-tier systems, it will make them generals in the army that snuffs out practices that are placing our planet in peril in their own unique way. It will add bandwidth, texture, and range to the Yellow revolution that awaits America. A Yellow superordinate memenomic goal must have elements of the all the superordinate goals of all the four cycles before it. Lessons from the *fiefdoms of power* era must be plugged into the same functional flow with the lessons learned from the *patriotic prosperity* era. Similarly, lessons of the *only money matters* cycle along with the emerging lessons of the *democratization of information* cycle must be plugged onto the same motherboard where they all serve a far greater superordinate goal. If it is representative of the values that Graves and Beck describe, and still serves as an economic model, it must simultaneously address three issues: People, Profit, and Planet. A superordinate goal for the United States that will define the values of a seventh-level system would have language similar to the following declaration: *Provide Global Leadership through Sustainable Economic Policies.*

Today, after Obama's re-election to a second term, many hot-button issues are still steering the passions of the First Tier ᵛMEMEs, but early signs of the emergence of Second Tier values are beginning to manifest in the most natural way. Yellow leadership, although thinly veiled, is beginning to be seen in government, the media and in the knowledge economy. In government, it is exemplified in the tenacity of political appointees like Paul Volker, whose ideas were originally sidelined for the fear that they would cause the collapse of the financial system.

SMART GOVERNMENT OF THE FUTURE

Volker exhibits the typical systemic Yellow thinking that understands the importance of the functional flow of a system. Orange toxicity had never been as widespread and dangerous as it was in the fall of 2008. As an objective observer, Volker understood the complexity of financial markets and understood the pathological problems causing the pressures from Wall Street within a historical context. Politicians and Wall Street insiders viewed the solutions offered by Volker's group as a dangerous prescription that would have collapsed the entire global economy when all it sought was simply the healthy functionality of the system. As an outsider Volker saw with stark clarity the extent to which the system was addicted to unhealthy practices. The begging for bailout money by politicians and Wall Street alike on Capitol Hill in front of the entire world had an eerie resemblance to a drug addict running out of recourses to support his habit. Volker's Yellow recommendations were paramount to a drug counselor's recommendation to abruptly begin a regiment to detoxify the system from its addiction. Much like an addict on a high would have responded by denying his need for rehab, Volker's recommendations were promptly rejected in favor of requesting more money to fuel the banking system's dependencies.

We will never know if the emergence of a new and more resilient monetary system was prevented from taking root from the ashes of financial collapse if the collapse had been allowed to happen, but it's clear to many critics and citizens alike that bank bailouts have further exposed the dysfunction in the system and added to the anger that is fueling the current social unrest. The Volker Rule, which is the top accomplishment of the Dodd-Frank Act, requires banks not to use depositors' money in their trading.[97] It remained open for public input till July 2012 before becoming a part of a deterrent fourth-level system that witnessed over three decades the deterioration of its power to regulate. Four years after the financial crisis, unhealthy Orange still firmly believes that the passage of the Volker Rule into law spells the end of the world for them. Volker sees far beyond Wall Street's limited interpretation of their world and has his eye on preserving the functional flow of capital to the economy many decades into the future. This is just one example of the kind of leadership needed for a regulatory ᵛMEME designed from the seventh level.

However, the dysfunction within the current system in all three branches of government has painted seventh-level leaders like Volker as lone wolves and destroyers of jobs instead of visionary exemplars representing the future of government. Although designing government from the seventh-level is beyond the focus of this book, it is clear the emergence of systemic Yellow is needed in order for the United States to take the quantum leap forward. Yellow leadership that fully understands the consequences of a subsistent existence must be present at all levels of local, state and federal government and in all three branches.

A smart second-tier government looking to regulate capitalism and the financial industry would look to place all competing first-tier subsystems on to a motherboard of healthy business practices for all. A second-tier government is a "Smart Government" that looks to establish institutions staffed by highly intelligent people who understand the intricate workings of the industry they're looking to regulate but are motivated by a far higher calling than the need to make a profit or the use of their positions as a springboard into the industry they seek to regulate. A *smart government* designed from Yellow is one that is far leaner and much less bureaucratic than anything we've seen. Since its purpose will be to pave the way in providing functional regulation of all the lower systems, it will replace much of the staffing needs at institutions like the SEC with smart technologies and algorithms that have the function to regulate. A *smart government* also balances its functional role to regulate with the keen awareness of how burdensome regulation was under the *patriotic prosperity meme* that relegated it to bureaucratic inefficiency and incompetence. This is regulation leading to a superordinate goal set by a Yellow economic policy.

Much like FDR's New Deal policies that transformed culture by setting a visionary path for Orange that transformed the entire nation, a Yellow visionary government must take inventory of the levels of complexity our culture has reached, and then design the next visionary system that inspires all the first-tier system stakeholders by the promise of the future. The super-ordinate goal of a planet with sustainable economic policies might not be a cause that Wall Street and the banking industry are excited to get behind at this stage, but once the toxic practices of their past continue to be exposed and the industry runs out of non-productive activities to exploit, the current expression of financial innovation will come to an end and banking will have to swallow the bitter pill of detoxification as it works its way back to serve a functional visionary role for our economy.

When it comes to detecting white-collar crime, the fourth-level system with its current diminished capacity has by default become reactive. In other words, it doesn't move in step with the innovative nature of the fifth level. Smart regulation designed from the seventh level, anticipates the direction of the fifth level and lays down the regulatory infrastructure to guide it on a healthy trajectory. As we languish in the decay stage of the current memenomic cycle it is of paramount importance that thought leaders with profound seventh-level values from the fields of finance, macroeconomics, technology, and the law, inform an emerging second-tier narrative of what constitutes smart government. It is only when government is seen as a smart player by the entire spectrum of values in first tier that a functional second tier platform for capitalism starts to emerge.

SEVENTH-LEVEL LEADERSHIP IN MEDIA

Early signs of Yellow are also appearing in the media. Before disappearing from the public eye in June 2012, Dylan Ratigan was a well-informed financial reporter who rejected the pathologies of Wall Street after reporting intimately on its inner workings for years. He has written about his insider experience in a book entitled *Greedy Bastards; How We Can Stop Corporate Communism, Banksters and Other Vampires from Sucking America Dry.* This is a Yellow second-tier book that speaks the language of the people. Ratigan's television show on MSNBC, from which he departed, was a platform that addresses the need for real solutions in our economy. By simply being a contrarian to the pathologies created by financial innovation, he is offering second-tier solutions that are informed by *life conditions* outside the world of finance and where America's challenges lie. His 2010 *Steel on Wheels* tour exposed his viewers to the untapped potential and the level of optimism that America's innovative genius holds in offering solutions to many of the problems in our economy from manufacturing to health care, education, and the public works sector.[98] The popularity of his show's last undertaking, the *30 Million Jobs* tour, which focused on finding functional solutions to our economic challenges, confirmed the desperate need for Yellow Second-Tier economic policies shaped by thinkers like him. Ratigan's own ability to see beyond the myopic dysfunction of the current expression of value systems was made famously clear in what became known as the "Dylan Ratigan rant." On the August 10, 2011 broadcast of the Dylan Ratigan Show he pointed to the universal dysfunction of the current system by saying:

> We've got a real problem! This is a mathematical fact! Tens of trillions of dollars are being extracted from the United States of America. Democrats aren't doing it, Republicans aren't doing it. An entire integrated system, financial system, trading system, and taxing system that was created by both parties over a period of two decades, is at work in our entire country right now. And we're sitting here arguing about whether we should do the $4 trillion plan that kicks the can down the road for the president for 2017, or burn the place to the ground, both of which are reckless, irresponsible, and stupid.[99]

If the hierarchy of value systems is correct, based on Ratigan's reasons for leaving and his affiliation with spiritual guru Deepak Chopra, these are efforts to deepen his understanding of humanity by exploring the deeper expressions of his Green ᵛMEME. Should he return to the media after such exploration he will be a far more effective Yellow leader than the one he already was. Media plays an influential role in shaping the thinking of our culture and will eventually come to the realization that Yellow thinkers like Ratigan have to populate key positions in it. From editors to producers and advertisers, the media has the responsibility to transcend its lower ᵛMEME practices and learn to include them in a platform that serves the non-exploitive needs of society in order to help it emerge.

SEVENTH-LEVEL ECOSYSTEM

Another promising sign of the rise of Yellow comes from Silicon Valley, one of the best examples of *life conditions* that are dominated by a healthy Orange and Green centers of gravity. Many of the companies here pride themselves on their Green work environments and the nature of what they do that has democratized the access to information throughout the world. One example of Yellow community reinvestment is Google's expansion outside the knowledge economy and into a sector that has long been the domain of government and non-profit institutions that are moving the knowledge economy into the seventh-level system. Google in the last few years has gotten involved in the development and ownership of affordable housing. It is playing a lead role in redefining corporate citizenship in big cities like Boston by providing a desperately needed supply of affordable rental property, while at the same time benefiting from tax credits offered through government programs.

This is not the type of news that makes the nightly headlines, but the fact that it happened at a time when access to capital, especially commercial construction loans, was at its worse in modern history makes it significant. Google could have hired some of the most intelligent hedge fund managers to take advantage of the collapsing housing market and followed the non-productive, unhealthy practices of Wall Street by investing in credit default swaps and make a far better return on its money. Instead it chose to invest in a desperately needed venture to shelter families. Win-win scenarios are nothing new to traditional business practices with an eye on corporate social responsibility, but if designed from the seventh level that has the flexibility and the resources to choose people over profit at the appropriate times, the outcome always results in a third win and that's the long-term sustainability of the planet.

Unlike many other traditional corporations Google fully embraces the values of the sixth-level system as it transcends but includes the healthy practices of all the other lower ᵛMEMEs. As a corporation whose unofficial motto is "don't be evil" and is run by the brightest engineers on the planet, Google holds the promise to spread Yellow functional form of corporate practices throughout the world. While it's still an infant when compared to traditional blue-chip fortune 500 companies it's forcing the corporate world to redefine their imbedded practices and outdated business models for ones that are functional and efficient.

In addition to direct investment in brick and mortar projects, Google is bringing disruptive practices to Wall Street. In March 2009 the company launched Google Ventures, which is the investment arm of Google. This is a fearless form of second tier style of creative destruction that is providing capital for Green-Yellow businesses that can potentially become part of a platform for a Yellow economy while at the same time forcing Wall Street to reexamine its non-productive activities that don't add value to economic output. Google Ventures invests in companies in a wide variety of sectors and stages and has committed to invest up $200 million a year in businesses run by passionate entrepreneurs who are bold and ambitious and are as excited as the guys at Google are about building disruptive companies.[100] When Yellow is committed to functional solutions that see with stark clarity the limitations of first tier values it becomes fearless and acts from that space in order to empower lower ᵛMEMEs to do the same.

Being born into the Green sixth-level system *life conditions* of Silicon Valley, and in absence of the old and tired values of the industrial-age business model, Google's rise to the Yellow seventh-level system happened naturally. There's much evidence that the Green values of Silicon Valley are playing a crucial role in defining a seventh-level Yellow system as the knowledge economy becomes the catalyst that distributes know-how and skills to the lower ᵛMEMEs to provide new employment opportunities in a variety of fields, including education, healthcare, and manufacturing. Google's second-tier functionality is discussed more in detail in the upcoming chapter on functional corporations. There is also much talk about a third industrial revolution that has all the marking of the distributed intelligence of a Yellow design that will be detailed in one of the upcoming chapters. As our society's focus increasingly turns away from the finance sector and the fallacy of Wall Street's practices becomes more exposed, more stakeholders will emerge as Yellow thinkers capable of starting change. This will eventually lead to a distributed intelligence whose natural function is to redistribute economic power and opportunity as needed, and in accordance with the needs of *life conditions*.

There are common patterns that are emerging among Yellow thinkers in Western society. First, in order to fix a system, articulate Yellow thinkers in any particular profession rise naturally and in response to an overwhelming need to provide guidance to a system that has lost its Blue order base. More often than not, Yellow leadership does not come from the regulators of a particular industry. These individuals tend to be thoroughly familiar with cutting-edge practices of industries of their own profession. Those are the insiders who are fully knowledgeable of the patterns of emergence within their industry's culture but have their sight set on the long-term viability of the entire macroeconomic system. Unlike the movement from one subsistence ᵛMEME to the next, a Yellow thinker doesn't throw out the entire industry and its practices in favor of practices centered in a higher first-tier ᵛMEME. He or she instead looks to transform and empower the best healthy practices of the entire industry and plugs them on a motherboard made up of all the subsistence ᵛMEMEs in order to expose their healthy expressions and create a diverse economic platform that's full of sustainable practices.

As we've seen with the natural emergence of Paul Volker in government and Dylan Ratigan in the media, a Yellow thinker naturally knows when industry practices become toxic and unhealthy and can easily draw the distinction between predatory and productive activity. The more imbedded and systemic the unhealthy practices are, the harder Yellow has to work to expose it in order to fit it into the needed functional flow. For every Paul Volker and Dylan Ratigan there are hundreds of Yellow thinkers who work behind the scenes, and their efforts often go unnoticed. In many circumstances, politicians and bosses who don't understand systemic Yellow thinking dilute their views in order to gain temporary favor and advance their own agendas. As more Yellow thinkers emerge in an open system, the dysfunction of the lower systems naturally becomes more exposed, allowing second-tier systemic thinking to spread from individual Yellow to one that allows for the successful creation of a functional economic platform.

The goal of the memenomics framework is to design for a sustainable economic future through the technologies provided to us by the emerging science of value systems. At a macroeconomic level this is undoubtedly a formidable task that requires a comprehensive understanding of the prevailing practices of current economic activity in a global economy that grows more complex by the day. Much of the value systems in the non-Western world are just experiencing their culture's entry into the fifth-level system and view these values as a birthright in their climb up the ladder of human emergence.

While the West has long resolved the debate over safety in the workplace and worker rights and faces daily struggles in addressing issues such as air pollution and environmental degradation, these concerns are not as high on the radar screen of China's or India's economic policy. They can't even begin to appear on the business-consciousness radar of many of the oil producing nations that claim to have some of the highest standards of living. Even different parts of the West seem to be at different cultural development stages that influence their economic policy. While the energy policy in the United States seems to be inconsistent and is often shaped by big oil, the Germans have moved to implement a policy of renewable energy that is pulling the plug on the historically monopolistic practices of the energy industry. This is yet another example of the type of smart government that is needed in shaping a Yellow seventh-level economic policy.

By acknowledging the inevitability of how the Western lifestyle is taxing the earth's finite resources, the Germans are able to contribute to ending the environmental degradation we have caused to our ecological systems since the dawn of the industrial revolution. The German economy has had one of the healthiest economic memestacks in the world since its industrial infrastructure was rebuilt after WWII and is poised to provide the world with a template on sustainable practices. Much like the United States was during the years of the FDR ideology, the goals of the German government today are very congruent with those of its people. Speaking to all constituents is an essential element in designing second-tier economic policies.

In designing a Yellow economic platform for the United States, one has to be inclusive of protective Orange values of industries, such as the extraction and oil industries that remain heavily invested in old technology with billions of dollars worth of infrastructure projects all over the globe. These companies are often run on a traditional command and control structure and any sudden change in their operations will have global systemic consequences. They obsessively guard against the potential loss of market share. They favor the status quo of not moving America into a green technology platform, as that would spell the end of their livelihood. There are many industries in the United States that resist change and are entrenched in old Orange practices that are increasingly protective of their technology in order to guard against their own demise. Compared to the distributed economic power that the knowledge economy is creating, these industries are attempting to concentrate power in the hands of the few and are using every tool at their disposal to shield themselves from an inevitable change. Their pervasive practices have become monopolistic by nature, as they have arrogated much political and economic clout to prevent change from taking place.

The United States banking industry and the energy industry have recently provided vivid examples of how an entire economy can be forced to remain in lower ^{v}MEMEs without Yellow leadership to guide it into new economic frontiers. A Yellow economic platform doesn't wait till old entrenched Orange practices disappear; it designs for the healthy emergence of these industries to enable them to see themselves playing a crucial part in a vibrant and sustainable vision of the future. Paul Volker's vision of where the banking industry needs to be in the future might not be shared by bankers who are addicted to non-productive but highly lucrative practices today. However, in a decade or so they will be glad that the Volker Rule redirected their resources towards productive practices that become aligned with overall changes in economic *life conditions*. Yellow always has the capacity to see into the systemic flow of the future and has the resources to design for that future accordingly. The post-modern vision of an economy is a Yellow vision that is empowered by the speed at which old Orange practices are being rendered obsolete.

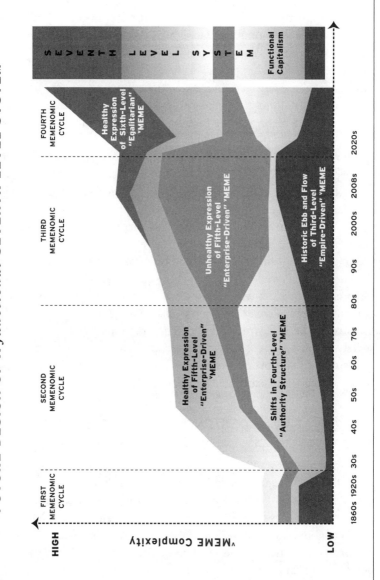

HISTORIC MEMESTACK OF ECONOMIC VALUE SYSTEMS AND THE
FUTURE DESIGN OF A *functional* SEVENTH LEVEL SYSTEM

Power, knowledge, and technology are being distributed to every corner of the world in an effort to design a sustainable, but highly distributed economic future that is empowered by change. A Yellow system of distributed economic intelligence has no room for "too big to fail." Failure of one entity in one segment of a Yellow economy will have no bearing whatsoever on the rest of the economy. Yellow is an open system, which anticipates the entropy of unnatural formations such as oil monopolies, big banks, and the healthcare industry, but doesn't work directly on ending their business models. It focuses instead on making their function a part of a natural flow that eventually allows them to see the shortcomings of their practices. This awakening to a higher calling might not transform their practices overnight since they would still have to answer to their shareholders and millions of employees, but it becomes a calling that eventually places the sustainability of the planet and its inhabitants on par with their need to make a profit.

As form follows function in Yellow design, some industries will need to maintain a command and control structure for as long as a Yellow economy needs it. If advancements in technology don't make oil obsolete, Yellow will empower oil producers to create the cleanest and most efficient form of fossil fuel to power high efficiency vehicles after extracting it with the least impact on the environment while at the same time empowering the industry to expand research and development into sustainable sources of energy. Although Yellow embraces the creative destruction of the knowledge economy and recognizes its greater role in distributing the economic intelligence to every corner of society, it must also recognize the economic needs emanating from existing *life conditions* and preserve some of the old structures in order to provide a transition that is as seamless and as painless as possible.

NATURAL DESIGN AND FUNCTIONAL FLOW

We have seen examples of early emergence of Yellow—what it looks like in individual leaders and how it might be reflected in corporate values as they relate to their sense of corporate social responsibility. The bigger and more complex question that will be answered here is how to design for overall cultural emergence into this systemic ᵛMEME. How do we identify the elements of a functional economic platform that resonates with Graves's recognition that we ought to design a system in order for all life forms and all beings to continue to exist?

This second tier approach is based on the principles of the concept called *Natural Design. It is* a large-scale systems change model of the Spiral Dynamics theory to naturally align people, resources, institutions, and processes to serve a superordinate goal, and can be applied to the large-scale economic policies in the United States and beyond. My earlier declaration of the viability of a seventh-level superordinate goal to achieve this must contain the proficiencies for reinterpreting our economic past through the lenses of value systems and the placement of those dynamics into a functional flow that serve this goal.

Since designing for this system has to take into consideration the triple bottom line of people, profit, and planet any restatement of economic policy has to include healthy people, just profits, and a sustainable planet. It has to be resilient, adaptable, and sustainable, while at the same time aim to provide long term, full employment. This is a system that embraces the advancements in science and technology and uses them as a function to serve that superordinate goal. Creative destruction is often blamed for eroding much of the labor-intensive employment base. But if it is placed in a functional flow of a second tier economic policy, it could serve as a catalyst to empower a new breed of entrepreneurs who are in business for themselves and in the process make the age-old debate between labor unions and corporations a more tempered and productive one.

The engineers who created robotics that replaced the factory worker a few decades ago are now being replaced by the newest advancements in artificial intelligence. The corporate business model is replacing humans with computers and mainstreamed processes at an exponential pace. Unless technology is embraced on the other side of destruction in a *natural design* way, it will continue to lead to a shift in wealth and employment away from the working and middle class. *Natural design* is always informed by the uniqueness of *life conditions* and not by elite policy makers who think they have the answers while beholden to the best thinking an Orange system has to offer. In the case of our political system that tried to export democracy to the Middle East, our best Blue thinking for governance met a tragic fate in Iraq. As a change model, *natural design* asks the simple question: change from what to what?

I have often observed Beck make the point of telling political and business leaders that "getting rid of what you don't want is not the same as getting what you want." The next appropriate system in cultural emergence cannot be more than one ᵛMEME above where *life conditions* of that culture are, but the new system cannot be designed from that next level. It has to be designed from systemic Yellow that anticipates the potential exploitation from all the first-tier ᵛMEMEs that hover above the level of where *life conditions* are. Our involvement in Iraq makes for a good example of this hypothesis. This was a second-level tribal culture whose emergence into a third-level feudal existence was halted by Saddam Hussein without alternative emergence channels.

The next stage for Iraq when the restraints of a tyrant were removed was the unhealthy expression of the third-level system. The United States didn't design an indigenous plan that channeled the energy of this repressed system, namely the civil unrest in quest for feudal dominance. Red was the obvious next stage for Iraq, not a fourth-level Blue democracy with obedience to foreign-imposed order and their rule of law.

Whether the issues are political, economic, or educational; or whether they are regional, national, or local, recognizing the stages of cultural development in *life conditions* is a crucial element in creating any Yellow model for change. In a Yellow economic platform, Orange gets plugged into the mosaic of life. The designers of this system are known as "Spirocrats," interested in the health of all the six first-tier levels, not Democrats or Republicans beholden to a narrow center of gravity in one or two subsystems. These designers are labeled as functionalists, not as socialists or capitalists. They are believers in most management theories and their function is to place these theories into a proper fit, a place that serves the overall superordinate goal of providing sustainable business models for all.

As a result of many decades of research and work in political hotspots around the world, Beck has honed down *natural design* to a simple formula. It simply poses the following question: HOW does WHO lead / teach / manage / design for WHOM to do WHAT and WHERE.[101] It seems to be a simple model to follow, but if the answer to these words of inquiry is designed from the second tier, it could hold the key to many complex issues that face the world today. *Natural design* is more interested in the simplicity that lies beyond the complexity where complexity is mostly brought on by highly developed forms of first tier expressions that become protective of their territory and often wonder into unhealthy and exploitative expressions of their ᵛMEME without detection. As a major tool of the Yellow seventh-level system, *natural design* simply asks the lower subsystems to plug the genius of those complex expressions into a platform that serves the health of the entire ecosystem and in the process makes them beholden to a far bigger vision of themselves. On a *natural design* platform, The four memenomic cycles become naturally focused on keeping the system in sync with *life conditions* for the longest time possible while anticipating change and incorporating it into the functional flow of the system before it becomes misaligned and needing *systemic change.*

A second-tier Yellow designer always starts by defining these questions in the reverse order in which they appear as an essential rank of relevance. We start with the "WHERE" first. In the case of designing a Yellow economic platform for the US, the WHERE is the *life conditions* in the United States.

This is the very diverse landscape from which Dylan Ratigan reported when his show is on the road. It was the mosaic of life painted in the vibrant colors of all the lower systems. It is the small hometown of the brilliant inventor looking to find capital to bring his invention to market. It is where the college student is looking for a first job. It is where the small business owner is looking to finance the expansion of his operations. It's where the hourly worker in the service industry struggles to survive on minimum pay and the owner of a growing factory looks to add another shift for his workers. It's where the head of a small community bank tries everything in his power to get his customer approved for an SBA loan so he can start a much-needed business in the community. It is the young Green value-system husband and wife with an Ivy League education who happily decide to settle in Vermont and start an organic farm. It is the streets of Detroit that see one of the highest levels of high school dropouts and chronic unemployment. It is also where the Internet geniuses in Silicon Valley and graduate classrooms in our universities are looking to create the next billion-dollar idea.

In short, the WHERE of the United States is what an up-to-the-minute US census report tells us about the demographics of the population and where they live. A Yellow, functional economy starts by designing for the needs of all the people in these *life conditions* with the full knowledge of the inventory of resources available to the culture from natural, human, and institutional resources. Of all the elements of the *natural design* formula, defining the WHERE is by far the most important element that will inform a Yellow economic policy. The geographic, memetic, cultural, and demographic contours of a society must play a crucial role in informing policy makers in order to design policies that are congruent with *life conditions*.

The next question that *natural design* asks is the WHAT. What are we designing for those *life conditions* that the WHERE identified? This is where the source of the superordinate goal comes from. Since our aim is to design an economic policy from Yellow, the WHAT is an economic policy that has all the qualities of a Yellow systemic design. It must aim to plug all the lower ᵛMEMEs and memenomic cycles into a sustainable and functional flow that serves the long-term viability of the system. Most of the qualities that have been described here as a Yellow economy go into defining the WHAT. The lessons learned from past economic history get reinterpreted through value-systems and functional flow in order to inform the WHAT of the future. This is the shape the design takes once it has been informed by the needs emanating from the WHERE. Certain economic policies need to take on different regional or local shapes in order to accommodate the local economies into the healthy expression of their value-systems.

If the WHAT is to design a superordinate goal for an economic policy, it declares that superordinate goal first in order to proceed to satisfy the requirements of the remaining elements of *natural design*. The WHAT redefines the superordinate goal for the seventh level that was declared earlier by adding the following: *To create the leadership that designs for economic prosperity through functional and sustainable policies that promote the health of the planet and empower full employment for generations to come.* This is an ambitious declaration that requires a wide macroeconomic and macromemetic perspective that examines many of the foundations on which capitalism stands. It will examine the value-systems that have lead to past dysfunction and look to place them into a functional flow that allows them to see a view of the entire system and brings clarity to their critical role in sustaining the system.

The next question in *natural design* that must be answered is the WHOM. For WHOM are we designing this economic policy? What are their value-systems priorities? What are their capacities? Are they an open, arrested or closed system? How do their *life conditions* vary from one region of the country to the next? Are they all realized in the fifth-level ᵛMEME on the trading floor of the New York Stock Exchange or are they teachers fully realized in a Blue value system living contently in a small town in the mid-West? Are they former gang members living in Detroit who are ready to exit the Red ᵛMEME but are waiting for job opportunities to leave that life behind? Are they Silicon Valley engineers realized in the Green vMEME who are looking to create the next social media craze and become billionaires before age twenty-five?

The WHOM seems to go hand in hand with the WHERE, but is more focused on assessing the individual capacities and memetic centers of gravity of individuals within a culture. When the post-industrial ideology declared the end of the Industrial Age and predicted the rise of the white color and technical class, it fell short on fully assessing our culture's capacities in a differential way that would have more profoundly identified WHOM in the post-industrial age it was designing for. The post industrial economy designed for the Orange-Green economic emergence but grossly misread the *life conditions* in states that were dominated by agriculture, steel manufacturing, and the auto industry. Because these states were left behind in identifying WHOM we're designing for, the stages of development of the local culture have downshifted and have struggled to emerge to a higher level of expression. The post-industrial policies treated the economy with a monolithic stroke of the brush as if the entire labor force was all made up of college graduates with identical value systems that couldn't wait to embrace white-collar work. The WHOM today still shows that only about one third of Americans hold college degrees and the most lucrative jobs that would have utilized the skills of the working, non-technical class have been outsourced as a result of an economic policy that was formulated by elite intellectuals who were out of touch with the needs of *life conditions.*

Although their thinking might have lead to that utopian place one day, no one bothered to design for the transition in education and training that would have paved the road to get the majority of the culture there and maintain a level of prosperity that was granted the working class under the industrial economy. By including the WHOM a Yellow economic policy would have designed for the next stage of transition for these industries and the hundreds of thousands of people they employed instead of leaving it up to unregulated Orange, which exported the jobs, hid behind the fallacy of providing prosperity to all through stockholder value, while shifting wealth away from a true representation of what *life conditions* reflected.

After identifying the WHERE, WHAT, and WHOM we move to identify the WHO. This is a description of the qualifications and the capacities of the people in key positions who will lead and design a future Yellow economic system. At levels that shape the regulatory structure of a Yellow economy, these individual will possess similar tenacities and a vision of the future similar to that of Paul Volker. They have no fear of reaction to their decisions from first-tier subsystems. In staffing key government positions with Yellow regulators, these individuals must possess systemic thinking that is intimately familiar with how business in their industry gets done. Yellow leaders always see the complexity of life in a world that is in danger of collapse and act and design accordingly. They understand that chaos and the need to change as par for the course in their appointed positions. Being familiar with cutting-edge innovation that is being used by Orange is a must in order to effectively regulate it. A Yellow appointee to the Federal Reserve, for example, must have the capacities to snuff out any practices that place the monetary system and the economy at peril. The individual must always think of designing structures into the massive bureaucracy that will make it evolve and change and always with an eye on the big picture, the superordinate goal.

The Securities and Exchange Commission, which received much of the public's anger after the financial crisis for failure to regulate activities of investment banks, can no longer by staffed by securities attorneys looking at their position as an internship into a lucrative career on Wall Street. A Yellow regulator with an eye on securing the functionality of the economy many decades down the road is not Machiavellian about his work. Although he or she will not hesitate to investigate and bring charges against lawbreakers, his/her primary function is to inspire all the lower ᵛMEMEs to act in the best interest of the long-term sustainability of the economy. Unfortunately, many high level government positions today still get filled based on political favoritism with little regard to the technical proficiencies of the appointees or their potential capacities for Yellow systemic thinking.

The WHO of *natural design* also affects the type of corporate leaders who get chosen to lead a Yellow economic platform. Much like the requirements for a Yellow regulator, a Yellow business leader has the ability to think and act systemically while at the same time keeping his/her eye on the three bottom lines of people, profit and planet. A wise Yellow business leader looks into the entire ecosystem of his economic activity and almost never chooses the quick and easy answer. When schools are not producing graduates with adequate skills to fill jobs, the leader becomes vocal in the community in order to remedy the situation. If financial markets continue to report record corporate profits while closing factories and streamlining operations he or she would sound the alarm on the effects these practices are having on the local community. Before deciding to automate a factory the leader ponders the future of employees and considers viable options for retraining or expanding market coverage so he doesn't have to let go of any employees. Profit margins are never the sole bottom line to the WHO in a Yellow economy. The leader is always aware of local *life conditions* and treats Main Street with the same level of importance as Wall Street.

On a national level, the WHO are those in a committee of Yellow economic advisors that will replace the current circle of economic advisors in the White House. These individuals will be empowered not by their own ego and credentials, but by their ability to listen to the challenges facing industries on Main Street and be able to enact economic policies that are representative of the WHOM, WHAT, and WHERE. The new systemic thinking will focus on the differential diagnosis of where certain blockages in the entire economic system are occurring and why. The primary focus will be a whole-systems approach to what's preventing jobs from reaching certain areas. Yellow thinkers at the national level always rely on local Yellow leaders who are familiar with the challenges and the uniqueness of *life conditions* to identify the economic challenges in varying parts of the country. Instead of a central command and control structure that has the pitfalls of a reductionist approach to economic solutions, a Yellow committee of economic advisors never paints national economic issues with a broad stroke. It invites the governors, mayors and business leaders from every city and state to provide information on the unique challenges they face. Once local economic challenges are identified they become a crucial part of the economic design process that employs an ecosystem approach to the resolving the problem.

The final piece of the *natural design formula* that needs to be uncovered is the HOW. These are the management procedures that a systemic Yellow thinker would need to employ in order to best serve the superordinate goal identified by a Yellow economic policy. Most economic decisions in the past have been made through a Blue-ORANGE decision-making processes that had little room for lower or higher ᵛMEME expression. The *patriotic prosperity* meme, although considered visionary in the 1940s and that lasted over four decades, was unaware of the burdensome effects that regulation and high taxation had on Orange innovation in the second memenomic cycle. The *only money matters* meme placed the destiny of the United States in the hands of financial innovation that crashed and burned much of the global economy. The new HOW is not informed by a modified fourth-level system Keynesian approach to economics, nor is it a Monetarist fifth-level system. The new management style of a Yellow economy is one of distributed intelligence. The new HOW is a management system that sees the health of the whole to be far more important than the wellbeing of some parts. The new HOW is the dawn of systems thinking in business, government, economics, education, and healthcare. The HOW is a management style that must have the capacity to understand where every ᵛMEME is in its stage of evolution and design for its healthy emergence to the next level. It must understand the different motivational techniques of every ᵛmemetic level and be able to design controls and levers appropriate for every level that allow the system to function at optimal efficiency. The HOW must possess the thinking that re-aligns the resources of the system, financial, human and otherwise to serve a Yellow economic superordinate goal.

In identifying the different elements of the *natural design* question, one can see the formidable task that lies ahead for all the stakeholders in our economy. The concept challenges most decision-making processes that dominate our business and political leadership today. It calls on politicians, policy makers, and business leaders to reframe their way of thinking and decision making from their current imbedded ways to ones that are aligned with the value-systems that represent *life conditions,* while at the same time being aware of the entrapments created by the past motivations of first tier systems. Most political leaders and policy makers know the elements needed to create a diverse economy and what is needed in order to continue to provide prosperity.

However, very few have the knowhow to keep the elements plugged in to a functional platform that is informed by the continuous changes in *life conditions.*

By committing to the use of *natural design* we are committing to the conceptual world of continuous change. As a primary macromemetic tool for a seventh-level system, it is empowered by what Graves calls the "Existence Ethic" that is rooted in the knowledge of all the different realities of all the lower ᵛMEMEs. Once the challenges of *life conditions* are identified, the formidable task that lies ahead is the alignment of culture at the large scale to that existence ethic that sees the future with undisputable clarity. *Natural design* then proceeds to sequence the elements of its design formula in picking new Yellow leaders who know the type of personnel needed for the job in every lower ᵛMEME. It is proficient in the language of these ᵛMEMEs and hires people with the proper value-fit in order to get the job done. Yellow leadership, whether directly or indirectly, makes the superordinate goal known to all the first tier systems to keep them functionally aligned in order to serve the efficient flow of the system while being empowered by a higher purpose. The same methodologies would be used to inform the design of new Yellow institutions. Yellow corporations will find themselves fulfilling a functional and sustainable role by following these principles in their hiring practices, their management philosophy, and in their overall relationships with their stakeholders from suppliers to stockholders and employees.

Functional forms directly influence the formation of Yellow economic entities that are at the base of a Yellow sustainable economy. By using *natural design* to identify the HOW, WHO, WHOM, WHAT, and WHERE, we'll attempt to articulate these functional forms to take *life conditions* from where they are now and design a functional economic platform that has many elements of sustainability and self-renewal.

However, to claim the ability to design such a system is not enough. Much of second tier economic design requires the awakening of consciousness of all the stakeholders in our culture today. It is an urgent call to arms to recognize the shortsightedness of the past and have an urgency to design for a sustainable economic future of a planet in peril. It is an economy that recognizes all the stakeholders, not just the stockholders. Second-tier economic design sees employment trends in corporate America and designs to empower a new entrepreneurial culture to become a catalyst for a distributed economic base for all to prosper. It is an economy that aims to align the genius of financial innovation onto a motherboard that serves the whole society. It is an economy that seeks to differentiate the powers of the Federal Reserve and central bankers all over the world by restating their mission through functional systemic alignment. It is one that embraces the return of manufacturing to Western economies while looking nothing like it did when it was outsourced. It is the differential reexamination of the mechanics of what defines a sustainable corporation beyond the current overused terms that define sustainability. It is the embracing of creative destruction as a part

THE MOMENTOUS LEAP	
Empowering a Yellow Economy	
FROM STRATEGIC ORANGE	**TO SYSTEMATIC YELLOW**
Hierarchical and Rigid	**Functional and Distributed**
Too Big to Fail	Failure occurs naturally without affecting the entire organism
Concentrated Wealth	**Distributed Prosperity**
Proprietary and Secretive	Collaborative and Open Source
Manipulate to Succeed	**Innovate and Disrupt**
Wall Street and Private Equity	Silicon Valley, Venture Capital, Direct Investors with hands-on knowledge; Crowd Funding
Subsistence-Exhaustable	**Sustainable-Renewable**

of the new economic model leading to long-term full employment. These are the elements that will define the quantum leap that human nature has been preparing for. These are the second-tier issues that will frame the dialogue and produce The Platform for Functional Capitalism.

NINE

Embracing the Values of the Knowledge Economy

f(knowledge)

You never change things by fighting the existing reality. To change something, build a new model that makes the existing model obsolete.[102]

—R. BUCKMINSTER FULLER

THE POST-INDUSTRIAL SOCIETY REVISITED: AN INFRASTRUCTURE OF KNOWLEDGE

Daniel Bell, the Harvard sociologist, hypothesized in 1974 that Western cultures would transition to a post-industrial society in several sequential stages. What he couldn't predict was how quickly the onset of these stages will take place and how long each would last. His work was often criticized for overlooking the economic devastation the transition would leave in its path and for not addressing the impending obsolescence of skills and institutions. *Life conditions*, it seemed, were not fully prepared to embrace this change. Bell asserted that once the values of this utopian, caring society are fully manifested it would be characterized by a culture with a well-developed base of theoretical knowledge, a well-developed information infrastructure and a thriving base of intellectual technology.[103] The journey along the road to the full manifestation of what Bell described in his manifesto was one full of twists and turns and painful adjustments along the way. The loss of many industrial jobs was chalked up as the inevitable change caused by progress. We all became prosperous again under a service economy and at the hands of a financial industry that liberated money from its arcane cages only to have it all collapse.

Were these the false starts and the exploitive Red and unhealthy Orange elements of society that hijacked the potential of a Green-Yellow knowledge economy, or were these necessary stumbling blocks that helped pave the way to a sustainable form of economic expression? Bell didn't know that what he was describing back then was the "Post-Finance New Economy." The building of the knowledge infrastructure that Bell spoke of was transforming Western economies and the rest of the globe in many profound ways. This is still an infant economy but has by far acted as the biggest catalyst in modern human history in bringing change to the world. It is moving cultural grouping up the emergence ladder at neck-breaking speed.

In the 1990s its Green ᵛMEME values spread the access to information to every corner of the world, becoming the ultimate educator of the globe. The global economy in its current form would not have been possible without the early development stages of the global information infrastructure. In the very early stages in the lifecycle of this industry, information and social networks represented the Green phase of the knowledge economy. Open source collaboration and the sharing of proprietary technological platforms helped put in place an infrastructure that was shaped by the values of the Green ᵛMEME. This was the healthy expression of Green that understood the unhealthy practices of Orange, but instead of taking to the streets to demonstrate about its abuses, it designed a Green system of information that allowed everyone with a laptop or a smartphone to become knowledgeable about Orange's abuses. The Green values of the Internet as they relate to economic emergence have completely and indirectly transformed the debate about what's next by simply making information available to global minds thirsting for knowledge.

SCARCITY VS. ABUNDANCE ECONOMICS

There is ample evidence that the egalitarian Green values of the knowledge economy have threatened the very foundation on which the traditional model for capitalism stands. It seems as though the economic ideologies of the Green ᵛMEME are diametrically opposite to those of the Orange ᵛMEME. One of the first things a student in microeconomics studies is price equilibrium, which is determined by supply and demand. If the supply of a certain product in the marketplace is scarce, the price tends to be high. The concept of scarcity has always driven a capitalist society that is defined by the economic metrics of the Orange system. Stock markets and businesses have mastered the skill of controlling the supply of a product, a commodity, or a service for no purpose other than to trigger the emotions underlying compulsive behaviors based on fears of scarcity. The fear of not having enough of a product triggers the Beige-Purple system of survival and the hunter-gatherer mentality in the consumer forcing him or her to pay a higher price. The scarcer the supply of a product, the higher its value. This scarcity mindset is imbedded in the way we think as humans. It is a part of our survival instinct. It controls much of the economic activity that makes the world go round.

For centuries, during uncertain economic times, people invested in gold because it is one of the most scarce and valuable precious metals. The precious commodity of diamonds is made even more precious by the extraordinary measures the industry employs to make sure supply remains scarce at all times in order to maintain the astronomically high prices. An oil painting by a famous artist sells for hundreds of millions of dollars because of the scarcity of his work. Billions in goodwill and value-added are created every day and become part of the economic landscape because of the perception of scarcity. Most commodity markets around the world create wealth based on the notion of scarcity and the limited supply of natural resources, regardless of whether the shortage of the commodity they're trading is real or just an illusion that serves the exploits of the trader. Economics of scarcity have been with us since the day tribes learned to exchange gifts and will be with us for many centuries to come. Both expressions of the Orange ᵛMEME, healthy and unhealthy, have perfected the practice of creating the illusion of product scarcity and limited supply in the consumer's mind, as demonstrated by the long lines at an Apple store when a new product is debuted or when the demand for gold skyrockets after we hear bad news about the economy and the fate of certain global currencies.

Strategic manipulation of prices and resources is a behavior that is in direct conflict with the egalitarian values of the Green ᵛMEME. With the onset of healthy Green ᵛMEME values, the knowledge economy has sought to transform an economy of scarcity to one of abundance. The "abundance economy" is a term often used to describe the values that drive the knowledge economy. The basic premise is that if abundance economics prevail over economics of scarcity, the whole world will then be a more prosperous place. It has been the mantra of many political and economic ideologies of the past, from socialism and Marxism on down to modern management theories that study the democratization of the workplace and employee-owned businesses. The utopian elements of a post- scarcity economy couldn't gain much traction in the past because the different values that motivated humans quickly dispelled the notion that we had the capacity to view the world in the same manner.

However, it was thought that things with the knowledge economy were going to be different. After all, this economy was creating systematic disruptions to imbedded Orange practices and the threat to the very survival of the Orange value system was real. Could the virtues of the knowledge economy form the Yellow economic platform lead the world to innovations in both prosperity and sustainability?

A good representation of the disruption this economy is bringing to traditional Orange establishments like the retail sector is best detailed in a 2006 book titled *The Long Tail: Why the Future of Business is Selling Less of More* by Chris Anderson, former editor-in-chief of *Wired* magazine. Anderson describes the *long tail* as an economy populated by consumers who live in a culture unfiltered by economic scarcity and where the *short head* represents a world taught to believe in the economics of scarcity based on a limited amount of retail shelf space, a limited number of television channels, and generally limited resources of all kinds.[104] Anderson makes a compelling argument that once the smoke and mirrors of artificial scarcity created by traditional Orange retailers is removed, the discovery of real prices can be reached to make a more efficient marketplace.

In an economy where consumer spending accounts for 70 percent of economic output, the knowledge economy seems to be acting as the catalyst for change through something as simple as an Internet connection and a few clicks on a keyboard. One of the primary goals of the online retail sector of the knowledge economy is to provide full transparency for everything a consumer wants to know about a product, from quality, availability, pricing, and the unbiased opinion of other consumers. Creative destruction in the retail sector not only brings larger variety and lower prices to consumers; it also gives away many digitally downloadable products such as books, music, and movies for free. The questions for the long-term sustainability of this model become: if there's little money to be made, is it an irresponsible representation of the egalitarian Green values that eventually have to come face to face with the real world? Or have Wall Street's astronomical valuations of these online retailers and websites turned them into unaccountable children who can't be bothered with the bottom line?

Anderson answers the questions with an observation that has systemic implications that threaten the very basis of the traditional capitalist model of production. He argues that the long-term sustainability of this new economic paradigm is being shaped by three rules: the democratization of the tools of production, the democratization of the tools of distribution, and connecting the supply and demand.[105] Does this thinking represent the coming of age of the knowledge economy? Many critics have argued that Anderson's theory is mostly limited to things that can be digitized, that *free* is not really free, and ultimately there will be a cost to pay for the Orange institutional obsolesce the knowledge economy is bringing to the new marketplace. Many of these arguments are coming from the brightest and most entrenched Orange establishment figures, such as Ivy League professors and prominent economists. This is a sign that the threats from the disruptive practices of the knowledge economy are real.

Similar criticisms have been leveled at the premise of the book *Wikinomics* where the authors proclaim that a new economic democracy is emerging in which we all have a lead role based on four powerful new ideas that are replacing the old tenets of business: openness, peering, sharing, and acting globally.[106] Although the book lays out in detail several case studies of how this new economic model can work, criticism from the Orange establishment has relegated it to a form of socialism and an anomaly that can't stand up to the rigors of the old capitalist model.

In today's economy the service sector accounts for over half of global productive output. Everything that has the potential of being digitized has the potential to revolutionize. The media and the publishing industry have gone through the whirlwind of this transformational change and have very little resemblance to their most recent ancestors. But, can this type creative destruction be brought to other segments of the global economy, such as manufacturing, government services, and the trade of global commodities and capital markets? To what point can the democratization of innovation and the shift from horizontal to lateral power replace the traditional structures in organizations and still provide for economic viability? If democratization of information were the ultimate goal of the knowledge economy, what incentive would traditional firms still have to invest billions in research and development? Can proprietary inventions and patent protection laws survive the relentless march of the knowledge economy that relies heavily on open-source collaboration and sharing?

While some industries have completely vanished as a result of this disruptive innovation, the effects this is having on traditional brick and mortar institutions appear to be seventh-level changes that are making their practices healthier and more transparent. The changes that are taking place in higher education in the United States provide a good example of how traditional institutions might transform themselves into Yellow systemic entities. A few decades ago higher education was centered on the physical campus of a college or university with limited student enrollment. Universities took pride in the small sizes of their classes and the one-on-one attention students received in a physical environment conducive for learning. For more than a century this was thought of as an indestructible model that would continue to grow, and the idea of online education was either inconceivable or thought of as impractical.

Today, there are over twenty million students pursuing online degrees, and that number is projected to keep growing.[107] An industry like online education is forcing the beneficiaries of the old economic model to adjust to this and in the process to become more competitive and transparent just to survive. The old model centralized the economic power around the physical presence of the institution of employees, administrators, and professors and a number of external economies that cater to them, such as apartment housing, print shops, and pizza parlors. The new model centralizes the decision making in the hands of the student-consumer and only gives a fraction of the old cost structure to the institution, with an even smaller fraction to the designer of the software portal that delivers the instructions and course materials. Since the student presence is a virtual one, no external economies are benefiting from the new model, and their survival has to rely on their degree of business savvy, not on the luck of being located close to the institution.

The greater threat from online education, however, remains to the institution as it forces traditional education to become more functional and efficient. This is a re-alignment that is preserving what is relevant in the old model while making the online model accessible to a much wider global market. This is a revolution dictated by the transparency the knowledge economy is bringing to the marketplace. Even for retail consumers who still prefer the in-store experience to passive Internet purchases, old Orange practices based on product scarcity are being replaced by an app on a mobile device that provides customers with instant price comparisons from competitors while they are in a store experiencing the product firsthand. As the knowledge economy matures and penetrates more segments of the economy that were thought of as impregnable just a few years ago, its primary function becomes the efficient utilization of the means of production to serve a far greater base of consumer-clients.

Since the dawn of the Industrial Revolution the patterns of creative destruction have experienced minor changes as only the content has grown more complex. The more entrenched the economic model is in the old system, the more it resists change. To use a metaphor from a highly specialized segment of the manufacturing sector, the current transition could be compared to an era in which the Orange establishment over many decades became fully entrenched in a macroeconomic model that invested trillions in prop engine technologies thinking it was the Holy Grail to end all future technological quests. As creative destruction moved forward, the industry created the far superior jet-engine technology that made the prop engine obsolete. Orange now finds itself in a place where it is spending an increasing amount of time, effort, and resources trying to convince the world that jet-engine technology is an illusion. The intersection of information, theoretical knowledge, and technology is making the defense of old Orange practices as preposterous as defending a prop engine in a jet engine world.

In value-systems studies, the debate among colleagues has been around which ᵛMEME the knowledge economy belongs to. Once it is fully vetted and has to answer to stockholder bottom line, will it be just another more advanced expression of the Orange 'MEME or is it the long-awaited entry into second-tier thinking that will eventually materialized in second-tier cultural values? Because of its heavy emphasis on the democratization of everything from information to production tools, and sharing and collaboration, is it just a Green 'MEME threat that is forcing Orange temporarily into healthy but costly practices in order to save the old system? Can the old hierarchical nature of Orange capitalism be saved? The paradigm shift into a new economic reality can no longer be denied nor can it be stopped, and the destruction it's leaving in its aftermath is real.

Beck often warns that entry into the seventh-level system threatens the existence of life on earth, as we know it. Well, that threat has come to our economic life. It has completely transformed the media, the publishing industry, and the retail industry. It has decentralized and externalized their business models and continues to chisel away on the structure of many storied industries that were thought to be safe from the digital revolution. It has made their products available in abundance and in greater variety at lower prices. It has completely turned the means of production and the methods of distribution upside down. Many questions will still have to be answered about whether this time creative destruction will lead to a utopian capitalist economy, or whether such a concept could exist and still be called capitalism.

What would an economy that has natural formations that automatically follow the virtues of *natural design* with sustainable and distributed economic systems look like? It would look like an economy in a new economic frontier that is local and global all at once. What is noteworthy is that most of the criticism of the knowledge economy came in the few years prior to the onset of the financial crisis when Red and unhealthy Orange values were running amuck. During this period what I call the perfect memenomic storm was loose credit combined with the economic model of scarcity to falsely reinforce the merits of the old system. Today, as that model continues to collapse, it is exposing the structural weaknesses of Orange in the face of rapidly moving digital world. The change is forcing historically imbedded Orange practices to embrace the virtues of the knowledge economy. As financial innovation assumes its functional role and becomes subordinate to real productive output, the intersection of information, knowledge, and technology will play a far greater role in defining what our next sustainable economic expression will be.

DISTRIBUTED INNOVATION (DI),
THE FOUNDATION OF A YELLOW ECONOMY

In describing the climb to the second tier of human existence, Graves prefaces the role that information and knowledge play in humanity's extraordinary climb into this level of consciousness. By the time of his death in 1986 he had no idea of how much of a crucial role technology would play in providing knowledge and information to people on such a global scale. Knowledge and the knowledge-economy are shaping the thinking of a world that has long suffered from the degradation brought by the subsistence ᵛMEMEs. Graves declares that knowledge and necessity will come to define the driving force behind this system as it seeks to correct and heal the damage caused by practices of lower complexity systems.[108] Knowledge is the catalyst that is building a vast infrastructure of informed global citizens who can lead the climb to second tier transformation. As the role of knowledge continues to mature, its natural progression is to discern the bits and bytes of information and shape them into more adaptable tools of innovation that answer to the needs of individuals and cultures in unique *life conditions.*

Distributed Innovation (DI) is the adaptation of *Natural Design* to the knowledge economy. It is a model that holds the potential to help cultures evolve by creating what's next in the application of new technologies and the distribution of memetically-honed information. It takes best management practices and enhances their content to fit the memetic contours of the local culture. It is not the same concept as democratization of innovation, which is a Green value concept that distributes the tools of technology indiscriminately. *DI* takes a systemic approach towards cultural and economic development. It is the proper honing of knowledge that will continue to be refined as it plays an increasingly integral role in shaping the future of this global, yet local, economy. It is the long awaited structural change that is transforming macro and micro economic practices. Unlike the traditional Orange models for economic prosperity that inevitably allow for labor and resource exploitation, the fundamentally different nature of *DI* is that it has memetically-honed tools of the knowledge economy and has a far better chance at a more fitting distribution of wealth than any economic model before it.

DI is a second-tier memenomics concept that is aware of potential abuses humanity can suffer should technology fall into the wrong hands of all the unhealthy expressions of different ᵛMEMEs. This is the systemic seventh-level system intersection of information, knowledge, and technology that is informed by the rules of *natural design*. It is a concept that is functional in nature in that it distributes proper technological uses to all levels of complexity and allows the content to be informed by the needs to fulfill the healthy expressions arising from the uniqueness of *life conditions*. It is the molding of information, knowledge, and technology into monetized units of exchange that are appropriate for each cultural value system with its unique indigenous expression. This seventh-level functionality lays down the blueprints for systemic alignment by properly informing the stakeholders in the system of the appropriate steps needed for economic emergence.

DI knows no national borders as the transmission of knowledge becomes more important than the transition of physical goods across physical planes. In a global economy that has to contend with a worldwide economic memes-tack and myriads of indigenous contents, *DI* acts as a natural catalyst that shapes prosperity through the unique expression of the local culture however and wherever it might be. Development-averse regions of the world have a far better chance at economic prosperity by easily tapping into the global information infrastructure than they did waiting on the old development model for projects to trickle down to their local villages. In most cases where the value systems are centered in the exploitive RED third-level system, corrupt leaders have bankrupted the traditional top-down economic development programs designed by global agencies like the IMF and the World Bank. Today, a group of women weavers in a remote village in Africa can find willing buyers for their garments anywhere in the world with nothing more than a satellite phone equipped with a good camera. This is how the knowledge economy can bring prosperity to a Purple ᵛMEME that would have taken decades, if not centuries, to reach under the old system. The use of memetically-honed tools that are a part of a *DI* toolkit will further enable cultures to build the necessary ecosystems around these distributed economic formations that become the foundation for a prosperous global culture.

In advanced economies, beyond the Orange applications in education, media, and retail, *DI* is making other ᵛMEMEs adapt naturally to healthier practices. The Internet has created a knowledge-sharing platform that informs the public about abuses inherent in old economic structures. This is where the digital age is filling in the gaps of a diminished Blue fourth-level system. Enforcement of some Blue ᵛMEME responsibilities have moved from the concentrated and often under-funded hands of government agencies to the hands of anyone with an Internet connection and a camera phone. Information uncovered by an investigative blogger who exposes the abuses of a municipal pension system of a big city becomes a catalyst for political change. A YouTube video taken of a Wall Street executive insulting the intelligence of bank regulators goes viral and costs him his job a few days later. An outspoken executive at a major investment bank quits his job and takes to the editorial pages of *The New York Times* about a corporate culture that views its clients in disparaging ways and sends the firm on a damage-control mission and in search of ways to change its image. Having an informed public does not always translate to dollars and cents as a measure of GDP, but the unintended non-commercial uses of information have become a collective tool for transparency that no traditional Blue structure can provide. In a world where the citizenry is fully informed, unhealthy practices of all kinds from all first-tier systems are naturally minimized. Once they are brought to the light, the design for healthy alternative practices and their supporting systems becomes possible. This is *DI* and the Yellow functional nature the promise of the knowledge economy holds.

The entrepreneurs who are the catalysts for the change that Joseph Schumpeter envisioned are the ones designing innovation in this new Yellow economy. These entrepreneurs are capable of making creative destruction an expression of healthy economic practices along the entire stack of value systems. This is a natural redistribution of the promise of capitalism that is stratified according to technical and entrepreneurial ability at all ᵛMemetic levels with the various contents that go beyond national borders. A Yellow knowledge economy distributes the wealth and the abundance of innovation to anyone willing to participate. Where there is economic repression, access to the Internet acts naturally to bring an end to these practices by providing information to the masses about healthy emergence. The model is naturally stratified and indigenously informed. Information becomes locally functional knowledge that serves purposes like mass collaboration and crowd mobilization for any purpose without being stopped by traditional barriers. In the Middle East today, access to information is taking on the form of distributed knowledge that is abolishing the old rule of repression and is bringing more development-prone values to the masses.

DI provides the technological knowhow to the user; however, the content and the shape of the final product relies on and is informed by local *life conditions* and thus takes on the form of *natural design*. Once the right groups leverage this distributed innovation, it becomes the foundation that creates the paradigm shift to an economy with distributed prosperity. *DI* provides the knowledge and the tools to create prosperity for every meaning making system throughout the world. If the goal is to feed a remote third world village in a sustainable way, *DI* will provide the latest in Western research for the design of that system. If it is to help a culture or a group transition from an unhealthy expression of one value system to the next, it aligns the political, economic and legal resources for the transition to happen by informing the group seeking the change. If it seeks to end the unproductive practices on

Wall Street, it exposes the entire toxic ecosystem that led to the formation of these practices, from politicians and lobbyists all the way down to the psychopathic trader risking billions on a single bet. Knowledge is revolutionizing the patterns of human emergence, and the memetically-honed tools of *DI* can expedite the process by unlocking the blockages that prevent real change from taking place. This is happening naturally as technology continues to distribute the enforcement of transparency to the general public. Once the blockages of greed, corruption and manipulation created by the old system are removed, prosperity becomes a byproduct of the proper functional flow of *distributed innovation*.

THE NEW ENTREPRENEURSHIP MEME

The knowledge economy has acted as a catalyst for Western value systems to enter the early stages of second-tier expressions, however much economic activity remains entrenched in the practices of the Orange system. As this creative destruction realigns Orange values towards a functional second-tier platform, new and memetically informed entrepreneurial leadership is needed to insure its long-term sustainability. The biggest challenge that this transition faces is how to empower future corporate and political leaders to acknowledge that we live on a planet that is in peril. How do we facilitate leadership transition from subsistence value systems limited to expressions of selfish interest to one that sees the essential need for all life form on the planet to continue to exist?

In order to create a Yellow seventh-level economy one must look at the complex ways Yellow individuals in today's economy think and attempt to assimilate these values into our schools, universities, management training programs and corporate boardrooms. These are the long resisted changes towards sustainable and renewable practices that have the continuity of all life on the planet as an overarching goal. Here, business leaders look beyond the traditional model that looks at maximizing stockholder value and the accumulation of vast individual wealth as their primary objective to see the proper distribution of wealth as a basic quality of life issue. Here is where *life conditions* provide business leaders with immediate feedback on whether their practices are congruent with the values outside the walls of their corporations and allow for a dynamic feedback system that harmonizes the two.

Graves prefaces the values of this cognitive existential state as one characterized by the dissolution of fear and compulsiveness and the marked increases in conceptual space that values life and focuses on the problem that its existence creates.[109] Here, the entrepreneur sheds the fear that Orange quantitative analysis is the sole metric to use in business practices. Traditional market analysis for product viability is replaced by a deep conviction that if you create a product that raises the conscious of the consumer, it will create its own new market. Because of its experiential nature, second-tier entrepreneurial leadership goes beyond the most common expressions of sustainable practices. Environmental programs that empower recycling and the use of renewable resources are just the tip of the entrepreneurial values of this ᵛMEME. Sustainability in all aspects of doing business becomes the driving force behind Yellow entrepreneurship. It places the stockholder on equal grounds with the stakeholder. Areas such as long-term economic sustainability rely on the long-term health and prosperity of the employees and the suppliers as key contributors to shareholder value.

Yellow entrepreneurship understands the interconnectedness of all life on the planet and acts accordingly. It redefines the best Orange models for corporate social responsibility and makes them healthier. A publically held Yellow organization does not stop at funding socially needed traditional programs; it also works on making business partners out of many local businesses that are willing to adopt its values. Because this is an open system that accepts the diverse nature of other value systems, it can easily plug them on to a healthy and sustainable business expression that can revolutionize the very nature of how business gets done.

Once actions of business leaders become informed by second-tier values, there will be little chance for a return to pure Orange practices. This is an attainment of a certain level of consciousness that represents the next stage in human evolution. It abandons the drive for amassing individual wealth to the detriment of others and embraces prosperity in relationship to the sustainability of life on the planet. Through *distributed innovation*, and the benefit of a well developed, cost efficient supply chain and a global information network, Yellow entrepreneurship empowers local communities and the return of the local business owner. This is the model that supports the movement from global hedge funds to localized, socially conscious funds and the re-investment in fully integrated local communities that needs to be taught at business schools. The knowledge economy has created millions of conscious investors with strong Green ᵛMEME values who aspire for Yellow business practices. Angel and super-angel investors with access to billions are sitting on the sidelines and waiting for the next paradigm shift that distributes wealth and opportunity to all. Yellow entrepreneurial values see the next frontier for small business and work on creating the investment infrastructure for conscious venture capitalists to come in and invest in community development initiatives through these businesses. This would naturally lead to a new small business-lending model that enriches the entrepreneur and the small venture capitalist without the involvement of the current banking system. This is an emerging model that will help establish a powerful and resilient economy that is re-distributed where the failure of one business has very little impact on the rest of the community.

Real-life examples of the patterns of Yellow leadership were shown in the previous chapter and they have all showed patterns of genuine concern for the long-term functionality of the system. Yellow entrepreneurship models should be taught in management schools and in corporate boardrooms with the urgency that the survival of the system is no longer confined to Orange institutions, but to the entire ecosystem we call home. The obsolescence of some Orange institutions on the hands of the knowledge economy should serve as a warning sign for traditional corporate practices to aspire for higher values and start embracing the virtues of Yellow entrepreneurship. The world can longer accept the teachings of strategic linearity to future business leaders. Beck often warns that an Orange system, which sidelines the need to be informed by Yellow values, tends to spawn the seeds of its own destruction. Today, that claim is playing out in glaring detail on Wall Street as the hubris of this system is rendering its business models unsustainable to the most casual observer.

TEN

The Case for Functional Financial Systems

f(finance)

I don't believe this is just a financial panic; I believe it represents the failure of the whole model of banking, of an overgrown financial sector that did more harm than good.[110]

—PAUL KRUGMAN
Winner Nobel Prize for Economics 2008

REALIGNING MONEY

The role that money plays in a higher cycle of human emergence cannot be understated. For centuries it has been the catalyst that propelled culture into the next stage of human development. From its earliest existences in the tribal value system over eight thousand years ago through today's mosaic of all the different value systems with the myriad of indigenous contents and codes, money has been an inextricable part of the human experience. As we saw in chapter three, money has historically played a dual value-systems role in advancing the plight of humanity. Cultures have moved from the second-level Purple values to the sixth-level Green values, while money remained a formidable presence in the Blue order system in whichever developmental stage each culture was in. Money was always backed by the most agreed-upon form of redemption as we transitioned through the different cultural development stages. Forms of payment have evolved from grain and fish, to precious coins, to gold bullion, to paper money backed by gold, and finally to the fiat currency that we have today that is backed by the word of national governments. These mediums of exchange represented the changing Blue content of money as it evolved over the centuries but remained, to a great extent a representative of human productive output.

The monetarist ideology during the *only money matters* era sought to change this historically proven relationship between money and humanity. In one of the most pervasive cases of the tail wagging the dog in modern history, the era of monetarism sought to make money a part of productive output.

This liberated it from its historic rigidity and gave it a place at the Orange fifth-level table. This was the beginning of the rise of the financial services sector and the slow shift in wealth. In two short decades innovations like securitization became pervasive. This was one of many concepts that sought to increase the value of the world's stocks and bonds by using newly liberated evaluation methods without having to add a single hour of human productive output to GDP. Central banks around the world embraced this direction of notional growth and provided financial markets with the liquidity needed to further encourage the creation of financial products.

Although this brave and historic experiment added wealth to many segments of society it had the potential to erode wealth if it ever decoupled from representing productivity and becoming its own independent sector. By the early millennial decade it became just that. In addition to liquidity from central banks, emerging economies flooded Western capital markets with so much cash that the financial services sector had no forms of productive output left to invest it in. This is when the *only money matters* era entered the decay stage of the memenomic cycle. Bets masquerading as complex financial instruments brought the global financial markets to their knees in 2008 and in the process brought a hastened end to Orange experimentation with money.

Pervasive financial innovation brought on bubble economies of all types. From asset bubbles to the dotcom bubble to the severest of all bubbles, housing, they all worked on eroding the relationship between productive output and money. Today the financial services sector finds itself running out of economic sectors to securitize and exploit. The tail can no longer wag the dog and we all have to pay the price. Today, as we languish in the greatest economic contraction since the great depression, new conversations about the future of money have already begun. Could this lead to a new paradigm that restores the credibility of major global currencies? Or would governments heed the calls of many critics to return to the gold standard in a desperate attempt to save the eroding value of their national wealth? Would Congressman Ron Paul get his wish to abolish the Federal Reserve Bank and hand its key responsibilities to the Department of the Treasury? Would an enhanced form of the monetarist ideology with some Blue accountability provide for a good model of financial governance? Would a Green policy of having a global or a regional currency temper the ambitions of leading economic powers and provide for a more equitable redistribution of wealth?

This is fertile ground to create a second-tier functional financial system that is informed by the memenomic experiences of the past century. All the questions posed here amount to value systems expressions of the first tier and have already been experimented with in one form or another. The return to the gold standard is impractical and because of its rigidity in having wealth tied to its value, going back on it will cause a prolonged economic contraction if not a worldwide depression. In absolute value systems terms, the gold standard is a false Blue that gives absolute economic advantage to the nation that holds the largest underground gold deposits with little regard to the merit of its workforce. The value of gold has a tendency to rise during economic uncertainty. The steeper the decline, the higher the value seems to be. Much of the talk about the return to gold has been generated by commodities dealers who create the classic economic apocalypse scenario in order to scare people into the safely of gold. For them it is just another opportunity to make money as the case is with all the other commodities they trade.

While the complexity of the global economy today has moved far past an antiquated system backed by gold, the search for the new model that holds the money supply accountable to a set of Blue rules continues. Ideas for what central banking of the future might look like have not been limited to strict Blue accountability and therein lies the danger in kicking the accountability can down the road. The paradigm to create a new global financial system that is not defined by dollars, euros, and other global currencies remains a utopian dream of a Turquoise eighth-level system that lays far ahead into the future. Before a new financial system designed for second-tier *life conditions* can be implemented, much needs to be done with first-tier values to align them on a healthy Yellow trajectory.

While the Federal Reserve's experiment with using Orange fifth-level values with the money supply proved dangerous, other value system experiments with it proved to be just as risky. Europe experimented with the money supply as a tool of Green sixth-level values. The European Central Bank imposed monetary policy on member states with the hope that it would bring integration and prosperity to the entire continent. In this case Germany -the primary backer of the Euro, entered the Green values-system out of the guilt it suffered from the last World War. This combined with France's blind pursuit of socialism, which ignored much of the Orange metrics needed to develop less complex European economies. As often is the case with Green, it doesn't see hierarchy. As a result of these Green values, Portugal, Ireland, Italy, Greece, and Spain were given billions in loans without ever addressing the deeper issues of differences in cultural values and productive capacities. These countries' failures to achieve what the Germans and French thought was possible has resulted in the European debt crisis, which is threating the unity of Europe. From a value-systems observer's point of view, this action was hasty and a good example of how Green's blind pursuit of equality can be very dangerous when it comes to economic policy. A true integration of a continent as complex as Europe would need decades, if not centuries, of cultural, political and fiscal integration in order to align the different value systems and their varying contents and codes on the same trajectory that serves the superordinate goal of equal prosperity. As often is the case with Green acting out of guilt, it resorts to easy and partially thought out solutions that feel good, but are not sustainable in the long term.

An example of a second-tier approach the ECB could have taken towards European economic integration, would have been the encouragement of manufacturers from Germany, France, and other advanced member states in Northern Europe to set up factories and research and development facilities in Southern Europe and Greece in an effort to inject a unified and sustainable work ethic to achieve some semblance of egalitarian prosperity. This would have fulfilled the purpose for creating the unified currency in the first place. This was yet another case of the tail wagging the dog, with the first being the US economy under the *only money matters* era. They both had disastrous consequences. The complexity of European economics is beyond the focus of this book, but this example illustrates yet again, the need to understand the role of money from a values-systems perspective. Its intended future use must remain representatives of productive output, a *functional* BLUE fourth-level role.

DESIGNING A SEVENTH-LEVEL CURRENCY

Experimenters with global currencies over the last four decades have mistaken the removal of the stringent BLUE of the gold standard with the notion that money can be used to finance whatever the desires of their value systems are without having to worry about a system of checks and balances. Although some lessons will be learned from the US's experiment with Orange currency, it will not serve as an effective model for all. Europe's experiment with Green currency will provide some lessons as well, but the model remains far from effective. Here lies the challenge in designing a second-tier approach that has systemic functionality both at the community level and at the global level. To the average person money still represents the Blue measure of hard work, but to world leaders dealing with complex financial issues the challenges are far greater than simple exchange. Because money means different things to the different value systems, the exchange of goods and services must be reflected as an expression of the local value systems. Many Green communities in the United States use complimentary currencies. These are agreed upon forms of printed-paper that accommodate daily commerce within those local communities. The barter system is another form of exchange that is used in both Green communities in advanced countries as well as rural Purple regions of the world. Many people in the Purple-Red value systems hoard gold and other precious medal because of their mistrust of paper currency. Yellow money for simple local exchange can take on whatever functional form the community decides it can be based on its value systems.

The bigger problem lies in designing a seventh-level exchange system for a complex global economy with global Blue accountability at its core. From a forensic value systems approach, what global leaders need to create is an evolved expression of the Blue "exchange for value" that money represents in light of the complexity of where *life conditions* are today. Under the current Orange system global GDP is measured based on productive output. GDP as a measure of productivity today does not differentiate between human productive output and non-human productive output, which in part explains the widening gap between Wall Street and Main Street. An evolved expression of the Blue accountability that money represents must have human productive output at its core. This is at the heart of a functional model that places the primary representative of productivity at the epicenter. All other economic activity derived from non-human output and by money employing money will be the complementary elements of the model. Gross Domestic Product must be replaced with Human Domestic Product.

This is not a Green economic concept for currency based solely on egalitarianism. This is a seventh-level system model at its best that aligns long-proven Orange metrics with the most widely known Blue representative of productivity, then adds a deep Green appreciation for humanity's talents and create a model for a functional currency. This concept doesn't look to equalize all human productive output. It is stratified in the sense that it will still place more value on the work of an engineer than it would on that of a construction worker. It will have an index—we'll call it the HDP index—that will assign certain agreed upon points to the nature of work being done by different people with different talents and capacities. At secondary and tertiary levels it will still include measures of non-human output that will limit the value of factory production and gains realized due to advancements in technologies. The current Wall Street model that places a bankable market value on a future product or service out of pure speculation will receive least priority in this new model. Most secondary measures of the HDP index will focus on new innovations that contribute to sustainability practices and better quality of life. The higher a country measures on the index, the higher the value of its exchange. Under this new Blue global mechanism for currency, money supply can only rise two or three percentage points above annual HDP in order to insure adequate investment in research and development into healthy innovative practices that insure a sustainable future. The natural operation of this model will no longer allow for financial innovation to decouple from productive output. This will ensure sustainable and real global economic prosperity for all.

Whether or not the real global currencies of the future have these specific mechanisms built into them is secondary to the function that the model should serve. Any naturally designed form of global exchange must place the largest emphasis on the value of human talent. When we're done asking the question *what does prosperity really want?*—and after we're done building the fastest computer and the most efficient factory, and have amassed vast amounts of personal wealth—in the end it is what we contribute to the improvement of the lives of others and to the long term sustainability of life on the planet that matters the most. What could account for a higher ideal for currency than a median of exchange that places human productivity above a process or a machine? Much work remains to be done before a new system gathers steam for a new paradigm. My hope is that these value system ideas inform the future narrative of what role currency plays in the conscious emergence of culture. Much remains to be done on how to make the current system healthy and to place it on a functional trajectory that makes it more receptive to values above its current expression. An essential element will be the need to focus on how to re-align the current policies of the Federal Reserve in order to serve the superordinate goal of funding The Platform for Functional Capitalism.

CENTRAL BANKS OF THE SEVENTH-LEVEL SYSTEM

The Federal Reserve today continues to borrow tools from the existing Orange system hoping that by throwing good money after bad, toxicity from ill-conceived financial practices will miraculously disappear. An audit ordered by the US Congress and released in late 2010 shows the Fed committing to $12.3 trillion in emergency funding for Wall Street banks, which brings the total bailout package for the financial crisis to $13 Trillion.[111] In a system that would have had any Blue accountability remaining in its values, this action would have caused a global economic calamity. The US dollar would have been substantially devalued and a rush to dump the currency would have unleashed an unstoppable worldwide panic. A central bank that turns on the printing machine without any moral reservation is a confirmation that the current system has reached the final stages of collapse. The institution and its policies have caved in under the weight of their own practices and have become obsolete.

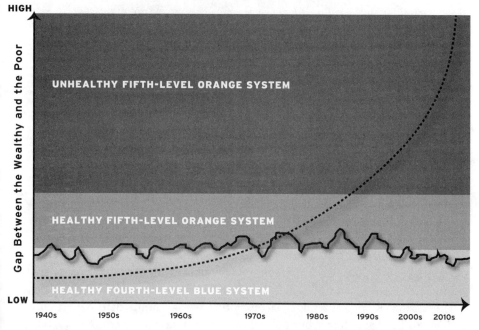

EFFECTS OF FEDERAL RESERVE POLICIES ON CULTURAL EMERGENCE

······ Enterprising (actual) fifth-level Orange system vs. /⌐ Functional (projected) seventh-level Yellow system

Exposing the fallacy of financial innovation with a fifth-level ᵛMEME Federal Reserve whose policies gradually decoupled from alignment with *life conditions* and shifted wealth away from the working and middle class vs. a seventh-level Federal Reserve that would have served the *function* of funding the various sectors of a fully diversified healthy fifth-level ᵛMEME economy with a firm basis in *smartblue*.

In designing a functional Fed, one must look at the value systems lessons learned from the current dysfunction, abolish toxic practices that can't be healthy, and plug the ones that can onto to a platform that serves the three bottom lines of a Yellow capitalist system; People, profit and planet. Getting rid of the toxicity will only happen over time as we continue to languish in prolonged periods of slow growth. More Wall Street funds will be devalued and more banks will suffer losses as we languish in a Japan-like malaise until the toxicity disappears and a new paradigm starts taking hold. Lawmakers looking to empower a new Fed with distributed Yellow intelligence will do things differently. They will first reexamine the wisdom of the 1977 Federal Reserve Reform Act from a whole systems perspective. A new system cannot place so much power for insuring full employment in the hands of the Fed Chairman. Under the Orange expression of money, the Fed replaced the views of a diverse group of economists working in specific industries by the singular view of one Alan Greenspan. Monetary policy was no longer a reflection of *life conditions* representing the unique financial challenges and the diverse business modalities of the entire economy. Opening the floodgates to the money supply became the model for the Fed. A rich diet of surplus capital everywhere for every industry was the sophomoric approach that made the entire global economy suffer from metabolic syndrome.

A seventh-level model that believes in the resilience of a distributed system will seek to reverse much of the direction the Fed has taken over the last three decades and do it in light of where *life conditions* are today. This is a *smart blue* model designed from the seventh-level that acknowledges the different capital requirements of every industry. It is a model that is informed by the leading economists specializing in every sector of the economy. There will be a return to the specialized economists who focus solely on the needs of their respective industry and professional trade organizations. Economists from the biotech sector, for example, would describe their specialized capital needs differently than those from the high-tech or the manufacturing sector. New monetary policies at the Fed will encourage the formation of special lending facilities that will accommodate the specific needs of every industry but only to the extent that borrower meets certain industry benchmarks. This new breed of specialized economists will work closely with the Fed to design specific industry lending programs and make them available through banks and other capital markets. Monetary policy will then be informed by the diversity of *life conditions* that are far more differentiated and resilient than their earlier Orange expression. The new model doesn't permit complacency and misalignment as capital needs will be regimented specifically for that industry and the failure of one entity will not risk the health of the entire industry or pose any systemic risk to the rest of the economy.

A distributed Yellow banking system will also seek to reverse bank consolidations, which was the main cause of the financial crisis and its prolonged aftermath. The too big to fail philosophy unfairly burdens all stakeholders in the system while giving a free pass for the ones causing the failure. Recently passed legislation like The Dodd–Frank Wall Street Reform and Consumer Protection Act of 2010 imposes comprehensive new regulations on the financial industry but falls short on completely separating activities of commercial banks from investment banks. Critics of the legislation also point to the fact that it doesn't address the too big to fail issue, and that in spite of the fact that the government has the power to do an orderly liquidation of a big bank, it doesn't rule out another bailout.[112] In value-systems terms, the recent legislation sought to give Blue a more effective role in regulating all aspects of the financial services industry, but did little to encourage the distribution of the check and balance mechanism to a diverse set of stakeholders. Empowering a diminished Blue in an environment that for decades has been dominated by exploitive Orange practices is like giving a soldier a pistol to fight off a tank and calling it financial reform. At best the legislation is a half step that only provides partial assurance against systemic failure.

A *smart-blue* system designed from the seventh level would have seen the financial crisis as an opportunity to start creating a new system for the long term to make the current system obsolete at the opportune time. Knowing that regulation from the current system can only achieve limited goals a new system would begin to encourage a new and distributed model for banking. It will promote the creation of small independent banks to the highest level possible. Under the current Fed, banks sought consolidation for two reasons, cost efficiency and growth. A seventh-level Fed will seek a distributed model with those same goals where efficiency has been realized by the help of technology. *Distributed innovation* that employs the latest advancements in banking, from efficient customer service operations to procuring large business loans, has leveled the playing field between small independent banks and large banks. The benefit in encouraging local ownership of banks is that they become stakeholders in their local communities knowing their customers personally and answering to their unique financial needs. As the model spreads it becomes a catalyst for local economic growth that has its own unique imprint of the local community. The more popular this new model becomes the lower the risk is to systemic failure. Its sustainability is based on its ability to address two concerns simultaneously: being able to provide whatever big banks can offer and taking on the unique and resilient form of a local business that is fully integrated into the community and provides for its unique financial needs.

SECOND-TIER CAPITAL MARKETS

The role the Fed played in the causing the financial crisis pales in comparison to that of Wall Street investment bankers. If the Fed's mistake was printing too much money, Wall Street's mistake was to falsely lead the world into thinking that that money was being used to grow the real economy. Since we are seeking to align the function of capital markets onto a healthy trajectory, it is important to remind ourselves of the original function that investment bankers serve. Under the traditional capitalist model investment bankers perform the crucial function of raising capital for companies to grow. We've seen how the infrastructure the financial sector built during the *only money matters* era shifted investor focus away from value investing (traditional Blue behavior) to the speculative promise of future performance of unproven notional assets (innovative unhealthy Orange-Red behavior). This has defined the psychology and the short-term temperament of the investor and the trader communities alike.

The perfect storm in 2008 pushed this system into the decay stage, as it was no longer able to sustain the fallacy of wealth creation. Many years after the bailout an astounding 85 percent of the investment activities of Wall Street's biggest banks remains unproductive.[113] This is a clear indication that the current system is incapable of voluntarily changing its habits and the current Blue structures are only partially effective in steering it on to a healthy path. The Dodd-Frank Act's legislation provides for transparency on trading activities in order to protect the consumer, but falls short on providing a way for Wall Street to pursue productive endeavors. The bigger problem that investment bankers and regulators face today is that the global economy is not creating innovative businesses fast enough to effectively employ all the excess capital around the world. This leaves the issue of Wall Street's re-alignment to productivity to be a function of market efficiency, which has to rein in much of the notional wealth created over the last three decades.

The next phase in the current economic contraction will be a slow trudge towards establishing a real value of all that is not notional, a painful but necessary step to return the system to an accountable Blue. This would have happened much faster if the Fed didn't provide a facility of $13 trillion for Wall Street to launder its toxic assets. In order for investment banking to reach a point where it has no choice but to pursue productive endeavors the Fed must stop all future measures for quantitative easing as these programs have proven to temporarily benefit Wall Street to the determent of Main Street. Without structural reform, quantitative easing has only increased the toxicity and the can for meaningful reform keeps getting kicked further down the road. Should the Fed stop all quantitative easing there will be a devaluation of all the toxic assets that remain on the books of banks along with many financial stocks, which will pull us into another recession. This will be the right recession to have, one of re-alignment where the stock market will move one step closer to becoming a true representative of real economic activity. A severe but temporary correction that realigns stock markets with actual productive output of the real economy will provide for a potential long-term solution for Wall Street as long as there are *smart blue* measures in place. In addition to asking investment bankers *are you being transparent* these new Blue benchmarks would also ask *how are your activities helping productive businesses raise to capital?*

The consequence for continuing with the way things are getting done has dangerous long-term implications. By printing money and buying toxic assets the US central bank has single handedly devalued the current and future value of the dollar to unprecedented levels. The reason we haven't seen the effects of that devaluation is because the rest of world is experiencing a recession as well. Other global currencies have been weakened just as much as the US dollar. Most of the economies that follow the Anglo-Saxon capitalist model are experiencing a systemic global devaluation of their currencies due to inflated assets everywhere. Central bankers around the world have convinced themselves that in order to save the global economy from a devastatingly long depression they have to cover up for the deeds of investment bankers. This is an erroneous and dangerous assumption that has the potential to substantially downgrade the purchasing power of Western currencies. All it would take is for countries like China, Taiwan, Brazil, and the OPEC countries that collectively own the majority of Western debt, to insist on alternative forms of payment—not in other forms of currencies but in actual physical commodities like gold silver and copper and other valuable raw materials that haven't been debased by a printing machine. Such a cataclysmic event would bring a swift end to fiat currencies and to Western stock markets, as we know them. Both investment bankers and central bankers are betting against the odds of this happening, but their actions that continue to devalue their currency show no signs of ending any time soon.

As we continue into the decay and collapse stage of the current cycle, structural changes that could represent signs of the emergence of the next system are beginning to appear. The field of financial innovation is attracting less interest from the labor force than at any time in recent history. This hasn't come about through soul searching but through clear indication that there's considerably less demand for financial services. *Bloomberg News* has reported that as many as 200,000 jobs in the financial sector were eliminated in 2012 alone.[114] While the system continues to languish in its final phases, much of the talent that shaped its recent history is being freed to seek other productive pursuits. The theoretical physicists and the math geniuses that were behind the creation of the Wall Street algorithms that caused the financial crisis were attracted there mostly because of the pay, not because of their conviction in serving humanity's best interests. Had these scientists gone into fields that properly utilized their talents, such as the knowledge-economy or rocket science at NASA, the economic landscape today would have looked completely different.

As Wall Street's nonproductive activities continue, our government has the opportunity to play a leading role that serves as a catalyst for change. A government designed from Second Tier sees the damage that nonproductive activity on Wall Street is causing and taxes it at the highest levels possible. This is not an unprecedented move. Taxing cigarettes has proven to be a very effective tool in reducing the use of tobacco products while raising billions in revenues from federal and state taxes. Just like the tax proceeds from tobacco, a *smart blue* design will safeguard the tax collected from Wall Street and invest it in research and development activities aimed at defining the next economic frontier. Just as the tobacco tax serves the superordinate goal of abandoning bad heath habits, a Wall Street tax will hasten the end of unproductive and toxic habits, enabling the realignment of the system with productive economic pursuits. The sooner the current value-systems expression of money comes to an end, the sooner finance can resume its boring but essential role of being a utility to the economy and not a shadow economy of its own.

Eleven

Designing for the Future of Manufacturing

f(manufacturing)

The world's largest economy can no longer count on consumer spending to drive demand, nor can it rely on Wall Street financial wizardry if it wants its population to continue to enjoy a high standard of living. The U.S. should work to have manufacturing represent about 20 percent of employment, more than double its current level.[115]

—JEFF IMMELT
CEO General Electric Co. & Head of President Obama's
Outside Economic Advisory Board
From June 2009 speech to the Detroit Economic Club

THE MANUFACTURING SECTOR AND VALUE SYSTEMS

To fully understand the role that economics plays in the human evolutionary process, it is essential to know the importance of manufacturing. On our road to higher expression of values, no economic sector has historically played a more crucial role in helping us reach that goal than the manufacturing sector. Before the industrial revolution cultures languished in a subsistent existence for thousands of years. While the merchant classes during the colonial era flourished, incomes of farmers barely increased from one generation to the next. With the creation of the steam engine came a set of industrial age values that forever changed the trajectory of human emergence. The dawn of the Age of Enlightenment with philosophers, scientists and industrialist at its helm has shown humanity the face of prosperity that continues to tantalize culture to this day. This was the dawn of fifth-level system values acting as a catalyst that moved culture from the subsistent Purple system through Red and Blue values in the fastest time imagined before becoming the universal paradigm for prosperity. On its road to that fifth-level Orange system, manufacturing had to go through its Red phase during the *fiefdoms of power* era.

As that system collapsed the *life conditions* of factory workers informed the Blue stage of the *patriotic prosperity* era of the measures that needed to be implemented under the New Deal policies in order to define the upward emergence of the system. During the era of the *patriotic prosperity meme* manufacturing established the United States as the global leader in defining the promise of the Enlightenment values. The first Industrial Revolution gave way to the second industrial revolution that created the assembly line and made mass production the new catalyst for prosperity and the focus of United States corporations. During much of this era the United State's superordinate goal was to win wars. This was a time where unprecedented advancements in science and technology were made through the coordinated efforts of government and the private sector. Economic development models during this era placed the strongest emphasis on the manufacturing sector if a country were to have a viable and sustainable economy. The United States, through the evolving values of the manufacturing sector, became the envy of countries seeking modern prosperity. The sector became synonymous with good paying jobs that defined the American middle class.

As the *patriotic prosperity meme* entered the decay stage, it announced the beginning of the end of US manufacturing. Along with the *only money matters* era came the post-industrial ideology that favored the rise of the technical and white-collar class of the service industry over anything else that had to do with manufacturing. Reagan's systemic deregulation of the economy encouraged manufacturers to abandon the values of shared prosperity for ones that placed the bottom line and individual success above all else. Suddenly corporation could claim that rigid Blue structures, such as regulations and labor unions, were forcing them to shut down, only to have their manufacturing operation re-appear in places like Taiwan and Mainland China.

Globalization became the catch phrase under which millions of US manufacturing jobs were sent offshore, outsourced, and streamlined. The demise of the US manufacturing sector seemed to be inevitable, as its contribution to the total economy seemed to be on a steady downward trajectory. This prediction was further reinforced by the rise of financial innovation that falsely relegated manufacturing to a lower expression of Orange values of emerging economies. As we entered the new millennium, manufacturing had become permanently stigmatized with images of environmental degradation, air pollution, and hard physical work. Since the onset of the monetarist ideology employment in the manufacturing sector dropped from over nineteen million workers in 1979 to just under twelve million in September 2012.[116]

While low-tech and modular manufacturing exited from the US to countries with lower costs, what remained was primarily the high value end of the industry. The auto and airplane manufacturers, the turbine engines and drug manufactures became the primary face of manufacturing. This is where the brightest in Orange innovation modernized and streamlined the entire manufacturing process. Advancements in production procedures through better engineering and industrial design gave us concepts like *lean manufacturing*, and *just in time manufacturing*. Innovations in the design of robotics and machines that have flexibility to produce multiple products continue to streamline the efficiency of the industry. Today, this is the face of manufacturing and it has very little resemblance to its older kin. Although manufacturing did not employ as many people as it did in past decades, it continued to add much to the GDP of the United States. A 2006 report by the Cato Institute shows that the United States remained the world's most prolific manufacturer—producing two and a half times more output than China and reporting a record year for revenues, profits, profit rates, and return on investment.[117] Up until the financial crisis, manufacturing was just another segment of the economy that was being defined to a large extent by Wall Street. During the *only money matters* era, levels of profits and the rise of stock prices substituted for concerns about levels of employment and pay within the sector. While the number of stakeholder got smaller with every passing year, stockholders were reaping the benefits of most of the advancements in innovation.

As the financial crisis exposed the weakness of the new direction of our economy, calls to reverse the fallacy of financial innovation and strengthen the manufacturing sector became increasingly louder. Jeff Immelt, CEO of GE and the head of President Obama's Economic Advisory Board, became an outspoken leader in acknowledging the dangerous predicament that financial innovation has put us in and stressed the urgent need to return to a manufacturing-based economy. In a June 2009 speech to the Detroit Economic Club, Immelt set a goal for manufacturing to reclaim 20 percent of employment by declaring:

> "The world's largest economy can no longer count on consumer spending to drive demand, nor can it rely on Wall Street financial wizardry if it wants its population to continue to enjoy a high standard of living."[118]

Whether Immelt realized it or not, the goal that he set for US manufacturing in that speech contain the elements that could realign the entire US economy on a second-tier trajectory in a few short decades. Achieving the goal of doubling the employment base of manufacturing presents a formidable task not only for Mr. Immelt and the Obama Administration but also for the entire culture. This is a long-term systemic challenge that requires structural changes to the institutions of our economy and to the many stakeholders within it. Much of our existing beliefs about what represents economic prosperity have to change. How can a segment of the economy that has become so highly automated reclaim 20 percent of employment? In light of where *life conditions* are today how can manufacturing reclaim its past glory of being the key industry that preserves national security, economic independence and a thriving exports sector?

SECOND-TIER MANUFACTURING

Mr. Immelt's 2009 declaration for having manufacturing account for 20 percent of employment should be regarded as the sector's seventh-level goal for fulfilling the criteria for The Platform for Functional Capitalism. The superordinate goal for the entire platform is for the United States to provide global economic leadership through sustainable practices. Designing the new manufacturing sector from second tier will provide the United States the unprecedented opportunity to reclaim global economic leadership for decades to come. In order for it to be sustainable it must be designed from a whole-systems approach. This is a long-term process that must take into consideration all current and future stakeholders. It is happening at a time when the decay of the current system is reaching its end point and a new paradigm is being born. The new system seeking to place manufacturing at its core must put an end to the debate that placed the values of the Industrial Age against those of the post-industrial or post-modern age and find a place for both ideologies at the same table. Each relevant value system in today's culture must be heard and allowed to contribute to the design. The new design scheme must serve the three bottom lines of a Yellow model for capitalism, which are people, profit and planet. If this is followed the outcome will be a new manufacturing sector that looks nothing like it did when it left the United States.

Contributions from a Smart-Blue System:

This is the era of the New Deal redesigned from the seventh level, where new policies have to serve *life condition* that are far more complex than they were during the Great Depression. It is not enough to create visionary Blue policies that serve Orange goals. Blue this time around has to be a *smart-blue* designed to be a catalyst that aligns existing talent, innovation, processes, systems, and value-systems on a trajectory to serve the superordinate goal. Benefits of hindsight that exposed the exploitive and unhealthy practices of past value-systems must be taken into consideration and preventative measures must be built into the design to prevent their re-occurrences. We must take into account past value systems dynamics that brought on the demise of the sector and take best practices from the innovation that was applied to what was left of it and combine it with a *smart-blue* government policy that insures it long-term sustainability.

The new advanced manufacturing has already started charting its own course and current Blue policies are not creating an environment sufficient enough for it to thrive. According to a manufacturing industry survey, more than 600,000 jobs in 2011 went unfilled due to a shortage of skills.[119] This is a confirmation that the rebirth of this fledgling field needs a different approach from the linear and outdated approaches of the past to accommodate its sustained growth. The new Blue must serve to nurture the emergence of second-tier *life conditions* through agencies like the Department of Education and the National Science Foundation. Past images of manufacturing might be stigmatized for older generations but there's a tremendous opportunity for our educators to shape a new narrative in manufacturing for anyone under the age of twenty-five who has never seen a factory.

The National Science Foundation in collaboration with the Department of Education and the National Economic Council can plant the seeds for this paradigm shift at a grassroots level that reaches every middle school and high school in the country. School science labs must have the newest innovations like 3-D printers that enable students to manufacture their own creations in the classroom by entering data and pushing a few buttons and in the process establish in their young minds the endless career possibilities these technologies can provide. This *smart-blue* collaboration wouldn't stop there. It will create a special task force that coordinates with employers on delivering a proficient and well educated labor force that meets their needs and remains ahead of the learning curve for future generations of workers.

A *smart-blue* approach would address the causes that made manufacturing leave the United States and finds a solution that serves the long-term and is insulated from the manipulations of first-tier value systems. It would work at limiting the reach of certain laws in areas of taxation, the workplace and the environment that have become antiquated and no longer serve their initial intended function. The US tax code should no longer favor companies looking to relocate operation to emerging economies. A *smart-blue* policy would offer a tax incentive for these companies to modernize and upgrade their factories while keeping jobs that might require retraining. The Office of Management and Budget must also reverse a disturbing trend in diverting resources away from Research and Development. R&D has been on a steady decline since 1965 when it accounted for just under 12 percent of government expenditure while today it accounts for less than 4 percent.[120]

In the last few decades R&D became the responsibility of healthy Orange corporations with little government input. What is needed today is not just Orange R&D that results in *esthetic change* that nudges the current system forward, but a whole systems R&D focused on *systemic change* that has to redefine an entire sector without biases to one subsector or another. Providing R&D funding to top research institutions that are on the cutting edge of science innovation and technology will insure the long-term sustainability of a thriving manufacturing sector and its perpetual self-renewal. A *smart-blue* would also address the issue of corporate taxes and work on lowering the rates to levels that give the United States the competitive edge over other countries. The regulatory structure at the EPA and the Department of Labor must be overhauled in light of advancement in new manufacturing processes and must reward businesses that achieve incremental successes toward reaching the sector's long-term goals.

The role of labor unions and OSHA should evolve and adapt to the new reality that the new worker in the new and evolved workplace is more likely to operate a computer or program a robot than he or she is to operate heavy machinery or stand at an assembly line. The Office of Science and Technology Policy, which was created to coordinate interagency activities of this nature, must be empowered by a new directive that sets incremental goals for all agencies to follow on the road to achieving the 20 percent sector employment goal. On the community level a *smart-blue* must encourage science fairs with competitions that exhibit the use of the latest innovations in manufacturing in efforts to spread this new meme. Industry recruiters should be making their case for new and prosperous career choices to students in high schools, community colleges and vocational schools. In short, the rebirth of manufacturing requires Blue to be considerably more involved than it has been in the past four decades. A Blue system designed from the seventh level will provide the needed leadership that accommodates *systemic change* by building visionary new structures that guide the new system for decades to come. With a sector as important as manufacturing, it is crucial for this new system to lay down a path that is resilient and adaptable to rapid change in order for it to accommodate the creation of millions of high paying jobs of the future.

Contributions from Healthy Orange and Muscular Green Systems

While the world was focused on making financial innovation the center of economic growth, traditional manufacturers had to adapt to changes brought on by globalization and the disruptive nature of the knowledge economy in order to survive. The information age brought profound structural changes to this sector of the economy. It has forced traditional representatives of manufacturing like the auto industry to abandon its traditional hostility to outside innovation and embrace a necessary change in direction—out with the old hierarchical formations that represented the hulking conglomerates of the past, and in with the Green values of the knowledge economy of collaboration and externalization. Part of the failure of the United States auto industry that required a government bailout could be blamed on its inability to adapt to change as quickly as its global competitors. This is an inherent danger in a traditional top-down system that believes in its ability to make innovative products while maintaining the command and control structure that tells its engineers, designers, and suppliers what to produce.

Proprietary systems of the past must give way to collaborative systems of the future. This is an emerging model that is digitizing the manufacturing processes and brining long-awaited disruptive innovation to it. The Orange model for scarcity that limits consumer choice and exploits natural resources, must give way to the muscular Green values of economies of abundance that guide the knowledge economy and invest in the continuous evolution of innovation. This must be the new model that the future of manufacturing is built on as the old model become more obsolete with every passing day. This is the coming era of digital manufacturing with a new paradigm that has to embrace the collaborative nature of an open system. Massive factories that do everything under one roof will be replaced by multiple assembly facilities located closer to their customers that put together modular parts manufactured by independent suppliers. In a manufacturing sector informed by the values of the knowledge economy these suppliers are a part of a vibrant ecosystem that shares the latest advancements in innovation while at the same time allowing healthy competition that removes all barriers from brining the best innovation to the consumer.

The full integration of the knowledge economy into second-tier manufacturing is inevitable. Because of its advanced disruptive nature manufacturing must attempt to duplicate the environment in which the knowledge economy operates. Much like the evolution of Silicon Valley, second-tier manufacturing must create an ecosystem made up of three major components that form its sustainable web of life. First the creators of this ecosystem must recognize the importance of being located close to the leading universities and research institutions that are heavily invested in second-tier Manufacturing R&D and produce innovation specific to that sector on a continuous basis.

Second, if the work at the research institute holds promise, it will naturally create an innovation pipeline made up of a cluster of small startups surrounding it, which will become its entrepreneurial extension. Collaborative thinking of a small group of genius engineers with compatible skills is what created the knowledge economy and there is no reason why this model won't work in manufacturing.

Third, if these startups are successful in creating viable products they will attract their own venture capital firms who specialize in understanding the funding needs of this emerging sector as it goes through different phases of product development. The seeds for this self-sustaining model can be sewn in different parts of the country with different manufacturing needs. Natural habitats could form around teaching hospitals and universities in Boston to provide for the needs of the biotech and pharmaceuticals industry. They could form around Detroit and the University of Michigan and help evolve the practices of the auto industry and in a number of other regions that are looking to establish themselves as leaders in alternative energy. Implementation of this model must take a long-term view, as it requires the participation of all stakeholders and the slow cultivation of a research-based ecosystem from the ground up.

RENEWABLE ENERGY AND THE FUTURE OF MANUFACTURING

If second-tier manufacturing is to heed Mr. Immelt's call for an economy that is less reliant on consumer spending then what goal does it need to set and what fundamental changes would stakeholders have to pursue? This is the *to do WHAT* part of the *Natural Design* formula that will have far reaching implications in defining how quickly the US emerges into a functioning second-tier economy. Some of the leading thoughts on what's next, not just for manufacturing but for capitalism as a whole, come from economist Jeremy Rifkin. His 2011 book *The Third Industrial Revolution: How Lateral Power will Transform Society* makes a compelling case for the WHAT part and introduces a viable goal for second-tier manufacturing. Mr. Rifkin claims culture can attain an ideal capitalist existence by what he coined as *Distributed Capitalism* by pursuing global renewable energy policies and, in the process, transform the capitalist system at its core.[121] After careful assessment of Mr. Rifkin's concept of *Distributed Capitalism* I have come to the conclusion that it represents the necessary Green values needed to transition economics to second-tier values, but it is not the same as *Distributed Innovation* or any other concepts of distributed capitalism that are parts of a Yellow platform for functional capitalism. The lessons learned from Rifkin's framework would inform a Yellow energy policy for advanced economies seeking energy independence

In patterns similar to the Green emergence of the information age that initially sought the democratization of information, Mr. Rifkin seeks the democratization of energy and in the process lays out a plan to achieve this goal. If the evolution of the information age is an example of how advanced Green ideas held the potential for disruptive second-tier economies, second-tier manufacturing should consider renewable energy as one of its primary goals. Since the energy sector accounts for a substantial part of the global economy today its transformation will not be easy. Brave second-tier leaders in government, academia, and industry must redefine the purpose of R&D in terms of evolutionary economics in a system with finite resources. Advancements in engineering, science, and information technology will be geared towards moving away from a carbon-based economy in pursuit of higher ideals that favor the long-term health of the planet and the sustainability of life, while still allowing for the attainment of reasonable profit and the overall health and happiness of humanity. The pursuit of this goal will help move the early stages of innovation in the field of renewable energy into exciting areas of exploration that will place it on a lower cost trajectory making it economically feasible for widespread use.

Infant technologies in areas like photovoltaic energy, hydrogen energy, battery storage, wind, and geothermal will all benefit from an R&D platform geared towards second-tier manufacturing with renewable energy at its core. Whether or not culture will achieve a new utopian existence through changes in energy policy is just a part of the focus of a functional seventh-level economy. It's the smaller goals it achieves along the journey and how these achievements interact with existing *life conditions* that determine how the future emerges. At every step in this process, the advancements in research will continue to lower production cost as workers needed in the manufacturing, distribution, and installation of these products will nudge the United States closer to achieving its future employment goals in this sector while safeguarding the three bottom lines of a Yellow economy.

ADDITIVE MANUFACTURING: A *DISTRIBUTED INNOVATION* MODEL

Because of high labor costs, the Orange value system outsourced many low-tech manufacturing jobs to China during the *only money matters* era. The disruptive nature of the knowledge economy is working towards reversing that trend. By digitizing and scaling the manufacturing process innovation is revolutionizing the sector to the point where the new factory worker becomes the factory owner. Additive manufacturing is also known as 3-D printing. This is a process of creating three-dimensional products from a computer-generated model. The machinery can be the size of a microwave or a small refrigerator that can fit in a garage. The early developmental stages of this technology have the potential of producing many of the low-tech consumer products that stack the shelves at a Wal-Mart or a local hardware store. Imagine a distributed manufacturing model that can be as easily operated as any of the application on a laptop today. Instead of sending a print command to generate a document one can generate actual products such as toys, rubber fasteners, or coffee mugs out of a block of raw material instead of an ink cartridge. Users with more advanced skills in creating 3-D graphics, can become their own custom designers and manufacturers who can target specialized markets.

The entrepreneurial possibilities with this technology are endless as it moves into the future. Beyond having a 3-D printer in every garage future adopters of this technology can form their own small factories with more complex printing that produces parts and components that complement the supply chain for heavy industry. The more digital the manufacturing process becomes, the lower the cost of 3-D printing. If the history of the personal computer is any indication of how disruptive technologies reorganize industries and improve lives, then digital manufacturing will bring much anticipated disruption to the way manufacturing is perceived today. 3-D machines of the future will be far less expensive and considerably more sophisticated than the ones that are currently on the market. As 3-D printing matures it will form networks of small businesses that can supply local communities with products that are less expensive and far superior to most things made in China today.

This is the distributed model of digital manufacturing and everything about its potential has second-tier properties. First and foremost it provides for lucrative manufacturing jobs that are externalized and can't be outsourced by a reductionist Orange CEO. This is an ecosystem of intelligent economies that move away from the toxic models of too big to fail to ones based on living systems where the death of one entity or organism in a natural part of the growth process. The model also has the potential of raising the entrepreneurial quotient of as many as 60 percent of the US population that does not have a college degree and has to settle for low paying service jobs. This is a model for prosperity where an individual's earnings potential is only limited by the amount of time and effort they put into it. The disruptive nature of this model has positive global implications, since it will contribute to lowering our carbon footprint through its efficient operation.

Traditional manufacturing uses machining techniques, which rely on the removal of material through methods such as cutting and drilling called subtractive processes that result in scrap material going to waist or to the recycling bins. Additive manufacturing creates products by laying down successive layers of material with no waste generated in the process. This model will also cut down on transportation and warehousing costs where efficiencies from Orange manufacturing principles such as *just in time manufacturing* are taken to the next stage through a distributed model that moves at the speed of light due to its close proximity to the products' retailer or end user. After a long journey that has lasted over three centuries, manufacturing seems to have come full circle. From the early days of the steam engine that announced the beginning of the Industrial Age to the dawn of desktop manufacturing that announces the beginning of the integral age, no other economic sector has played a more crucial role in moving humanity up the emergence ladder.

TWELVE

Defining the Sustainable Corporation from Stockholders to Stakeholders

$f(corp)$

"I believe the purpose of any business can evolve over time. This evolution of purpose is the result of the dynamic interaction of the various interdependent stakeholders with each other and with the business itself. Customers, employees, investors, suppliers, and the community all influence business purpose over time."[122]

—JOHN MACKEY
Co-founder & co-CEO
Whole Foods Market

THE CORPORATE ᵛMEME STRUGGLE

The corporation as we know it today has come to symbolize everything that has gone wrong with capitalism. Greed, power, and political influence seem to be synonymous with the values that define corporate America, especially after the financial crisis of 2008. It seems that all large corporations have aided and abetted in moving more financial resources to the hands of the wealthy and taking jobs away from the ones who need them the most: the working and middle class. While the average American continues to suffer through the worst economic downturn since the Great Depression, corporations continue to report record profits with record levels of compensations for their CEO's.[123] These disparities have provided a great source of discontent that has fueled the Occupy Wall Street movement and the hundreds of spinoffs like it all over the world. Although the protests might have died down, the movement has forever imprinted in the minds of most Americans the simple realization that 1 percent of the population controls almost half of the financial resources of this country.

Has the American dream become a nightmare as a result of how corporations manipulate resources? The promise of prosperity for the many has become the exclusive domain of the very few. Is this capitalism that has run amuck on the hands of corporations with unlimited power that have lost their sense of social responsibility and greater purpose? Has the pervasive culture of *only money matters* lulled corporate executives, CEOs, and members of their board of directors into such a numbing comfort zone that empathy for others is simply an emotion that can't exist? An informal online survey conducted in October 2011 asked participants the following question: What would you do to change corporate America, Wall Street, the government, and capitalism in general. Not surprisingly, the majority of respondents opted for imposing more regulation across the board, from restrictions on CEO pay and more taxation on corporate profits, to the enactment of laws that disallow speculative corporate financing and the discouragement of corporate monopolies.[124]

As we've seen, the dominant *life conditions* in the United States indicate that we are painfully exiting the Orange ᵛMEME center of gravity in search of higher meaning. We've also seen how corporations that were born into the Green ᵛMEME *life conditions* of the knowledge economy have adapted well in helping parts of society emerge into the Green-Yellow value systems. It seems that the more innovative the knowledge economy gets in perfecting its *distributed innovation* the more protective traditional Orange corporations become. Nowhere are these practices more evident than in the energy industry. While Europe and China focus on refining renewable energy technologies, our coal, oil, and natural gas industries focus on pursuing controversial new technologies that extend the life of the non-renewable fossil fuels industry in efforts to limit consumer choice.

Hydrofracking is the newest and, by far, the most controversial way these corporations extract energy out of the ground. The process uses pressurized water mixed with undisclosed chemicals to force underground layers of rock to break down and release oil or natural gas trapped in it. Many concerned groups including the United States National Institute of Environmental Health Sciences found this practice to pose substantial health risks. The list of dangers these practices pose to the environment is inexhaustible and ranges from ground water contamination, degradation of air quality, surface contamination caused by the migration of gases and hydraulic fracturing chemicals that are brought to the surface, on to a number of other risks caused by spills and flow back into the water supply.[125]

Public anger seems to be at its highest towards industries like the energy industry and the corporations within it that have evolved into natural monopolies which are granted privileges and exemptions from state and federal laws. Over the years the culture of these corporations evolved to focus on strengthening relationships with lawmakers in order to preserve their monopolistic hold on markets instead of embracing advancements in technological innovation. While the motto in non-monopolistic, purely market-driven industries is "innovate or die" the motto with natural monopolies seems to be "secure political influence or die." This is blatantly apparent in how the fracking industry obtained EPA exemption status in what a *New York Times* editorial called the "Halliburton Loophole" that was dubiously tucked into the 2005 energy bill at the behest of Vice President Dick Cheney.[126] This type of political influence is a confirmation that industries like energy have become a closed system when compared to industries of the knowledge economy. For Halliburton, which is heavily invested in extraction contracts, equipment, and infrastructure, it is much easier to pursue changes in environmental laws through lawmakers who are friendly to it, than it is to pursue long-term research and development into renewable energy. This seems to be a common pattern that arrests the movement of traditional Orange industries up the spiral of emergence thus making their practices toxic and increasingly archaic in the face of the knowledge economy that embraces innovation at neck breaking speed.

Can traditional corporations survive these changes in *life conditions* where the majority of the population has less than a favorable image of the values these entities project? While political influence seems to be the standard operating procedure for corporations in industries like energy, finance and healthcare, not all traditional Orange corporations fall into the same ᵛMemetic profile as the ones that form these natural monopolies. Many businesses, large and small, are best run by Orange values, and it would be a disservice for society if they were run from lower or higher first-tier systems. As long as it is the healthy version of the ᵛMEME guiding the mission of that corporation and operating in an open system, it is more likely to fall into the *natural design* scheme that informs its business model. A corporation informed by Yellow systemic values seeks to employ the most proficient ᵛMEME, whether in the selection of employees, suppliers, partners or independent contractors who do the job based on the value systems of the stakeholders that corporation serves. The urgency for any corporation in any industry is to embrace open systems that place people, profit, and planet on equal footing in their pursuit of their corporate mission. Based on the trajectory of technological advancements that are a result of the intersection of information, knowledge and technology, it is just a matter of time that creative destruction will make the corporate model of many closed systems obsolete.

THE CURRENT FUNCTIONAL MISALIGNMENT

The pursuit of productive output is the driving force behind capitalism, but somewhere along the line large corporations abandoned their functional interests as their primary purpose and aligned themselves with a new goal of maximizing shareholder value. The perfect ᵛMemetic storm that caused the financial crisis was an anomaly that exposed speculative and short-term thinking that attempted to re-align the natural function of many corporations with the fallacy of notional wealth. During the *only money matters* era the pursuit of long-term investment in research and development gave way to marketing strategies that repackaged the same products with the primary objective of meeting Wall Street analysts' expectations. Product innovation gave way to market capitalization. Satisfaction with work gave way to satisfaction with pay. CEOs with technical and industry knowledge gave way to ones with charisma and financial knowledge who knew exactly what capital markets wanted in order to drive up the price of their company's stock.

As this realignment of values continued, quarterly financial results became the primary drivers of corporate goals. Stock options and pay packages lured financially savvy CEOs from one company to the next. Creative accounting schemes such as booking future revenues for the current accounting period based on projections and a number of other financial innovations refocused corporations away from long-term sustainable practices to the all-important quarterly financial results. CEOs with barely a few years at the helm began to retire after engineering astronomical rises of share values and cashing in their stock options worth millions. It seemed that in less than a decade American ingenuity which is an expression of a healthy Orange ᵛMEME in an open system, gave way to an unhealthy and toxic expression that strategically pursued money and very little else. It was just a matter of time that this realignment proved to be greatly misguided. In the aftermath of the financial crisis, many investors are angry at the losses they incurred and continue to question the wisdom of many CEOs.

Today many traditional Orange-run corporations find themselves having to relinquish the short-lived values of financial engineering and restructure their organizations in order to re-align with their functional purpose. Four years after the financial crisis the global economy is still experiencing an economic contraction that must rein in the extravagances of the *only money matters* era. During these sobering times, many old Orange corporations, especially commercial and investment banks, will go through prolonged periods of adjustment as they realign with their natural functions. This is a painful systemic process that must deal with the consequences of the bursting of asset bubbles of all types. It requires time and patience and considerable reflection on the ᵛMemetic patterns of behavior that steered corporate leadership to abandon their long-term virtues for unsustainable, get rich quick schemes.

To get an idea of how costly this misalignment could be, one only needs to examine another prominent economy that has experienced a systemic bursting of bubbles of all types. In the 1980s Japan was on a trajectory to become the leading economic power in the world as its government and its banks were doing everything under their discretion to accommodate that goal. Japan's realignment to the *only money matters meme* took up all of the 1980's decade. As its banks' valuations of assets decoupled from economic reality and the house of cards came crashing down, it was left with what is known as a "zombie economy" that has lasted well over two decades.[127] As the innovation of the knowledge economy moves forward at lightning speed, the Japanese economy finds itself unable to catch up as it continues to dig itself out from under the misguided policies of the 1980s. Consumer electronics that made the Japanese economy superior in the late 20th century might have been its last claim to functionally aligned economic leadership as it continues to struggles with structural reorganization of its institutions. The damage that bubble economies leave behind is prolonged and systemic, and there will be no escaping these effects in the United States.

However, unlike Japan, there are two major factors in the US economy that, out of necessity, will speed the functional realignment of old Orange practices. The first factor is the presence of an angry American electorate that is opposed to any additional taxpayer bailouts and has very little trust in Wall Street, which will force the failure and the subsequent unwinding of insolvent entities. The second and more optimistic factor that holds the promise to move culture up the ladder of human cultural emergence, is the innovative nature of the knowledge economy that continues to create technologies that are making old Orange practices obsolete. As the virtues of the knowledge economy spread the memes of their corporate culture to the rest of the economy, a return to functional areas of competencies will again become the guiding principle of capitalism to force old Orange practices back into healthy open systems out of necessity and the need to survive.

THE *FUNCTIONAL* SEVENTH-LEVEL CEO

The knowledge economy didn't just bring creative destruction to the way corporations do business; it is forcing society to rethink the very nature of business leadership under the capitalist model. In studying the history of corporations and their intended functions, one quickly comes to the realization that their role as an investment vehicle for the common good has not always served their intended purpose. Criticism of the legal, social, and management structures of corporations goes back hundreds of years to the days of the British East India Company, which has served as the historic example of critics for its exploitations and resource manipulation and for placing enormous wealth in the hands of the merchant class.

The father of capitalism himself, Adam Smith, warned in *The Wealth of Nations* that when the actual production process required to obtain capital is moved from the hands of the owners and into the hands of management, the latter will inevitably begin to neglect the interests of the former, creating dysfunction within the company.[128] The corporation has gone through many forms of existence since the days of Adam Smith, but his moral philosophy towards capital production and the need to have the active involvement of the owners in management and leadership positions, still holds true today. What would Thomas Edison think of how General Electric is being run today? If current *life conditions* informed his genius would he approve of GE's diversification into non-scientific and non-manufacturing areas like finance and insurance, or would he advocate the functional pursuits of his company's primary areas of competencies?

If Edison's values were running GE today, would the technologies for solar energy and wind turbines have the United States closer to energy independence and a green energy economy, and would this form of leadership at a systemic level have placed the United States at the global forefront in defining a sustainable global economy? It is futile to speculate on how corporations would have emerged differently had they continued to be guided by the genius of their founders. Many well-established companies even with those visionary founders at the helm have struggled and disappeared and have become the subject of many leadership case studies as they fade into history. But many others have succeeded spectacularly and in the process changed corporate leadership at its core.

The obvious question to ask from a values-systems perspective is: Do successful founder CEOs naturally exhibit systemic seventh-level thinking, and can their ^VMemetic profiles provide some answers in designing functional corporate leadership? The unique management styles of these leaders have not only helped their companies weather economic cycles; they are providing for a new level of consciousness in business practices that have all the markings of systemic sustainability. Are corporations like Apple, Starbucks, and Whole Foods guided by Yellow seventh-level visionaries who see their businesses operations within an ecosystem of a natural habitat of the seventh level in a marketplace predominated by fifth-level system values? Was Howard Schulz's action in firing Starbucks' CEO Jim Donald in 2007 justified?

A value-systems examination of Starbucks at the time provides a good example of how the brightest fifth-level Orange thinking can become reductionist in its pursuit of higher returns. A few years prior to the firing of Donald, Starbucks had embarked on its largest expansion, the brightest in Orange metrics targeting efficiency and cost-cutting that should have pleased Wall Street. Instead the strategy had the effect of diminishing the appeal of Starbucks' experience as a coffee house, and the company was forced to close hundreds of underperforming stores. As Chairman, Schulz took full responsibility for the temporary misalignment in values and resumed the CEO position while righting the ship back to what he called its core values.[129] The misalignment in this case was in placing the highest priority on fifth-level system goals with little regard to the intrinsic values that made the Starbucks experience so unique.

In a July 2010 Interview published in the *Harvard Business Review*, Schulz hinted at the realignment of values that are putting his company on an open Yellow functional path. First he spoke of how the leadership had to stand up in front of the entire company and confess their failure to 180,000 employees And the second came at what Schultz considers a watershed moment for the company when he took 10,000 store managers to post-Katrina New Orleans for a character-and-values boot camp where they logged more than 54,000 volunteer hours, and invested more than $1 million in repair projects in the ravaged city. "If we hadn't had New Orleans, we wouldn't have turned things around. It was real, it was truthful, and it was about leadership. . . . We reinvested in our people, we reinvested in innovation, and we reinvested in the values of the company."[130] Since Schulz's comeback as CEO, Starbucks practices have become more aligned with Yellow sustainability practices than they ever were. Starting at home with the Create jobs for USA program, which supports agencies that provide financing to underserved community businesses and to global outreach programs that have raised millions of dollars for access to clean water in developing countries and creating sustainable ecosystems that support farmers throughout the globe who grow their coffees and teas.[131]

What is noteworthy about Starbucks' realignment and the deepening of commitment to its values is that its customers and shareholders alike revere its new direction. Conscious investors who believe in Starbucks' commitment to its founder's principles were generously rewarded by having their share prices increase more the five times in the four short years since Schulz was reinstated as CEO. By making Starbucks an open system in a habitat that supports all the stakeholders, he raised the consciousness levels of the stockholders and made them all wealthier participants in global sustainability practices that embrace people, profit and planet. A question remains: Would a non-founder CEO who doesn't necessarily view his position as his life-long endeavor and the sole pursuit of his future legacy have done the same thing?

Many other founder CEOs exhibit leadership qualities that are not necessarily as predictable and easily understood by the casual observer. The late Steve Jobs provides for a great example of visionary leadership that transcends the prescribed Orange metrics of the most successful non-founder CEO. In 2009 *Fortune Magazine* named him CEO of the decade for radically and lucratively transforming four industries: music, movies, mobile telephones and his original industry, computing.[132] Since 2009 Apple has played a major role in transforming digital publishing and tablet computing. Although he was a reclusive man, Jobs in his trademark black turtleneck and blue jeans was known the world over for the elegance he put into Apple's products. His biographer Walter Isaacson describes his most salient quality as his intensity and ability to focus his attention like a laser in his drive towards perfection.[133] The functional alignment in Jobs' case was to provide beauty and simplicity of use in everything he created and all other values within Apple, its numerous partners and suppliers had to align to his vision.

Through many years of trials and errors including an earlier ouster from the company he founded, Jobs refined his long-term vision and honed in his craft. The result was the complete transformation of a company from one that was just another maker of personal computers to one that became the world leader in innovation and in the process it profoundly transformed several other industries. The financial rewards for following a founder's vision in Apple's case is even more compelling than that of Starbucks as evidenced by the long lines at an Apple store every time a new product is released and the astronomical rise in value of Apple's shares that have made it one of the most valued corporations in the world.

To understand founding CEOs' visions and the different functional alignments they have compared to non-founder CEOs is to begin to understand how Yellow systemic thinking in an organization works. Functionality differs greatly from one industry to the next, but what makes it a tool of seventh-level values is its drive to go beyond the artificial limits and pressures imposed by the predominant Orange *life conditions* of Wall Street and an investment community that expects short term results. A 2007 research study by Rüdiger Fahlenbrach of the Department of Finance of the Fisher College of Business at Ohio State University determined that founder-CEO firms differ systematically from successor-CEO firms with respect to firm valuation, investment behavior, and stock market performance.[134] It also found that because these founder-CEOs consider their firm as their life's achievement, they have an intrinsic motivation and a long-term approach that encourages them to pursue an optimal shareholder-value maximizing strategy instead of concentrating on short-term actions. They also have a different attitude towards risk and make more focused mergers and acquisitions.

This is a functional ethic that was abandoned during the *only money matters* era when mergers and acquisitions were based mostly on financial reasons instead of a functional alignment that synergized companies with complementary skills, shared values, and common goals. Fahlenbrach also found that these CEO's have shaped their organizations from inception, and thus the impact of differences in managerial characteristics on corporate behavior and performance is particularity strong. The findings point to consistently higher rates of return of founder-CEO run companies over those that were run by non-founder CEO regardless of industry. One of the hallmarks of healthy Orange practices that align long-term corporate functionality is investment in research and development and in future production capacity. Fahlenbrach's research confirmed that founder CEOs spend up to 22 percent more on R&D and up to 38 percent more on capital expenditures. [135] This is an ethic that contradicts the trends of recent CEO behavior that seems to concern itself with immediate liquidity and daily fluctuations of their stock price than long-term strategic planning that invests in employees and innovative products.

In designing Yellow functionality for corporate leadership one can tap into the rich reservoir of knowledge about the character ethic of these successful founder CEOs and discover the different roads they have taken in arriving at values that inform their long-term decision-making. Founder CEOs are known to be eccentric and unorthodox in their approaches, which adds to the intrigue of a world centered in the often reductionist values of the Orange fifth-level system. Many might argue that the so-called sustainability practices are nothing more than the healthy expression of the Orange system that insures long-term profitability. For Yellow, a value system that is interested in the functional flow of all other value systems, healthy Orange is a part of that design scheme. It matters little that the practices might not be accepted by other systems, but once long-term sustainability of a corporation becomes its guiding force it naturally seeks to make its practices aligned with a Yellow functional trajectory in the long run.

The theory of Spiral Dynamics describes a seventh-level CEO as a functionalist who believes in the long run of time rather than his or her own life and establishes his or her core motivational and evaluative systems from that perspective thus becoming relatively immune to external pressures or judgment.[136] In today's corporate culture, especially in the financial services industry, concern for continuity of life on the planet and the natural habitat might sound alien to many corporate leaders. What the fifth-level system leadership often fails to see is that continuity of corporate life on the planet is directly related to and highly intertwined with our ability to sustain future generations on a planet with finite resources. Beck often describes a seventh-level leader as one who possesses contextual authority and runs the gamut of being gentle or ruthless, a conformist or non-conformist based on the circumstances, and one who replaces anything artificial or contrived with spontaneity, simplicity and ethics that make sense. These characteristics seem to describe Yellow leadership in both the knowledge economy and in a new emerging consciousness in old industries that still engage in the trade of physical goods. While knowledge economy firms by their functional nature are bringing an end to many entrenched old Orange practices, leaders in the retail industry that can't be digitized who fit Beck's description of seventh-level leadership are setting a new standard of practice that old Orange retailers are scrambling to adopt.

THE EVOLUTION OF OWNERSHIP

Since the utopian days of Adam Smith's moral philosophy, the management of enterprise has evolved into a science reflecting greater levels of complexity and varying schools of thought on who or what represents the most valuable assets of a business. Nowhere has this debate been livelier than on the issue that defines the term "ownership" and what it means to the corporate bottom line and the long-term sustainability of a corporate business model. Studying the history of memenomic cycles, one can see that when *life conditions* were predominated by the third level Red system, ownership meant complete control by the owners. This was the era of the Gilded Age and the robber barons before the system collapsed during the Great Depression from the toxicity of its own values. During this period the owner of a given enterprise had full control over how labor and capital were utilized. Even if a corporation was publically held, the sense of possession of the enterprise was limited to a small circle of family members and a few trusted associates who strictly upheld the values of the owners. Workers were viewed as nothing more than units of production with no sense of possession or access to ownership.

FDR's New Deal policies and the values of the *patriotic prosperity meme* attempted to redefine ownership by introducing a series of labor protection laws and plugging management and labor on the same motherboard of patriotism that sought to win wars and establish the middle class for what it is today. During this era the prominence of labor unions redefined what became known in the annals of management science as the psychology of possession—not necessarily through actual possession of property and stock, but through psychological ownership of bargaining rights for better wages and work conditions. As this memenomic cycle came to an end under the weight of its values, ownership was again redefined during the early stages of the post-industrial era.

The prominence of the technical class and the white color worker ushered in a new era of both psychological possession and physical possession of ownership in a corporation. Employee stock options, 401Ks, and defined benefit plans became the preferred ways to attract and keep talent in a corporation. Distribution of ownership in the form of financial rewards became the hallmark of the *only money matters* era. As this meme spread to systemic levels, ownership became more associated with financial gains and less with the functional alignment with the products and services a corporation produced. As the model for financial innovation entered the decay stage in 2008, the values of the knowledge economy started to come into full view. These values that initially sought to democratize access to information are laying the ground for a new and functional form of ownership. Suddenly the engineers, who were creating the foundation that sought to spread the values of the information age, were the ones being financially rewarded for doing what they do best.

As this functional leadership continues to emerge and the knowledge economy continues to differentiate its bits and bytes into new and informed business models that reflect the total needs of an evolving culture, it will continue to revolutionize the very nature of how ownership is viewed. This is the integration of all types of possession that serve as a self-renewing and sustainable business model. This is the coming of age of management science where the integration of physical, psychological, and functional ownership becomes the catalyst for a new and efficient style of execution that propels the global economy into the systemic and functional values of the seventh-level system.

This is *natural design* that first seeks to identify the needs of *life conditions* through the prism of value-systems that penetrates through the deepest layers in order to understand the motivation of stakeholders and plugs them on a motherboard that serves a new superordinate goal. That goal is to provide global leadership through sustainable practices. This type of functional leadership is at the heart of the seventh-level corporation that makes it radically different than that of any model before it, in that it provides for decentralization of decision-making based on optimization of function. The sustained emergence of this model has the potential to redirect corporate leadership away from the sole pursuit of profit to a distributed Founder-CEO ethic that naturally motivates every stakeholder to give him or her a fully integrated sentiment of ownership in the pursuit of a new and sustainable superordinate goal.

GOOGLE'S SYSTEMIC DISRUPTION

In today's economic environment, companies like Google that are on the cutting edge of innovation provide a glimpse of what the future of corporate functionality might look like as the knowledge economy matures into a full and purposeful expression of the seventh-level system. Not only is this company leading new innovation into what's next in its own industry. It uses the values that made it successful to fund innovative start-up ventures that have the potential of making many industries in the closed Orange system obsolete. Google was born out of its cofounder Larry Page's original idea for his PhD thesis about wanting to quantify the underlying mathematical characteristics of the World Wide Web.[137] In doing what many in this industry call the reverse engineering of the Internet, the founders of Google, Larry Page and Sergey Brin, have placed the knowledge economy on the right path to functional second-tier practices. Within a few years of the company's founding, algorithms behind obscure innovations like PageRank and AdWords began to quietly revolutionize the advertising industry.

Googlenomics, a term coined by writer Steven Levy in his book *In the Plex: How Google Thinks, Works and Shapes Our Lives*, is becoming the model that is sending waves of disruptive innovation throughout the online advertising world. Google's business model has become a source of great angst for executives on Madison Avenue and it won't be long before similar models begin to force corporate boardrooms in traditional Orange corporations to reexamine the very basis on which business gets done. Levy summarizes the disruptive paradox that is Google's business model this way:

> What could be more baffling than a capitalist corporation that gives away its best services, doesn't set the prices for the ads that support it, and turns away customers because their ads don't measure up to its complex formulas? Google's success is not the result of inspired craziness but of an early recognition that the Internet rewards fanatical focus on scale, speed, data analysis, and customer satisfaction. A bit of auction theory doesn't hurt, either.[138]

So what aspects of Google's successful software development, management, and business model are indicative of seventh-level system intelligence? I asked that very question to my colleague Kevin Kells at the Center for Human Emergence, who holds a PhD in Electrical Engineering and is an insider to the Silicon Valley culture. He offered an explanation to the idea of reverse engineering of the Internet in more layman terms. "Google did something that no other search engine was able to do before. It crowd-sourced the self-quantification of the World Wide Web. In essence, it asked each entity the simple question: Hey, who are you? And the answer was: What you are is based on what all the other entities think of you, some stronger than others.

For someone who's thoroughly familiar with the theory of Spiral Dynamics and the work of Don Beck, Kells believes that Google's culture, execution, and management style evidence aspects of the seventh-level Yellow system. Kells has been in this industry for two decades and has seen the knowledge economy emerge up the spiral after IBM's Blue stage all the way through the Greening of companies like Motorola, where your manager was your friend. According to Kells, what Google took into its innovation platform is a management style that takes best practices from the Blue stage, the Orange stage, and the Green stage. It is the weaving of best practices from the different management value systems that make its economic model successful: "Give away useful features for free, then charge fees for advanced business features."

In Google's skillful handling of the constant—and sometimes self-contradictive—flux of Blue (accounting, rules of the engineering and design road, non-disclosure agreements, management hierarchy), Orange (marketing, creative individual impulses, project management, strategic decision making), and Green (respect of freedom to speak, and needs of its designers, engineers, management, and creative impulses), Kells acknowledges seeing signs of seventh-level Yellow system thinking. The essence of second-tier Natural Design is reflected in Google's marginal advantage on an internet-fueled massive scale that simultaneously manages all three value systems, Blue, Orange and Green, in a functional flow towards a superordinate goal, respecting each, embracing the healthy aspects of each and aligning each towards company goals, project goals, and Google's overarching social goal of not being evil.

Google's workplace is a fast track for what Kells calls an *innovation pipeline* where myriad ideas are given a low-pressure chance to compete with each other and iterate themselves into something better, sometimes getting beaten out by other incremental innovations. This is a radical version of research and development that gets fed by a rich diet of ideas for innovation that battle each other in a low-key way in Google's internal market first in order to move up to the next stage of evolution, "public release as beta." By releasing a product early in the development stage and repeating the process often, Google leverages "the crowd" for feedback and working out the bugs within a certain product. This release often philosophy optimizes the features of the product more quickly and adapts more precisely to market demands. Google understands the *innovation pipeline principle* of the information age in a superior way. This is the knowledge economy's equivalence of a new product development process of the industrial age. Much of the Blue and Orange support structures that are part and parcel of the traditional process are implemented through software supported team processes, freeing human creativity towards innovation. By recognizing and encouraging this pipeline and optimizing its software-supported implementation, Google is like an industrial plant made up of powerful servers, programmers, engineers, and designers who constantly and at near zero cost experiment with any product and adapt the virtual production process as needed.

Not only is Google's Orange superior to traditional Orange when it comes to research and development, its Green values are far more muscular than any previous expressions in companies within the knowledge economy. With a corporate campus that replicates the Green *life conditions* of a university the work environment becomes a very conducive place for learning, creativity and sharing of new ideas. Management at Google is able to create a superior work environment by understanding how the brains of engineers and designers function. What evolved naturally was the formation of small groups with similar interests, motivations, and complementary talents that work on certain projects or parts of a project and see it to its successful conclusion. This was a model that was far superior to previous Green values at the workplace that is naturally functional for that particular work environment. Another insight into Google's muscular Green values in a work environment is how their culture views "down time." Giving the brain a rest during the workday is looked upon as one of the most productive times that reignite creativity.

This is reflected naturally in a management philosophy that believes in allowing engineers and designers one day out of the workweek to work on whatever projects they want. These management tools that are the result of what emerges naturally in a collaborative work environment become a catalyst that fuels creativity that continuously feeds the new knowledge-economy model. This is what moves this economy from the earlier expression of Orange-Green values that produced occasional innovation that made companies disappear when better innovation came along to one that is far more resilient. Imagine a continuous innovation incubator that is empowered by an army of the brightest engineers and designers that constantly introduce products to the marketplace without worrying about cannibalizing their own success.

When it comes to how Google views growth, Kells has a unique view on its approach. When Orange corporations pursue a growth strategy they do it mostly through the acquisition of other corporations. According to Kells, Google takes that Orange model to the next stage by adding a natural and systemic approach to its acquisition model where all the stakeholders are winners in the long term. In part, this is a return to healthy Orange practices that promote complementary acquisitions specific to the industry in which a corporation operates in order to increase market share. However, when the targets for acquisition are mostly start-ups, as in the case of Google, the focus shifts away from immediate market share to long-term capacity to produce products.

Kells points out that software startups sometimes work with the goal of being acquired by larger companies like Google after developing an initial product and increasing what he calls their *brain bank* value. When acquiring smaller software companies, Google doesn't just look at that company's product. It studies the history and the future trajectory of the individual talent behind the making of the product. Then, as an additional evaluative step, it studies the collective team and team intelligence—both human-product and human-human—behind a product before it decides which innovations and companies to acquire. Google views this process as a natural mechanism in recruiting exceptional talent in order to remain on the cutting edge of changes in *life conditions* within the knowledge economy. The biggest asset in the knowledge economy is the present and future value of that brain bank within every venture, large and small.

The culture that makes up Google's operating brain bank provides these viable startups with work conditions they simply cannot recreate on their own. The pools of talent, knowledge, relationships, experience, and the unique management structure are so attractive to these startups that they naturally want to be absorbed into this constantly evolving and growing system. By pursuing natural next steps to retain its competitive edge Google is creating value for all of its stakeholders. This model for business acquisitions is purely functional as it aligns the talents of the brightest engineers and designers with a proven business model while constantly challenging their creativity and knowhow. Unlike the Orange model of the millennial decade when the primary pursuit of mergers and acquisitions was to increase short-term stockholder value, this is a functionally sustainable long-term model that grows stakeholder value by increasing the size of the brain bank. This is the catalyst that transforms both the workplace and the monetization of talent of the knowledge economy into an open system in perpetuity. Only time will tell if this model will be replicated or replaced by one that better optimizes the talents of the genius class in a capitalist culture. Regardless of how the future of the knowledge economy changes, Google has provided a template for disruptive innovation in the pursuit of growth and the creation of exceptional work environments that set the standards for adopting functional values in corporate practices.

So, how do second-tier values in a workplace like Google affect culture at a systemic level? I pondered the value-systems meaning of what my colleague said about Google's self-quantification of the web. What kept coming to me is that in itself is the seventh-level functionality that the world is craving. The users of the Internet continually reporting back to Google about who they are is one of the widest models of *life conditions* informing a search engine about themselves, and it's being delivered in the most efficient way without the results ever being manipulated by human input. In designing its search engine, Google believed that human beings, not the number of random hits, is the best judge of what a good web page is. In asking the question of who are you, they knew precisely how to ask it and just as importantly how to receive the answer. Far more weight in searching for the response is placed on the number of other websites linking to a particular webpage than on the subjective inclusion of a particular webpage based on the number of hits it randomly received.

In other words, if I want to know who you are, I would ask you and a number of other people who can be completely objective about whom they think of you are. Then in shaping the response I would place far more weight on the latter. This is the difference between an employer believing everything a potential candidate for a job says about his or her experience and the actual verification of that candidate's job history. The validity of the decision on the fate of the applicant becomes directly related to the degree of unbiased transparency received from the public domain and not just simply what the candidate tells the employer, making the decision process far more scientific and objective. Often the self interest of the entity seeking the data clouds the purity of the research by steering the respondent in the way questions are phrased and how the responses are tabulated in order to serve the needs of the entity. Full transparency without these biases would represent an accurate reflection of the entire spectrum of *life conditions,* providing for the best possible data that informs a systemic decision maker.

To add further clarity to this point as a Second Tier concept of functionality, here is a distinction that I often hear Beck use in his lectures. When speaking to global change agents about brining real change to the world he restates a famous Gandhi quote. Beck questions Gandhi's declaration to *be the change you want to see in the world*, which is subjective first tier, most likely Green that doesn't recognize the hierarchy of value-systems. Because of its First Tier subjectivity Beck asks what if that's not the change the world needs. (Imagine an Al-Qaeda-like Red organization becoming the change it wants to see in the world). He then rephrases the statement in simple, functional, Second Tier, Yellow terms as follows: *Do the change that the world needs done*. The rephrasing that transcends the subjective self-interest of First Tier values through the unbiased observation of what needs to be done is a functional approach that has the health of the entire system in mind. Transparency when providing data to advertisers is what's at the heart of Google's business model. This is how Google's revenue generating algorithms work. They removed their biases from data provided to the advertiser, giving full transparency on what the web reports on where people shop, and in the process became the leading generator of web-based ad revenue: a disruptive model that became a platform that's making a venerated industry scramble to save an old model from becoming obsolete.

Google has extended its disruptive practices beyond the world of advertising. Many years after its own initial public offering its IPO model still offers the potential to bring disruptive innovation and far more efficiency to capital markets. By using what is known as a Dutch auction Google introduced mathematical algorithms to set a fair price for its IPO. A typical IPO for a web-based venture is similar to the recent Facebook IPO. For months, investment bankers Like Goldman Sachs create hype with institutional investors about the potential of the stock. They still use the same metrics and values that result in the change they want to see instead of the change the investment world needs done. Google stock, on the other hand, was offered to the investment community at large. With a few restrictions, private investors had as much access to Google stock as did investment bankers. The result was a share price determined by the full transparency of the marketplace with little biased manipulation by investment bankers typical of most IPO's.

Since its initial public offering Google stock has gone up more than 900 percent and has a following of not just investors, but stakeholders who believe in the company's future, while Facebook's share price have fallen by more than 45 percent since its IPO in May 2012 leaving many disappointed investors behind.[139] If one is to look at the distribution of wealth in these two models, The Google IPO has made millionaires and billionaires out of anyone who invested in the stock with a nominal initial fee paid to investment bankers. The overvalued Facebook IPO on the other hand has taken tens of millions of dollars out of the pockets of investors while investment bankers still earned their brokerage fees as a percentage of the much higher initial stock price offering.

Google is creating disruption with everything it touches, and its investment arm, Google Ventures, holds great potential in redefining many entrenched old Orange industries that were discussed earlier in this chapter. Google's investment arm represents the early stages of evolution of venture capital into second-tier capital markets. Before the launching of this model, if an entrepreneur wanted to raise capital for business expansion there were two general places to do so, based on the nature of the business. If the venture dealt with bits and bytes, Silicon Valley was the place to go. If it were anything else Wall Street and private equity was the destination. It seemed that these two realms were worlds apart; the latter representing traditional Orange ways for business expansion, while the former represented the knowledge economy that moves at the speed of light and is powered by the wealth and knowhow of the genius class.

Through its investment arm, Google has extended its unique business model that's a cross between a university and a corporation to every entrepreneur who believes in the disruptive nature that's at the heart of Google's mission. When visiting the home page of Google Ventures the visitor is welcomed with the words "A radically different kind of venture fund that invests $100's of millions each year in entrepreneurs with a healthy disregard for the impossible."[140] Google doesn't seem to be making such a statement just to be critical of current practices of venture capitalists; it backs up an entrepreneur's disregard for the impossible by providing a complete infrastructure of support. Design and engineering know-how along with staffing and marketing knowledge that made Google so resilient become a part of the venture's business model going forward. This fully integrated approach to venture capital has resulted in the creation and expansion of over a hundred companies that are, like Google, on the cutting edge of innovation in industries like energy, life sciences, mobile applications and gaming.[141]

The question remains: Is this model for funding resilient enough or large enough to create systemic disruption on a large scale? One thing it has created for sure is a model that Wall Street and VC markets are incapable of providing for startups and that is full access to Google's constantly evolving brain bank—from engineering to marketing—which provides for a fully integrated second-tier approach to how ventures of the future will be launched.

THE DIFFERENT WHOLE-SYSTEMS APPROACH OF WHOLE FOODS

Seventh-level corporations today seem to be divided into two distinct types, the digital and the non-digital. Unlike the handful of corporations that were born into the Green *life conditions* of the knowledge economy, the success of Whole Foods Market stands as a testament to how functional values of the seventh-level system can make a business model thrive in a industry dominated by old Orange practices. This is one industry that is in no danger of being digitized or rendered obsolete anytime soon. As a result, it sees little need to evolve its management practices in order compete. In contrast with the disruptive nature of the knowledge economy that forces imbedded industries to redefine themselves in order to survive, Whole Foods sets new standards of practice for the rest of its industry to follow.

While Google represents the disruptive innovation of the genius class in the seventh-level system, Whole Foods represents the conscious evolution of an industry as old as modern humanity itself. This is a corporation that represents an ethic that is reflective of a future place in time where second-tier values dominate the economic landscape. Unlike the model for the workplace in the knowledge economy that requires high proficiency in technical skills and advanced degrees in math and engineering, Whole Foods' model engages the widest distributed network of anyone who shares its core values or is willing to prescribe to them. From local growers, producers, suppliers, customers, and employees, and all the way to its stockholders, this is a distributed model that meets more of the needs of local *life conditions* than any other Yellow model that has emerged so far.

Whole Foods management style tips the organizational chart upside down in places where needed. It adopts best practices from traditional Blue-Orange grocers, combines them with Green values of local farmer's cooperative, and injects them with a set of principles that are redefining the future of prosperity, and to a larger extent, the virtues of capitalism itself. Its management structure is unlike any other in its industry in that it believes in radical decentralization where small teams are responsible for most key operational decisions. On the surface this looks like a peer-based Green model that works peculiarly well at all levels and in every unit of operation from front-line recruitment all the way to national headquarters.

Take the example of new hires that are assigned to a team for a period of four weeks. After the trial period is over, team members vote on the future of the recruit who must receive a two-thirds majority vote in order to stay on full time. This practice is uncommon not only in the grocery business but in the most evolved forms of Orange management practices. Looking past the Green recruitment process, the small team unit becomes a pivotal model that represents the *distributed innovation* that is at the heart of Whole Foods' success. Once these teams who represent the procurement process for each store are empowered by a sense of ownership and the freedom to be creative, they become the representatives of a distributed Yellow system with the most accurate reflection of the needs of their local customers. Consider the choice of which groceries go on the shelf. In the case of a traditional grocer that decision is made somewhere within the corporate hierarchy with little or no input from front line employees. At Whole Foods, it's left up to team members, who are most in touch with what appeals to the local customer, and stocking decisions don't have to go beyond consultation with the local store manager.

Store and regional managers are empowered through a natural combination of autonomy and structure. The company divides the United States into a dozen unique and decentralized regions that balance Blue accountability and Orange efficiency with the desire to satisfy the uniqueness of regional tastes. There are regional oddities: Venice, California, has a kombucha bar; Portland, Maine, is the only store that carries live lobster; in Dallas, you can hit "The Spa by Whole Foods Market" while a team member shops for you.[142] If the mission of a grocer is to provide an exceptional customer experience then what better way to meet those needs than having employees in direct contact with that customer making the decision to satisfy the unique shopping desires of the local population and having regional and local suppliers align with the fulfillment of those desires. Once these local growers subscribe to Whole Foods' values in using natural and organic methods in their production processes they become a sustainable microcosm of thousands similar suppliers who make up the unique and diverse web that defines a big part of the systemic functionality of Whole Foods' philosophy.

Green values alone at the workplace don't make much for a business model, but once endowed with a sense of ownership and accountability to the bottom line they become a steppingstone into second-tier values. The successful team model at Whole Foods does not come without accountability. Although in-store teams have a significant degree of discretion over staffing, pricing, and product selection, they are also held accountable for the profitability of their various departments. Teams are assessed against monthly profitability targets, and their performance is visible across the entire company. When they meet those goals, team members receive a bonus in their next paycheck.[143] This is a model that combines a healthy muscular form of Green with Blue-Orange metrics within a group dynamic that is empowered with decision-making and the ability to compete with hundreds of peer groups within the system that has a superordinate goal of providing exceptional customer experience.

Many management practices claim to place happiness of customers and employees above all else; however, very few go the extra mile to empower their front-line employees with critical decision making that reinforces that claim to make it a functional part of the management model. That process in turn plays a crucial role in picking the choice of which growers, producers, and suppliers to partner with making it a reflection of the values of the local community. Once combined with the Orange metrics of efficiency, Blue sense of accountability, and the need to make a profit, it transforms Whole Foods' management style to a perpetual open system that is functionally decentralized and most in touch with the needs of its stakeholders.

Much of Whole Foods' values are a reflection of the business philosophy of its cofounder and current co-CEO John Mackey. When it comes to the integration of the three forms of ownership that determine the character ethic of a Founder-CEO, Mackey embodies all three. In a 2010 interview with *The New Yorker* magazine he establishes the possession part of ownership as he views his company as his child and himself as a father to his fifty-four thousand employees.[144] The well being of the company and its employees cannot easily be separated from Mackey's personal mission in life. Part of Mackey's functional ownership of the Fouder-CEO ethic is discussed in the preceding section on the management style at Whole Foods, but what drives that functionality lies within the philosophical leanings of the man himself. Mackey believes that business can pursue profits and a higher purpose simultaneously. He sets out to define how the two can coexist through what he calls Whole Foods' "core values" that aim at the fair treatment of all stakeholders. In a sixteen-page manifesto, entitled *Conscious Capitalism: Creating a New Paradigm for Business*, Mackey defines a new frontier for capitalism where business consciousness takes a huge leap forward and transcends the confines of its current values.

In an observation common to most second-tier leaders who are interested in the continuity of life beyond their own, he identifies a far bigger set of stakeholders, which he claims are irrevocably interdependent and can help capitalism move into a second-tier expression. The first group of stakeholders is made up of four: customers, employees, investors, and suppliers. Most reputable Orange companies now include all four as a part of defining the reach of their corporate social responsibilities. The other three that form the second group are the health and well being of the population, the food system and the planet.[145] In a narrative that reinforces the interdependence of these stakeholders, Mackey introduces a transformative model that has far-reaching cultural implications, while at the same time attempting to tame the beasts of two competing value systems that have been at odds with each other for over fifty years.

Just convincing corporate America of the very simple premise that it ought to be responsible for things that don't directly impact its products, was, and remains, a monumental task. In today's corporate reality these are two separate sets of stakeholders that don't coexist in mission statements of publically held corporations. The former is what defines the Orange value system while the latter the Green value-system. Critics see the former as having taxed the earth's resources while the latter has proven ineffective in stopping it. The primary client in the first group has remained the stockholder with secondary but necessary attention paid to others in that group. The ladder group of stakeholders is a reminder of John Lennon's song "Imagine"; it's a great utopian goal to aspire to, but in no uncertain terms has it been or is it now a big part of corporate social responsibility. While the ladder group of stakeholders believes the former is taxing the health of the planet, the former rejects the premise that its responsibilities include these vastly non-profitable endeavors. Getting these two subsistent value systems to agree represents the greatest difficulty that the conscious evolution of business faces today.

Green believes that its own values are the highest levels of consciousness humanity can reach. It rejects the pursuit of profit as a lower value and looks down at everything that corporations represent. To the unhealthy expression of Green the way Whole Foods and Mackey approach the solutions for a healthy planet are rejected because of their own strong rejection to Orange values. Since Green doesn't have the lenses to see things systemically, it perceives Whole Food's desire to make a profit as another representation of corporate greed. For the Orange value-system Whole Foods' core values and the mixing of the two stakeholder groups have remained a paradox that defies explanation.

While these two conflicting value systems have been at the heart of the fight that has arrested the upward emergence of capitalism, Mackey's argument for systemic prosperity might provide the answer to how business can move into second tier. What *Conscious Capitalism* has done is create a platform that plugs the systems that have competed for decades on a motherboard that simultaneously works on growing the healthy aspects of both Green and Orange values while pursuing a new bottom line that's atypical of a first-tier enterprise: People, passion, purpose, profit, and planet. The shift to second-tier consciousness in Mackey's model comes when he refocuses the purpose of capitalism from the *pursuit of self-interest* to the *pursuit of the public good.* By widening the focus of business to include the health of the food supply, people, and planet, and having a proven system in place that is capable of meeting these challenges, Mackey's *Conscious Capitalism* lays down a new road map for the business world to follow.

This transcendent goal is at the heart of Mackey's philosophy that challenges the current wisdom of management practices. The paradigm shift that has interdependence through commerce at its core becomes an essential part of the pursuit of the public good and moves the idea from being an inspiration to a business model that is guided by sustainability and growth simultaneously. As articulated by Mackey himself, the core values in this case are measures that keep balance between the happiness of customers and the wellbeing (financial and otherwise) of team members, stockholders, suppliers, the community, and the environment.[146] The fact that interdependence is acknowledged as one of the highest values and is proven through practice within a highly decentralized model that views growth within the context of the public good makes Whole Foods a leading model for distributed prosperity of the seventh-level system.

Transparency in Mackey's *Conscious Capitalism* model in everything a corporation does is the driving force that makes it a functional tool of second tier. Nowhere is this more apparent than in how it addresses the issue of corporate governance. In the aftermath of the financial crisis, some of the most hot-button issues that have steered the passions of the general public have been CEO pay, executive compensation, and the distribution of stock options. In 2012 successful corporations operating within an open system like Starbucks and Apple rewarded their CEOs with compensation packages in the tens of millions of dollars. These are standard acceptable practices within a system that rewards success, healthy Orange values at their best. Very little attention is paid to executive compensation as long as the corporation is profitable and adapts the latest in best practices such as sustainability and other trends that define corporate social responsibility.

While accumulation of personal wealth is still at the heart of first-tier capitalism, *Conscious Capitalism* places the public good as its primary benefactor. Mackey leads on this issue by example. Any founder and CEO of a company with a market capitalization the size of Whole Foods, is expected to be worth billions and have an annual compensation package worth millions. Not John Mackey. According to the company's latest financial information, he owns less than 1 percent of the total outstanding stock and received an annual salary of $1.[147] While compensation experts and management gurus scratch their heads in trying to interpret these facts and other random attributes of Whole Food's compensation philosophy, Mackey and his board of directors continue to alter this crucial area of the Orange landscape for the better. Executive compensation is capped at nineteen times the average pay of a full time employee, and it doesn't stop there. According to a 2005 study cited by Mackey, his company offered an unprecedented 93 percent of its stock options to non-executive employees, while the average offering in all other publically held corporations in the US was just 25 percent.[148]

To understand the wide-ranging implications of Whole Foods' distributed compensation model and still have executives who are very content with their jobs is to begin to understand the difference between first-tier and second-tier leadership. Yet another philosophical perspective that is far different than any seen in a typical Orange organization, is the issue around secrecy of employee compensation. All team members at Whole Foods know what everyone earns. On the surface this might look like an egalitarian Green value, but Mackey believes it reduces resentment and creates a basis for healthy competition and advancement in a workplace. Because team members are the crucial connection that completes the model's web of interdependence, they enjoy a great degree of flexibility in picking many other benefits—making it a highly adaptive, self-organizing model that is functionally second tier.

Since Mackey first articulated the core values of *Conscious Capitalism* in 2006, it has become a beacon that has attracted a new breed of business leaders. Conscious Capitalism, Inc. today is a non-profit organization whose primary goal is to advance the integration of consciousness and capitalism.[149] Executive leaders from some of the most successful corporations ranging from Southwest Airlines, to Nordstrom's believe in its virtues as they relate to the interconnected web that is life on this planet. To advance these virtues at the grassroots level, Conscious Capitalism Institute was created. It constitutes a rapidly growing global community of scholars from leading business schools, corporate executives, and CEOs, along with groups of consultants, entrepreneurs, and thought leaders who together form the most important stakeholder for the future of capitalism: the change agent. It is this systemic approach to change that will influence *life conditions* into thinking and doing things differently that will determine the success or failure of capitalism as an ideal.

THE CORPORATION OF THE FUTURE

So would corporate governance from second tier still be known by the same name? Would the current criticism of corporate practices disappear should executive compensation be capped and employees offered the lion's share of stock options? This will be a good place to start, but most corporations today still have a long way to go to be considered second tier. To the mainstream, companies like Whole Foods are often a contradiction, especially when the language used to explain their philosophy lacks proficiency in second-tier thinking. For most corporations the path to second-tier emergence will be similar to Whole Foods, not to Google or the disruptive path of the knowledge economy. This requires the entire culture to evolve its thinking. This is a long and arduous road that must take on the mantle of the development of human cultural and economic emergence through the process of raising the levels of consciousness of entire societies and setting an example for the whole world to follow.

Fundamental changes are needed in how we view ourselves in relationship to our environment and to our fellow human beings. When corporations begin to see themselves as a part of a living organism, concepts like *Conscious Capitalism* will be much easier to accept. By making our defenseless planet the ultimate beneficiary of our economic activity, we align our values with a different set of motivations. When we begin to see life as an interdependent mesh, we place the survival of the human species on equal footing with our economic interests and ourselves.

So, why would *Conscious Capitalism* serve as the ideal model to follow, and what is so different about its approach that so much time was dedicated to it in this chapter? From a value systems perspective, functionality in this model is informed by a different set of metrics than any other second-tier model discussed earlier. When all the stakeholders identified in it are treated as *holistically interdependent*, a whole different set of values that is far more conscious begins to rise. Suddenly every stakeholder is meshed into an inter-woven web that regards the planet as one ecosystem. This is the singular organism that all stakeholders plug onto to insure its long-term health. From this perspective germinates a whole different set of *distributed innovation* that the theory of Spiral Dynamics calls "Holons," which is representative of the eighth-level Turquoise value system.[150]

This is not to be confused with the notion that capitalism, and society in general, are entering Turquoise. We are just now beginning to see the problems of entering into second tier values and will spend decades addressing structural reforms in first-tier capitalism before it emerges into Yellow. Turquoise, in this case, is informing a platform called *Conscious Capitalism* on how to functionally align first-tier systems on a Turquoise trajectory through a Yellow path. Much still needs to be made healthy in the first tier and much of corporate values remain misaligned with the needs of *life conditions*. Corporations must embrace the healthy form of Green first before they can make the great leap to Yellow where they can objectively see the damage first tier-values have inflicted on the planet.

Command and control corporate structure is out. Collaboration, decen-tralization and empowerment of small groups and the human spirit is in and is functional. It is that functionality that is guided by second-tier values like Google's "don't be evil" and Whole Food's "holistic interdependence" that will transform the guiding principles of today's corporate governance and reach beyond their subsistence value systems This will be a new frontier where corporate consciousness is informed by the delicate balance of Earth's ecosystem where all stakeholders understand the urgency for the continuity of life on a planet with finite resources.

Endnotes

1 Clare W. Graves, *The Never Ending Quest,* eds. Christopher Cowan and Natasha Todorovic (Santa Barbara, CA: ECLET Publishing, 2005), 161.

2 Clare W. Graves, "Introducing the Theory," 1974. http://www.clarewgraves.com/theory_content/audio/CG_clip1.mp3

3 Global Center for Human Emergence http://www.humanemergence.org/home.html Retrieved Jan 3, 2010.

4 Said E. Dawlabani, "Economic Policy and Global Value Systems," *Integral Leadership Review,* August, 2009.

5 Don Edward Beck and Christopher C. Cowan, *Spiral Dynamics: Mastering Values, Leadership and Change.* (Malden, MA Blackwell Publishing 1996, 2006), 29.

6 Svenja Caspers, Stepahn Heim, Mark G. Lucas, Egon Stephan, Lorenz Fischer, Katrin Amunts, and Karl Zilles, *Moral Concepts Set Decision Strategies to Abstract Values,* PLOS ONE Website, http://www.plosone.org/article/info%3Adoi%2F10.1371%2Fjournal.pone.0018451. Retrieved Jan 20, 2013.

7 Ayn Rand, *The Objectivist Ethics,* The Ayn Rand Institute, http://www.aynrand.org/site/PageServer?pagename=ari_ayn_rand_the_objectivist_ethics Retrieved Jan. 3, 2010. [Original Source: Paper delivered by Ayn Rand at the University of Wisconsin Symposium on Ethics in Our Time in Madison, Wisconsin, (February 9, 1961)].

8 "Irrational exuberance" is a phrase used by the then-Federal Reserve Board Chairman, Alan Greenspan, in a speech given at the American Enterprise Institute on December 5, 1996 during the Dot-com bubble of the 1990s. The phrase was a warning that the market might be somewhat overvalued.

9 Greenspan, Alan *The Age of Turbulence: Adventures in a New World* (New York: The Penguin Press), 2007, 20.

10 Greenspan, 21.

11 Greenspan, 48.

12 Schumpeter, Joseph A., *Capitalism, Socialism and Democracy (London: Routledge,1942,1994),* 82–83.

13 Greenspan, 40–41.

14 Extracted from a brief description by Rand at a sales conference at Random House, preceding the publication of *Atlas Shrugged* in 1957 after being asked by the book salesmen to present the essence of her philosophy.

15 Frum, David (2000) *How We Got Here: The '70.s (New York, New York: Basic Books),* 292–293.

16 Harriet Rubin, *Ayn Rand's Literature of Capitalism* (September 15, 2007). http://www.nytimes.com/2007/09/15/business/15atlas.html? Retrieved May 3, 2010.

17 Edmund L. Andrews, (October 23, 2008) "Greenspan Concedes Error on Regulation", *The New York Times*. http://www.nytimes.com/2008/10/24/business/economy/24panel.html. Retrieved June 16, 2010.

18 Frederick J. Sheehan, *Panderer to Power: The Untold Story of How Alan Greenspan Enriched Wall Street and Left a Legacy of Recession* (New York: McGraw Hill, 2010), front flap.

19 "Guru, Abraham Maslow," *The Economist*, Oct. 10, 2008, (http://www.economist.com/node/12383123), Retrieved March 5, 2010.

20 United States Department of Labor, Bureau of Labor Statistics http://www.bls.gov/cpi/home.htm. Retrieved July 7, 2010.

21 Herbert A. Simon, "A Behavioral Model of Rational Choice," *Quarterly Journal of Economics* 69 (February 1955): 99–118.

22 Humergence, exploring Clare W. Graves, Emergent-Cyclical theory of human nature. http://humergence.typepad.com/the_never_ending_quest/2006/03/graves_and_masl.html. Retrieved June 4-2011.

23 Clare W. Graves, "Summary Statement: The Emergent, Cyclical, Double Helix Model of the Adult Human Biopsychosocial Systems," Boston May 20, 1981.

24 Beck and Cowan, 27–33.

25 Beck and Cowan, 31.

26 Don Edward Beck, Spiral Dynamics Integral, Level 1 Course Manual (Denton, TX Spiral Dynamics Group, 2006).

27 Clare W. Graves, *The Never Ending Quest*, eds. Christopher Cowan and Natasha Todorovic (Santa Barbara, CA: ECLET Publishing, 2005), 163.

28 Beck and Cowan, 50.

29 Beck and Cowan, 53.

30 Beck and Cowan, 55.

31 Beck and Cowan, 63.

32 Beck and Cowan, 168.

33 Beck and Cowan, 42.

34 Beck and Cowan, 76–80.

35 Beck and Cowan, 34–47.

36 Graves, 202.

37 Beck and Cowan, 203–214.

38 Beck and Cowan 215–228.

39 Beck and Cowan, 229–243.

40 Beck and Cowan, 245–259.

41 Beck and Cowan 260–265.

42 Beck and Cowan 274–276.

43 Beck and Cowan 286–289.

44 Witt, Ulrich."evolutionary economics." The New Palgrave Dictionary of Economics. Second Edition.Eds. http://www.dictionaryofeconomics.com/article?id=pde2008_E000295. Retrieved June 20, 2011.

45 Beck and Cowan, 59–61.

46 Michael V. White and Kurt Schuler, "Retrospective, Who Said 'Debauch the Currency': Keynes or Lenin?" *Journal of Economic Perspectives*, Volume 23, Number 2, (Spring 2009) 213–222.

47 Merrill C. Tenney, ed., *The Zondervan Pictorial Encyclopedia of the Bible*, vol. 5, "Weights and Measures," (Grand Rapids, MI: Zondervan), 1976.

48 Sheila C. Dow (2005), "Axioms and Babylonian thought: a reply," *Journal of Post Keynesian Economics* 27 (3), 385–391.

49 William A. Shaw, *Select Tracts and Documents Illustrative of English Monetary History 1626–1730* (London: Wilsons & Milne, 1896) [reprint: (New York: Augustus Kelley Publishers, 1967)], 166–171.

50 Adam Smith (2002) [1759]. Knud Haakonssen, ed., *The Theory of Moral Sentiments* (Cambridge University Press), xv.

51 Adam Smith, *The Glasgow edition of the Works and Correspondence of Adam Smith*, vol. 3, 26–7, edited by W.P.D. Wightman and J.C. Bryce (Oxford: Claredon Press, 1980).

52 Michael Hudson, *Super Imperialism: The Origin and Fundamentals of U.S. World Dominance*, 2nd ed. (London and Sterling, VA: Pluto Press, 2003), 63–68.

53 M. Bordo, (2002) *Gold Standard, the Concise Encyclopedia of Economics http://www.econlib.org/library/Enc/GoldStandard.html. Retrieved July 10, 2010.*

54 United States Department of Labor, Bureau of Labor Statistics, 1980, http://data.bls.gov/pdq/SurveyOutputServlet. Retrieved August 3, 2010.

55 Board of Governors of the Federal Reserve System, *The Federal Reserve System Purposes & Functions*, Washington: Federal Reserve Board Publications, 2005, 1.

56 Ibid., 3.

57 Phillip Cagan, 1987, "Monetarism," *The New Palgrave: A Dictionary of Economics*, v. 3, Reprinted in John Eatwell et al. (1989), *Money: The New Palgrave*, pp. 195–205

58 Niskanen, William A.,*Reaganomics; The Concise Encyclopedia of Economics.* http://www.econlib.org/library/Enc/Reaganomics.html. Retrieved August 3, 2010.

59 United States Department of Labor, Bureau of Labor Statistics, 1980–1984 tables, http://data.bls.gov/pdq/SurveyOutputServlet. Retrieved August 3, 2010.

60 Graves, 247.

61 John D. Buenker, John C. Burnham, and Robert M. Crunden, *Progressivism* (1986), 3–21.

62 "Coolidge's Legacy," Calvin-coolidge.org. 1926-03-05. http://www.calvin-coolidge.org/html/coolidge_s_legacy.html. Retrieved October 3, 2010.

63 Conte and Carr. *Outline of the U.S. Economy.* N.p.: U.S. Department of State. http://economics.about.com/od/useconomichistory/a/post_war.htm. Retrieved October 5, 2010.

64 Ibid.

65 Neil B.Lillico, Neil B. *Television as Popular Culture: An attempt to influence North American Society? An Ideological analysis of Leave it to Beaver (1957–1961).* A memoir submitted to the School of Graduate Studies and Research in partial fulfillment of the requirements for the M.A. degree in History. University of Ottawa, 1993.

66 Arnold B. Barach, *USA and its Economic Future* (New York: Macmillan Company, 1964), 90.

67 Barach, 57.

68 Conte and Carr. *Outline of the U.S. Economy.* N.p.: U.S. Department of State. http://economics.about.com/od/useconomichistory/a/change.htm. Retrieved October 7, 2010.

69 "BEA: quarterly GDP figures by sector, 1953–1964". Bea.gov. Retrieved December 17, 2011.

70 "Statistical Abstract of the United States: Historical price indices". Retrieved December 17, 2011.

71 "Statistical Abstract of the United States, 1964" Retrieved December 17, 2011.

72 www.census.gov/hhes/www/income/data/historical/ Retrieved December 20, 2011.

73 http://www.usgovernmentrevenue.com/breakdown_1961USbt_13bs1n Retrieved December 20, 2011.

74 Frum, 295–298.

75 Frum, 298–300.

76 Forex as an investment of the future, What is Forex, what is investing, what is the future?" The Market Oracle http://www.marketoracle.co.uk/Article13053.htm.

77 Daniel Bell, *The Coming of the Post Industrial Society.* New York. Harper Colophon Books, 1974. P13.

78 "The Prize in Economics 1976 - Press Release". Nobelprize.org. 3 Jan 2012 http://www.nobelprize.org/nobel_prizes/economics/laureates/1976/press.html.

79 William A. Niskanen, *"Reaganomics".* The Concise Encyclopedia of Economics. Retrieved 2-2-2012.

80 Ibid.

81 Steve Early, (2006-07-31). *"An old lesson still holds for unions".* The Boston Globe. Retrieved 2-4-2012

82 University of Virginia Miller Center *"Remarks on the Air Traffic Controllers Strike August 3, 1981."* http://millercenter.org/president/speeches/detail/5452. Retrieved 2-4-2012.

83 United State Department of Labor. Bureau of Labor Statistics. http://data.bls.gov/pdq/SurveyOutputServlet. Retrieved 2-4-2012.

84 *"To Treat the Fed as Volcker Did". The New York Times.* 2008-12-04. Retrieved 2-6-2012.

85 Nathan Gardels, *"Stiglitz: The Fall of Wall Street Is to Market Fundamentalism What the Fall of the Berlin Wall Was to Communism". The Huffington Post.* September 16, 2008. Retrieved 2-7-2012.

86 The National Bureau of Economic Research. *"Author F. Burns",* NBER 1949 http://www.nber.org/books/burn49-1. Retrieved 2-8-2012.

87 Bell, 17–18.

88 Bernanke, Ben (February 20, 2004). "The Great Moderation" *federalreserve. gov.* Retrieved 2-12-2012

89 John C. Edmunds, "Securities: The New World Wealth Machine," *Foreign Policy,* no. 104, Fall 1996, 118–123.

90 Charles Ferguson, Director (May 16, 2010). http://www.imdb.com/title/ tt1645089/Inside Job (Television Documentary (DVD). Sony Pictures Classics. Event occurs at 17:20. http://www.imdb.com/title/tt1645089/.

91 Christopher L. Culp and Robert J. Mackay: *Regulating derivatives, the current system and the proposed changes,* CATO Regulation: The Review of Business & Government. http://www.cato.org/pubs/regulation/regv17n4/reg17n4b. html. Retrieved 3-1-2012.

92 Bank for International Settlements, *OTC Derivative Market Activity for the first half of 2008.* http://www.bis.org/search/?sndex=alike&_st=false&c=10&q= derivatives&mp=any&adv=1&sb=0&fn1=date_range&fv1=2008. Retrieved 3-1-2012.

93 This American Life, "The return of the giant pool of money," http://www. thisamericanlife.org/radio-archives/episode/390/transcript. Retrieved 3-2-2012.

94 Don Edward Beck, PhD, *Stages of Social Development, the Dynamics that Spark Violence, Spread Prosperity and Shape Globalization,* Spiral Dynamics, Integral http://www.spiraldynamics.net/DrDonBeck/essays/stages_of_social_ development.htm Retrieved 3-12-2012.

95 Graves designated levels of existence in alphabetical pairings with A through G representing existential problems, or Life Conditions and N through U representing the adaptive intelligences in the brain. G-T is the 7th level system or the YELLOW vMEME in Spiral Dynamics.

96 Clare W. Graves, "Human Nature Prepares for a Momentous Leap," *The Futurist,* April 1974, 84.

97 Dave Clarke & Alexandra Alper, (October 11, 2011), "U.S. reveals Volcker rule's murky ban on Wall St. bets", Reuters. Retrieved 3-28-2012.

98 The Ratigan Report, *MSNBC* http://ratiganreport.msnbc.msn.com/_news/ 2012/01/06/10008698-launching-the-30-million-jobs-tour. Retrieved 3-25-2012.

99 Dylan Stableford, "Video: MSNBC's Dylan Ratigan has a meltdown over the meltdown". *Yahoo News,* 8/10/2011. http://news.yahoo.com/blogs/cutline/ video-msnbc-dylan-ratigan-meltdown-over-meltdown-031046281.html. Retrieved April 3, 2012.

100 Google Venture-Where We Invest, http://www.googleventures.com/where-we-invest Retrieved April 26, 2012.

101 Beck and Cowan, 145.

102 Richard Buckminster Fuller Quotes http://www.goodreads.com/author/quotes/165737.Richard_Buckminster_Fuller. Retrieved 05-7-12.

103 Bell 1974, 17–33.

104 Chris Anderson, *The Long Tail: Why the Future of Business is Selling Less of More*, (New York: Hyperian Books, 2006–2008), 50–53.

105 Anderson, 52–57.

106 D. Tapscott & *A.D.*Williams, *Wikinomics: How Mass Collaboration Changes Everything* (New York: Penguin, 2007), 15–20.

107 The Sloan Consortium, Going the Distance: Online education in the United States in 2011. http://sloanconsortium.org/publications/survey/goingdistance_2011 Retrieved 05-12-12.

108 Clare W. Graves, "Human Nature Prepares for a Momentous Leap", *The Futurist*, April 1974, 81.

109 Graves, 369.

110 Paul Krugman, "The Market Mystique," *New York Times*, Mar 26, 2009. http://www.nytimes.com/2009/03/27/opinion/27krugman.html. Retrieved 9-3-2012.

111 A Report from the New Economy Working Group, "How to Liberate America from Wall Street Rule." http://issuu.com/newgroup/docs/.

112 Charles Gasparino, "Too big to fail grows, the failure of banking reform." *The New York Post* online. July 24, 2012. http://www.nypost.com/p/news/opinion/opedcolumnists/too_big_to_fail_grows_cVFocOFPEAJyQ4LgCR2ilO. Retrieved October 18, 2012.

113 John Cassidy, "What Good is Wall Street?" *The New Yorker*, Nov. 29, 2010, 50.

114 Hyman Simeon, Financial Sector Job Cuts Announces: 200,000. Bloomberg.com, Jan. 30, 2012. http://www.bloomberg.com/portfolio-impact/2012-01-25/financial-sector-job-cuts-announced-200-000.html. Retrieved October 17, 2012

115 David Bailey and Soyoung Kim, Reuters. June 26, 2009. http://www.reuters.com/article/2009/06/26/us-ge-immelt-idUSTRE55P4ZT20090626. Retrieved Oct. 14, 2012.

116 US Department of Labor, Bureau of Labor Statistics. http://data.bls.gov/pdq/SurveyOutputServlet. Retrieved October 14, 2012.

117 Daniel J. Ikenson, Thriving in a Global Economy: The Truth about US Manufacturing and Trade. Cato Institute. August 28, 2007. http://www.cato.org/publications/trade-policy-analysis/thriving-global-economy-truth-about-us-manufacturing-trade. Retrieved October 14, 2012.

118 Bailey and Kim, Reuters. June 26, 2009.

119 Nick Schulz, "Hard Unemployment Truths about 'Soft' Skills,"WSJ.com, Sept. 19, 2012. http://online.wsj.com/article/SB10000872396390444517304 577653383308386956.html. Retrieved October 17, 2012.

120 The White House Office of Management and Budget. http://www.whitehouse. gov/omb/budget/Historicals. Retrieved Oct. 17,2012.

121 Jeremy Rifkin, The Third Industrial Revolution: How Lateral Power Will Transform Society (Excerpt). *The Huffington Post*, Sept. 28, 2011. http://www. huffingtonpost.com/jeremy-rifkin/the-third-industrial-revo_b_981168. html. Retrieved Oct. 18, 2012.

122 John Mackey, *Conscious Capitalism: Creating a New Paradigm for Business*, JohnMackey'sBlog,http://www.wholefoodsmarket.com/blog/john-mackeys-blog/conscious-capitalism-creating-new-paradigm-for%C2%A0business. Retrieved 10-18-2012.

123 US Department of Commerce, *Bureau of Economic Analysis*. http://www. bea.gov/newsreleases/national/gdp/2011/gdp4q10_3rd.htm. Retrieved April 3, 2012.

124 Survey Central, *What would you do to change corporate America, Wall Street, the government and capitalism in general*. http://surveycentral.org/ survey/33473.html. Retrieved April 3, 2012.

125 Valerie J. Brown, February 2007). "Industry Issues: Putting the Heat on Gas". *Environmental Health Perspectives* (US National Institute of Environmental Health Sciences) 115 (2): A76. PMC 1817691. PMID 17384744. April 5, 2012.

126 "The Halliburton Loophole", *New York Times*, November 2, 2009 (http:// www.nytimes.com/2009/11/03/opinion/03tue3.html?_r=1&adxnnl= 1&adxnnlx=1338218432-fg6KaStIZcp+GyJXLr+suQ). Retrieved April 5, 2012.

127 Rick Newman, "How to Survive a 'Zombie Economy,'" *US News and World Report*, August 23, 2010 http://money.usnews.com/money/blogs/flowchart/ 2010/08/23/how-to-survive-a-zombie-economy. Retrieved May 23, 2012.

128 Adam Smith, *An Inquiry into the Nature and Causes of the Wealth of Nations*, (Clarendon: Oxford 1776), 741.

129 Aaron Pressman, "The Coffee Wars IV, Schultz rallies Starbucks baristas," Bloomberg *BusinessWeek*, February 23, 2007. http://www.businessweek. com/investing/insights/blog/archives/2007/02/coffee_wars_iv.html. Retrieved May 23, 2012.

130 Ignatius Adi "The HBR Interview: We had to Own the Mistakes", *Harvard Business Review*, July, 2010 http://hbr.org/2010/07/the-hbr-interview-we-had-to-own-the-mistakes/ar/1. Retrieved May 23, 2012.

131 Starbucks (2012) Responsibility:values,goals,progress.http://www.starbucks. com. Retrieved May 23, 2012.

132 Adam Lashinsky, "The decade of Steve: How Apple's imperious, brilliant CEO transformed American Business," *Fortune Magazine*, November 5, 2009. http://money.cnn.com/2009/11/04/technology/steve_jobs_ceo_decade. fortune/index.htm. Retrieved May 24, 20102.

133 Walter Isaacson, *Steve Jobs* (New York: Simon & Schuster, 2011), 561.

134 Fahlenbrach Rüdiger, Founder-CEOs, *Investment Decisions, and Stock Market Performance*, Ohio State University, Fisher College of Business, August 8, 2007. http://www.ssrn.com/abstract=606527. Retrieved May 27, 2012.

135 Ibid.

136 Beck and Cowan, 282.

137 John Battelle, "The Birth of Google," *Wired Magazine*, August 2005.

138 Steven Levy, "Secrets of Googlenomics: Data-Fueled Recipe Brews Profitability," *Wired Magazine*, May 2009.

139 Carol Kopp, *"Rediscovering Google,"* Market Watch/*Wall Street Journal*. http://www.marketwatch.com/story/rediscovering-google-2012-09-26. Retrieved September 26, 2012.

140 Google Ventures. http://www.googleventures.com. Retrieved September 27, 2012.

141 http://www.googleventures.com/companies. Retrieved September 27, 2012.

142 Nick Paumgarten, "Food Fighter: Does Whole Foods CEO know what's best for you?," *The New Yorker* Jan. 4, 2010. http://www.newyorker.com/reporting/2010/01/04/100104fa_fact_paumgarten. Retrieved October 8, 2012.

143 Gary Hamel, "What Google, Whole Foods do Best," *Fortune*, Sept. 27, 2007. http://money.cnn.com/2007/09/26/news/companies/management_hamel.fortune/index.htm. Retrieved October 9, 2012.

144 *The New Yorker*, Jan. 4, 2010.

145 John Mackey, *Conscious Capitalism: Creating a New Paradigm for Business*. http://www.wholefoodsmarket.com/blog/john-mackeys-blog/conscious-capitalism-creating-new-paradigm-for%C2%A0business. Retrieved October 11, 2012.

146 John Mackey, *Conscious Capitalism*, http://www.wholefoodsmarket.com/blog/john-mackeys-blog/conscious-capitalism-creating-new-paradigm-for%C2%A0business.

147 http://www.reuters.com/finance/stocks/overview?symbol=WFM.O. Retrieved October 12, 2012.

148 John Mackey, *Conscious Capitalism*, http://www.wholefoodsmarket.com/blog/john-mackeys-blog/conscious-capitalism-creating-new-paradigm-for%C2%A0business

149 Conscious Capitalism Institute, http://consciouscapitalism.org/institute/. Retrieved October 14, 2012.

150 Beck and Cowan, 289.

Acknowledgments

Nestled high above the banks of the Umpqua River in western Oregon is a slice of heaven called Lighthouse Farms. It was there during a meditation retreat in the middle of the financial crisis of 2008 that the idea for this book was born. Writing was never an easy process for me, but with the support and the extraordinary inspiration from so many great people around me it was turned into a labor of love. I thank Don Beck for his brilliant foreword to the book. Don is one of the most conscious leaders I know, who is decades ahead of our time. I also owe a debt of gratitude to Jean Houston who at the first sight of the book outline urged me to drop everything else and finish it.

I have a deep gratitude for all my teachers past and present. I am thankful for the advice of my college professor, Gustav Schachter who always encouraged me to look past economic data in order to affect change, counsel that has guided me for over thirty years. I want to express great appreciation for my dad, who at age ninety is still the sharpest person I know, and for my mom for always providing the best home life a kid could ask for. I owe a special thank you to my wonderful siblings, Nassif, "*Dr. D,*" who dedicated his whole life to helping inner city kids, and Nick "*little Dr. D,*" and his young family, and to my sister, Nuha, and her family who provided inspiration.

I also want to thank Richard "*the Crawdaddy*" Dance for setting me on the road to self-discovery. I am also thankful to Dr. Ichak Adizes and Dr. Laura Frey Horn for their generosity and the many opportunities I have had to teach their graduate students. I am thankful for Jeff Salzman of the *Integral Center* in Boulder for affording me the first opportunity many years ago to present my work to the integral community. My gratitude also goes out to my colleague and friend, Kevin Kells, who always understood the simplicity beyond the complexity in bringing a better understanding of the world.

I also owe many thanks to my agent, Bill Gladstone, who believed in the transformational nature of my work and represented me accordingly. Much gratitude goes out to my publisher, Kenzi Sugihara, at SelectBooks, Inc. for his vision of what my book can become, and to my editor, Nancy Sugihara, for her collaboration in making my message clearer.

To all my previous colleagues, employees, and partners from the real estate and homebuilding industries, thank you all for being my teachers. I'm especially thankful for my assistant, Lil Buddha, our four-legged King Charles Cavalier who warmed my feet throughout the many months of writing.

Finally, to all my colleagues in the Spiral Dynamics community, this book would not have been possible without our daily exchanges that kept my thinking pure and my message on target. You are my Turquoise tribe and together we can move mountains.

Index

About the Author

SAID DAWLABANI is the leading expert in the value-systems approach to economics. He is the founder of The Memenomics Group, an advisory organization that reframes economic issues through the prism of value systems and offers sustainable solutions based on this emerging science. For the past decade he has worked closely with renowned global geopolitical advisor Dr. Don E. Beck, one of the architects behind South Africa's transition from apartheid and co-author of Spiral Dynamics, the most authoritative theory on value systems.

A real estate developer turned social entrepreneur, Dawlabani has a prominent 25-year career in the brokerage, development, and investment counseling sectors of the real estate industry. He structured hundreds of complex planning, development, and historic restoration projects and advised notable clients such as the Resolution Trust Corporation, the FDIC, US Bankruptcy Court, and the Bank of New England on asset disposition strategies. In addition to his development and brokerage work in Boston, Scottsdale, and San Diego, he advises a select circle of clients on long-term investment strategies.

Said is a descendent of the Bishop of Antioch Philexinos Yohana Dawlabani, publisher of more than seventy works and translations of mysticism and esoteric Christianity and among the few early 20th century scholars to translate the Bible from Aramaic and Greek to Arabic and Turkish.

He is also the COO and member of the Board of Directors of The Center for Human Emergence Middle East, a think tank that frames the political and economic issues facing the region through the prism of value systems. He's a guest speaker on the topic of transformational leadership at several academic graduate programs, including the Adizes Graduate School in Santa Barbara, CA and the University of Virginia.

For more information visit memenomics.com